GODZILLA
RULERS OF EARTH

STORY BY **CHRIS MOWRY** AND **MATT FRANK**

WRITTEN BY
CHRIS MOWRY

ART BY
MATT FRANK AND JEFF ZORNOW

INK ASSIST BY
MOSTAFA MOUSSA
(CHAPTERS 2 & 3)

COLORS BY
PRISCILLA TRAMONTANO

LETTERS BY
SHAWN LEE

SERIES EDITS BY
BOBBY CURNOW

COVER ART BY **MATT FRANK**
COVER COLORS BY **JOSH PEREZ**

COLLECTION EDITS BY **JUSTIN EISINGER** AND **ALONZO SIMON**
COLLECTION DESIGN BY **CHRIS MOWRY**

ISBN: 978-1-63140-172-5
17 16 15 14   1 2 3 4

Special thanks to Yoshiko Fukuda and everyone at Toho for their invaluable assistance.

Ted Adams, CEO & Publisher
Greg Goldstein, President & COO
Robbie Robbins, EVP/Sr. Graphic Artist
Chris Ryall, Chief Creative Officer/Editor-in-Chief
Matthew Ruzicka, CPA, Chief Financial Officer
Alan Payne, VP of Sales
Dirk Wood, VP of Marketing
Lorelei Bunjes, VP of Digital Services
Jeff Webber, VP of Digital Publishing & Business Development

Facebook: facebook.com/idwpublishing
Twitter: @idwpublishing
YouTube: youtube.com/idwpublishing
Instagram: instagram.com/idwpublishing
deviantART: idwpublishing.deviantart.com
Pinterest: pinterest.com/idwpublishing/idw-staff-faves

www.IDWPUBLISHING.com
IDW founded by Ted Adams, Alex Garner, Kris Oprisko, and Robbie Robbins

THE STORY SO FAR

Near the Monster Islands research facility (a chain of islands housing some of the planet's captive giant monsters), the undersea creatures known as the Devonians unleash their monsters in an all-out attack against the humans at the surface. Using Mechagodzilla, Jet Jaguar is able to defeat the vicious monster Destoroyah. But beneath the surface, Godzilla has his hands full with Gezora, Manda, and Titanosaurus as the four kaiju head straight toward the Devonian kingdom below.

The Cryog Commander disguises himself as a Devonian refugee and, while eventually betraying his human hosts, convinces them to launch a final nuclear strike against the monsters and Devonians on the ocean floor. The resulting explosion does little to destroy the monsters, but buries the Devonians—and Godzilla—in a massive underwater cavern. Neither have been seen since.

Lucy Casprell, still recovering from being lost at sea and washing ashore on the home of Mothra, Infant Island, stays at the Monster Islands facility, continuing her studies of the giant monsters. Little does anyone know however, that a new threat is on the horizon. With Godzilla missing, the time has now come for a final push to rule the Earth!

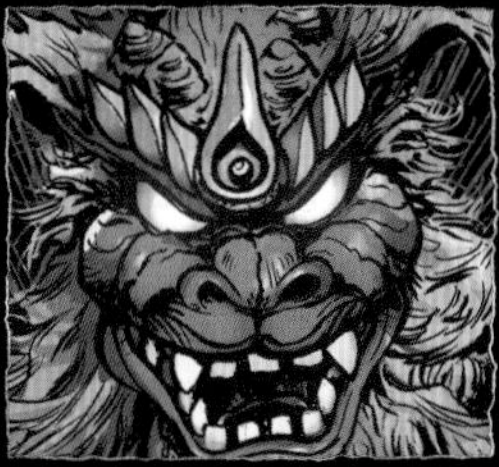

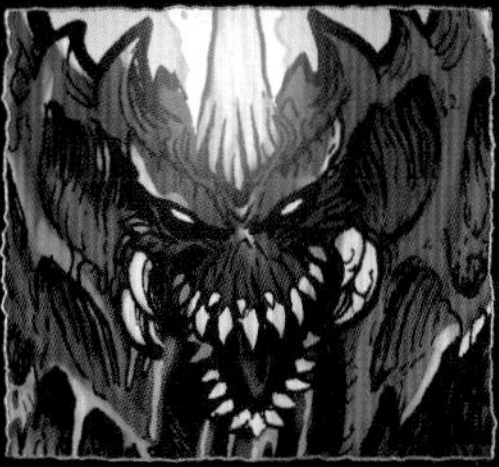

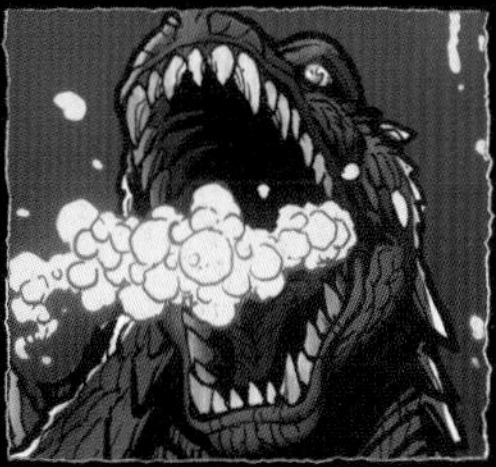

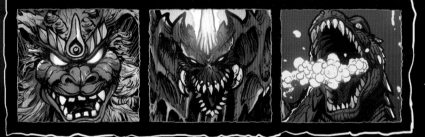

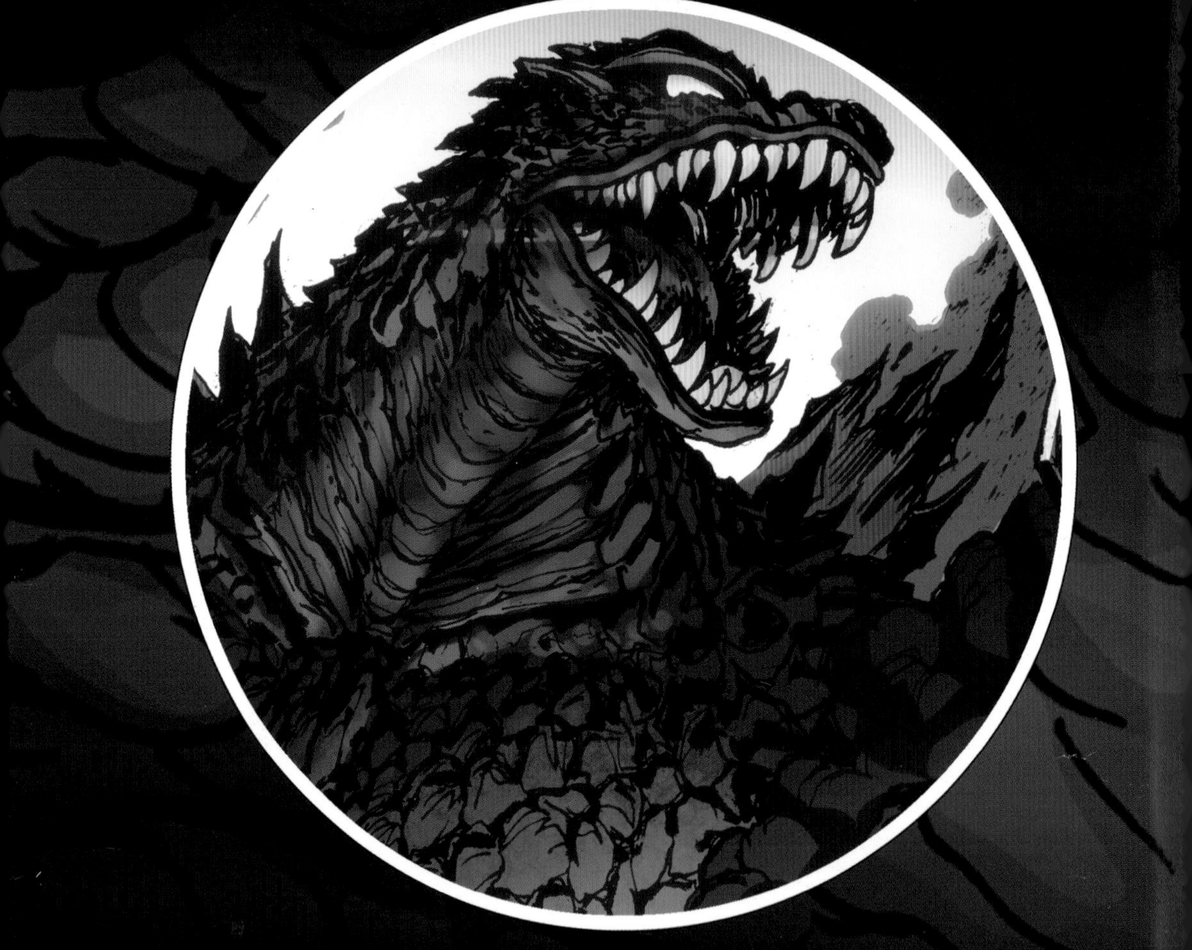

CHAPTER ONE:
CHANGING OF THE GUARD

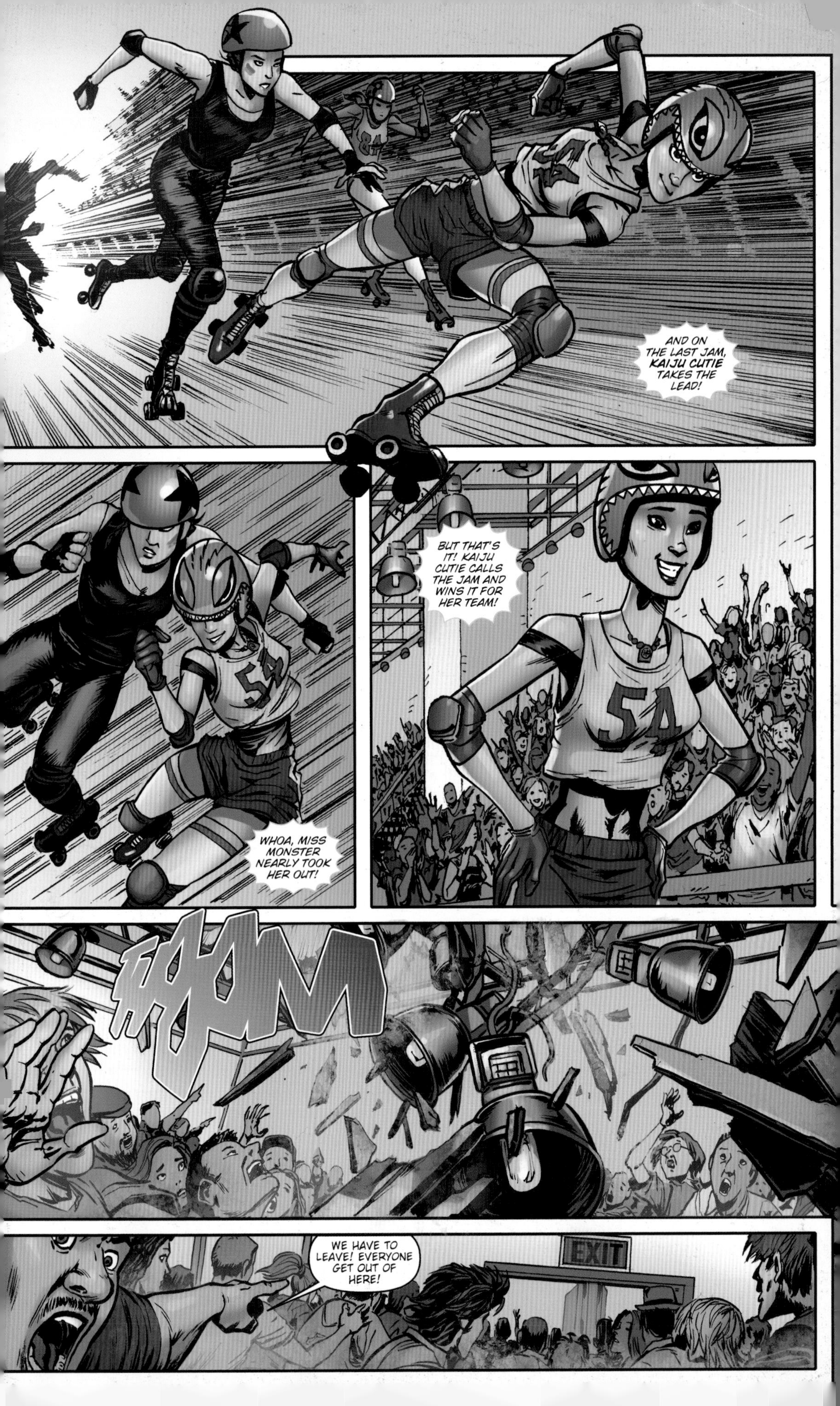
AND ON THE LAST JAM, KAIJU CUTIE TAKES THE LEAD!
WHOA, MISS MONSTER NEARLY TOOK HER OUT!
BUT THAT'S IT! KAIJU CUTIE CALLS THE JAM AND WINS IT FOR HER TEAM!
FOOM
WE HAVE TO LEAVE! EVERYONE GET OUT OF HERE!
EXIT

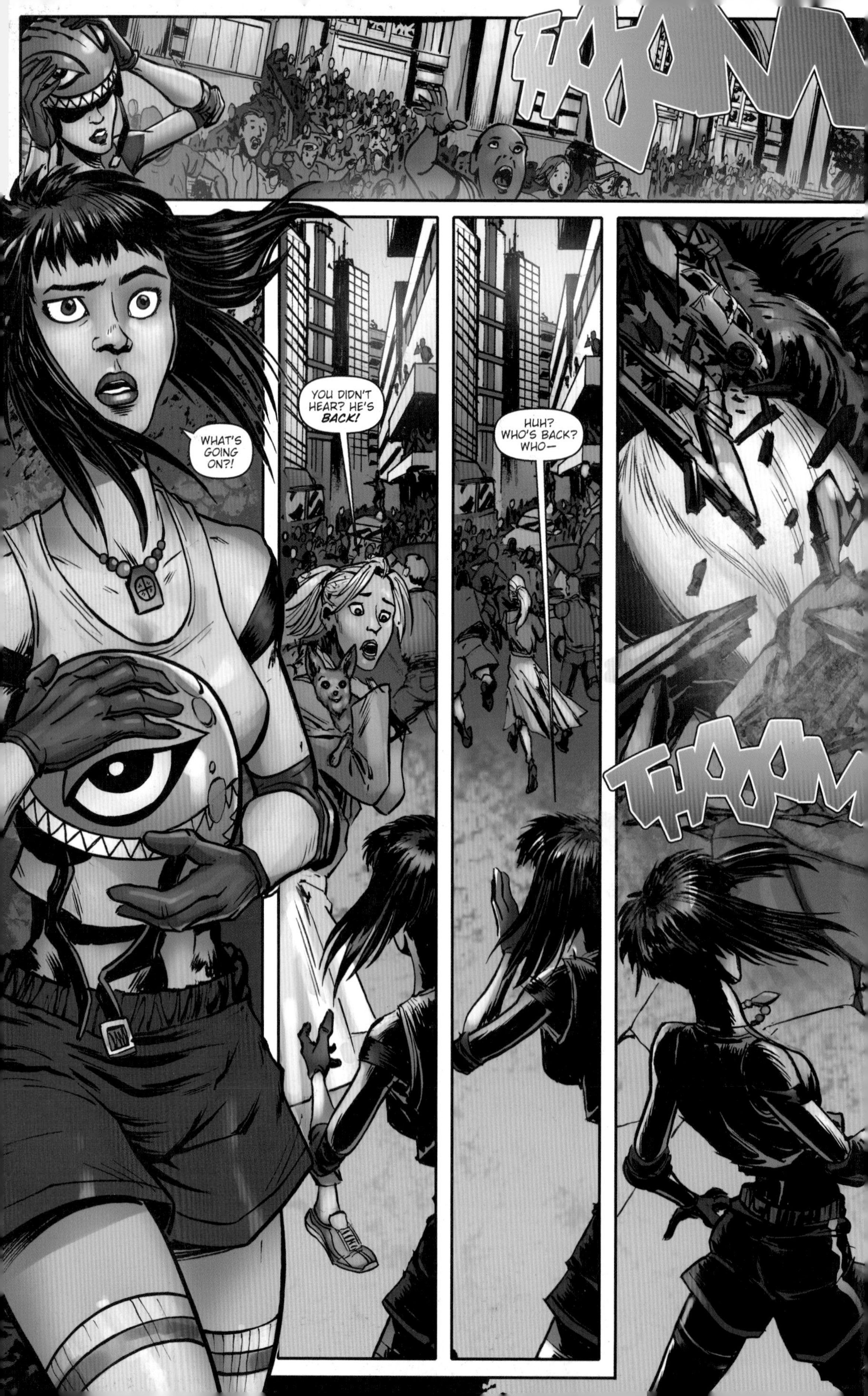
THOOM
WHAT'S GOING ON?!
YOU DIDN'T HEAR? HE'S *BACK!*
HUH? WHO'S BACK? WHO—
THOOM

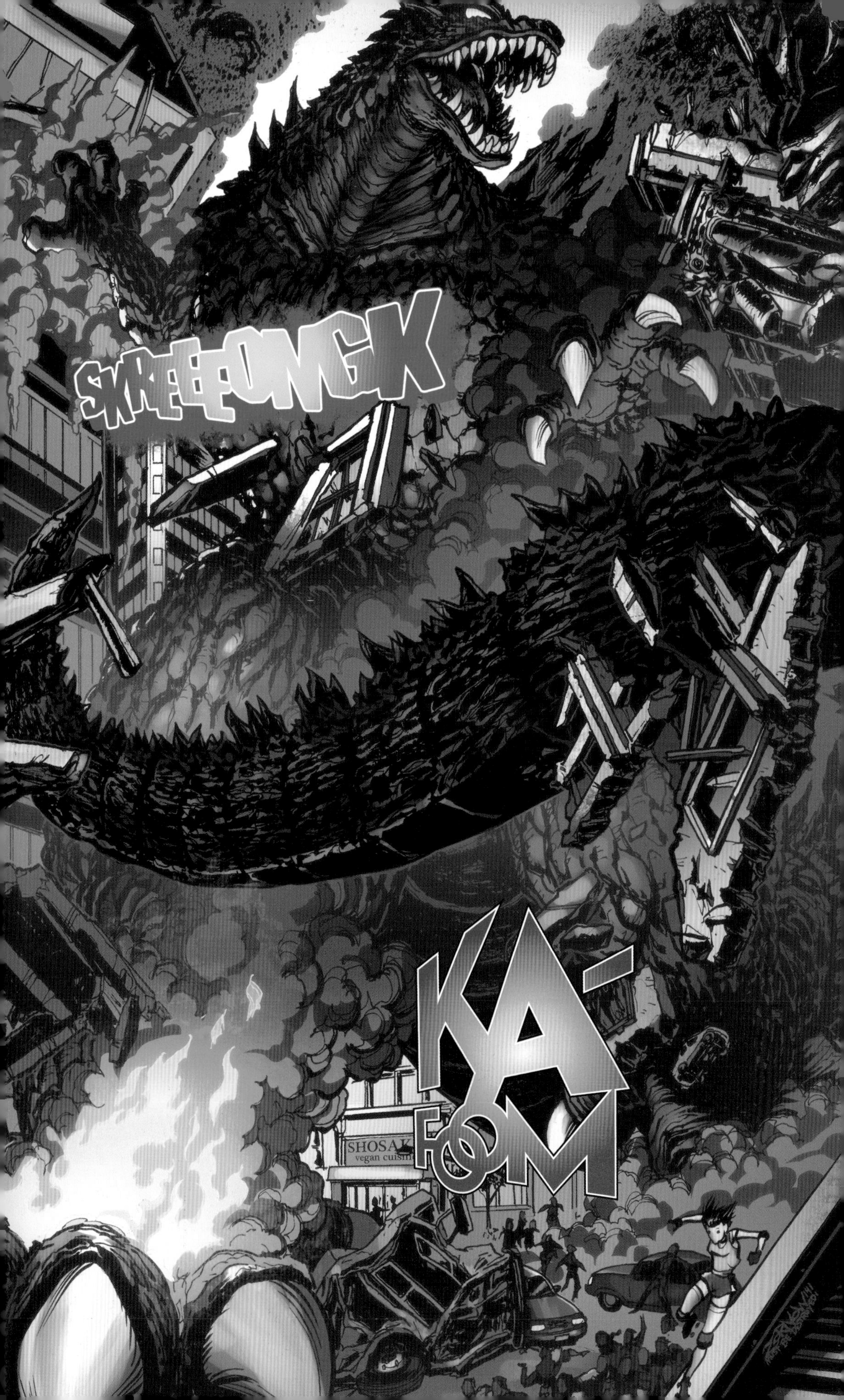
SKREEEONGK
KA-FOOM
SHOSAK
vegan cuisin

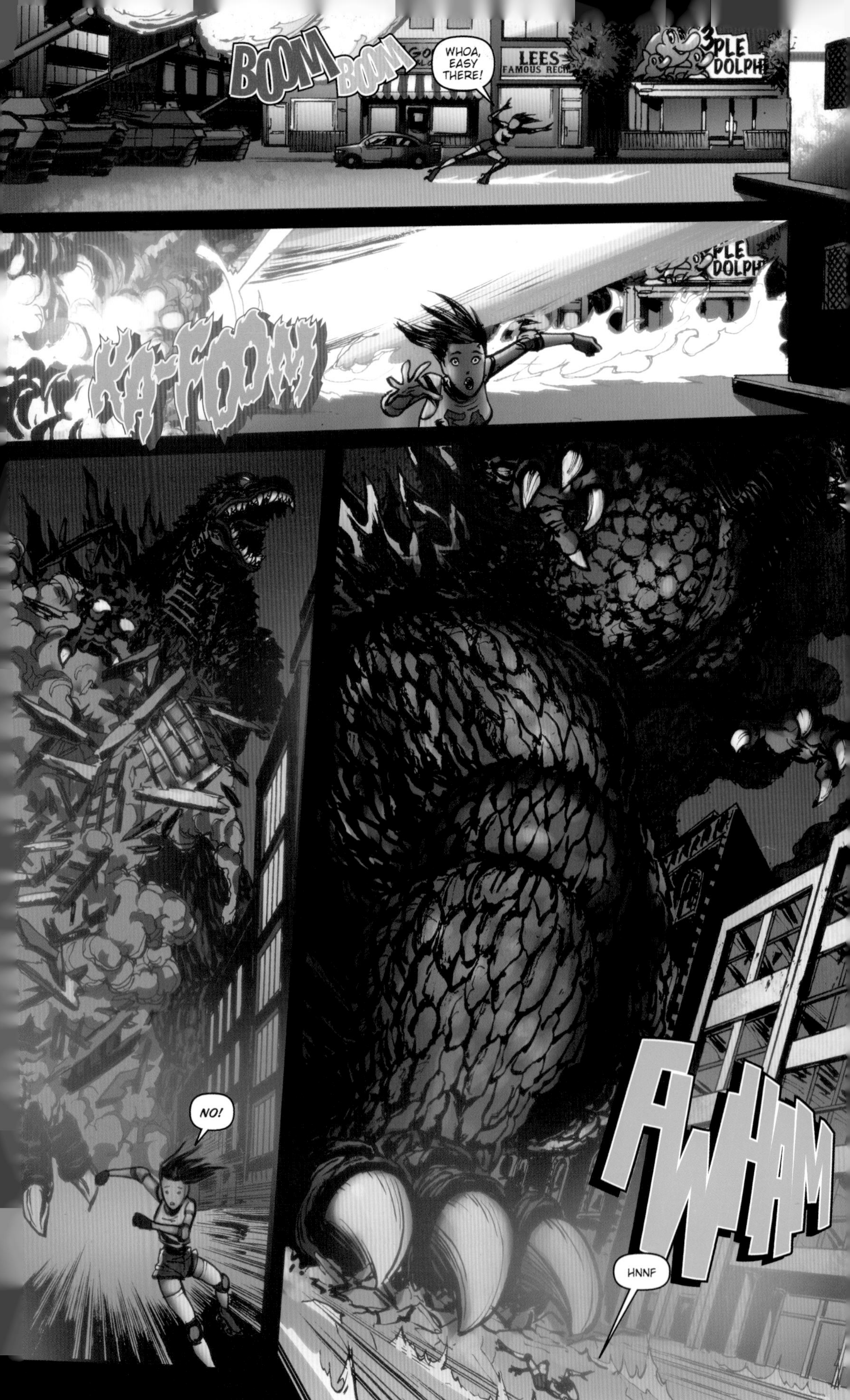
BOOM
BOOM
WHOA, EASY THERE!
LEES
KA-FOOM
NO!
FWHAM
HNNF

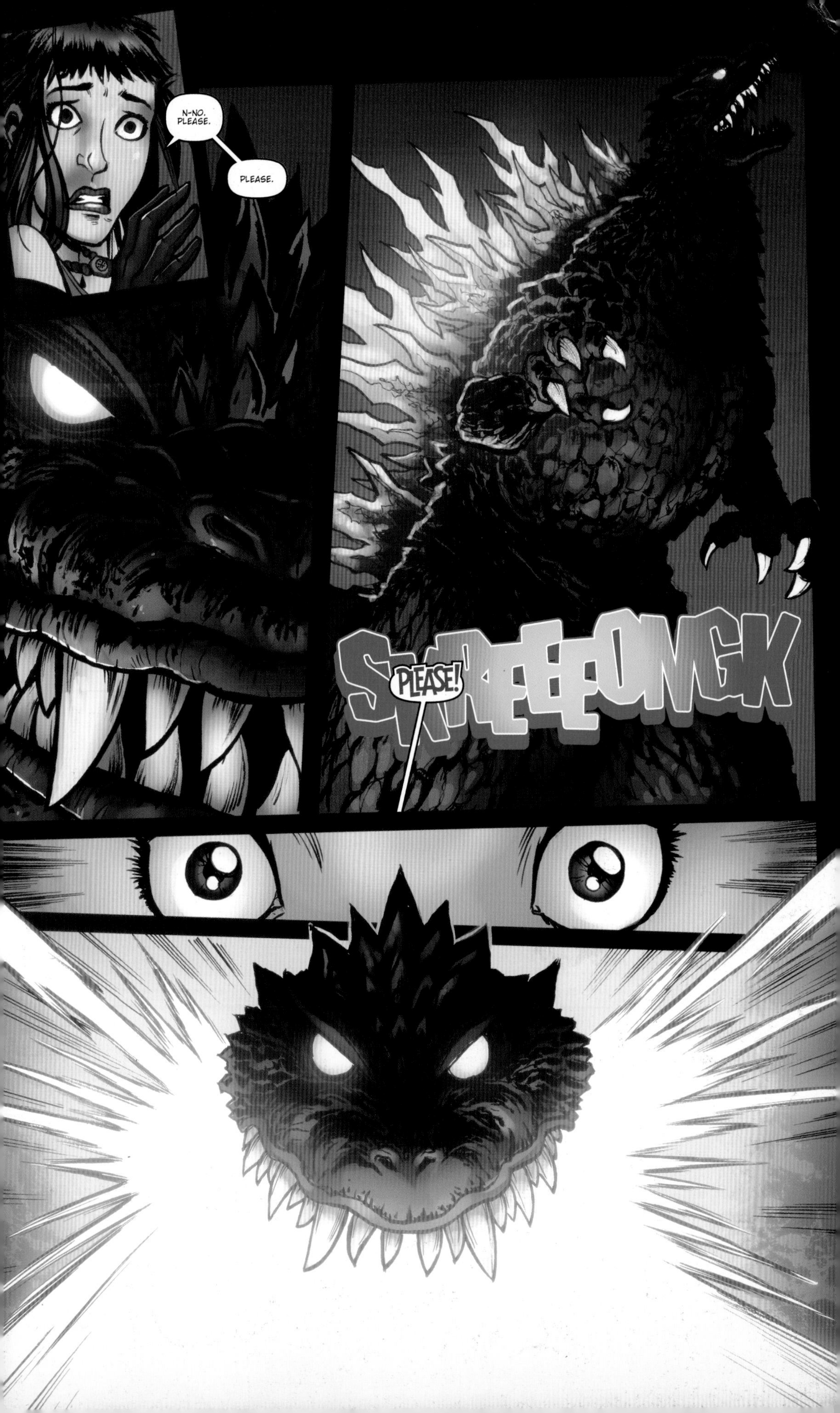
N-NO. PLEASE.
PLEASE.
SKREEEONGK
PLEASE!

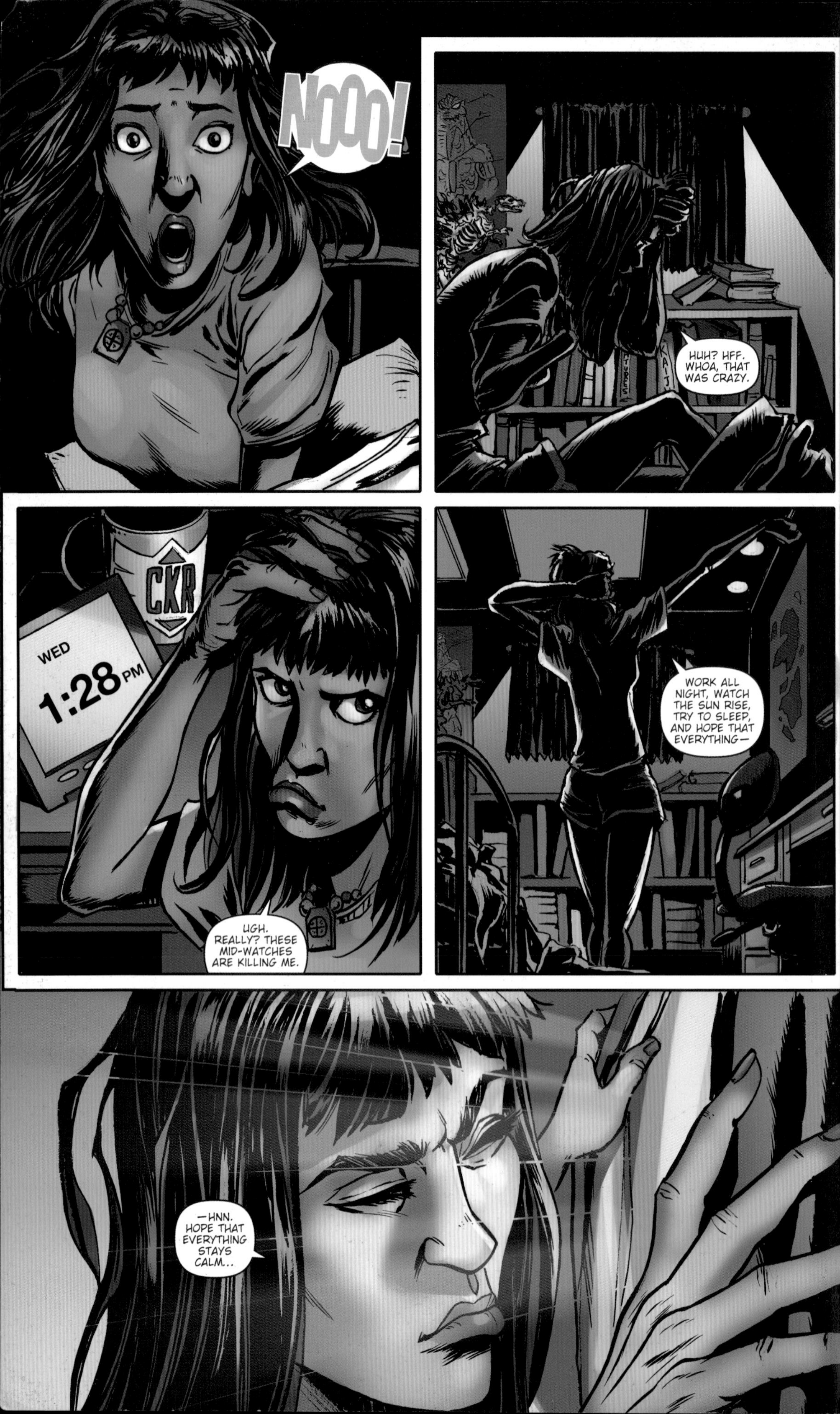
NOOO!
HUH? HFF. WHOA, THAT WAS CRAZY.
KAIJ
TUBES
CKR
WED
1:28 PM
UGH. REALLY? THESE MID-WATCHES ARE KILLING ME.
WORK ALL NIGHT, WATCH THE SUN RISE, TRY TO SLEEP, AND HOPE THAT EVERYTHING—
—HNN. HOPE THAT EVERYTHING STAYS CALM...

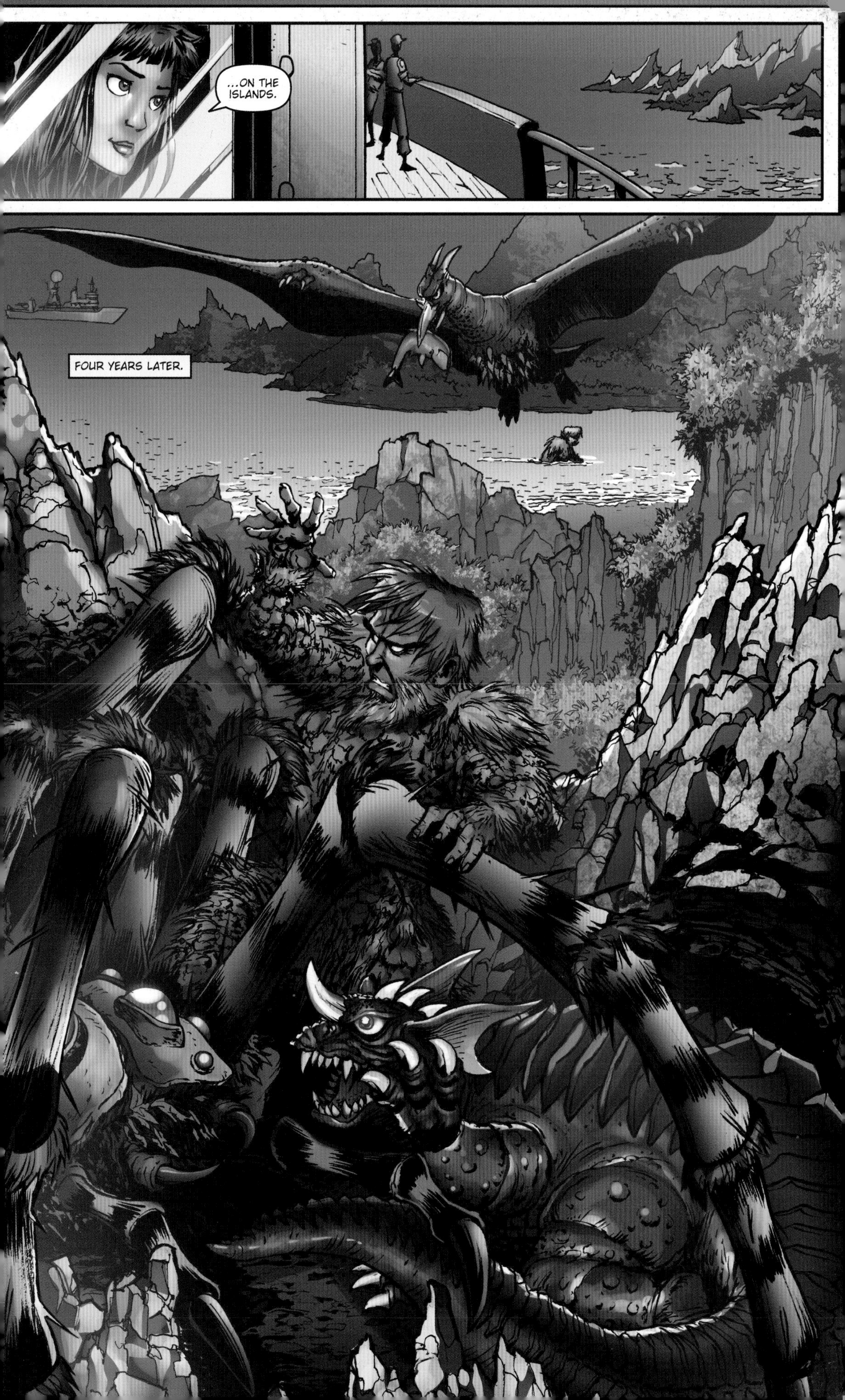
...ON THE ISLANDS.
FOUR YEARS LATER.

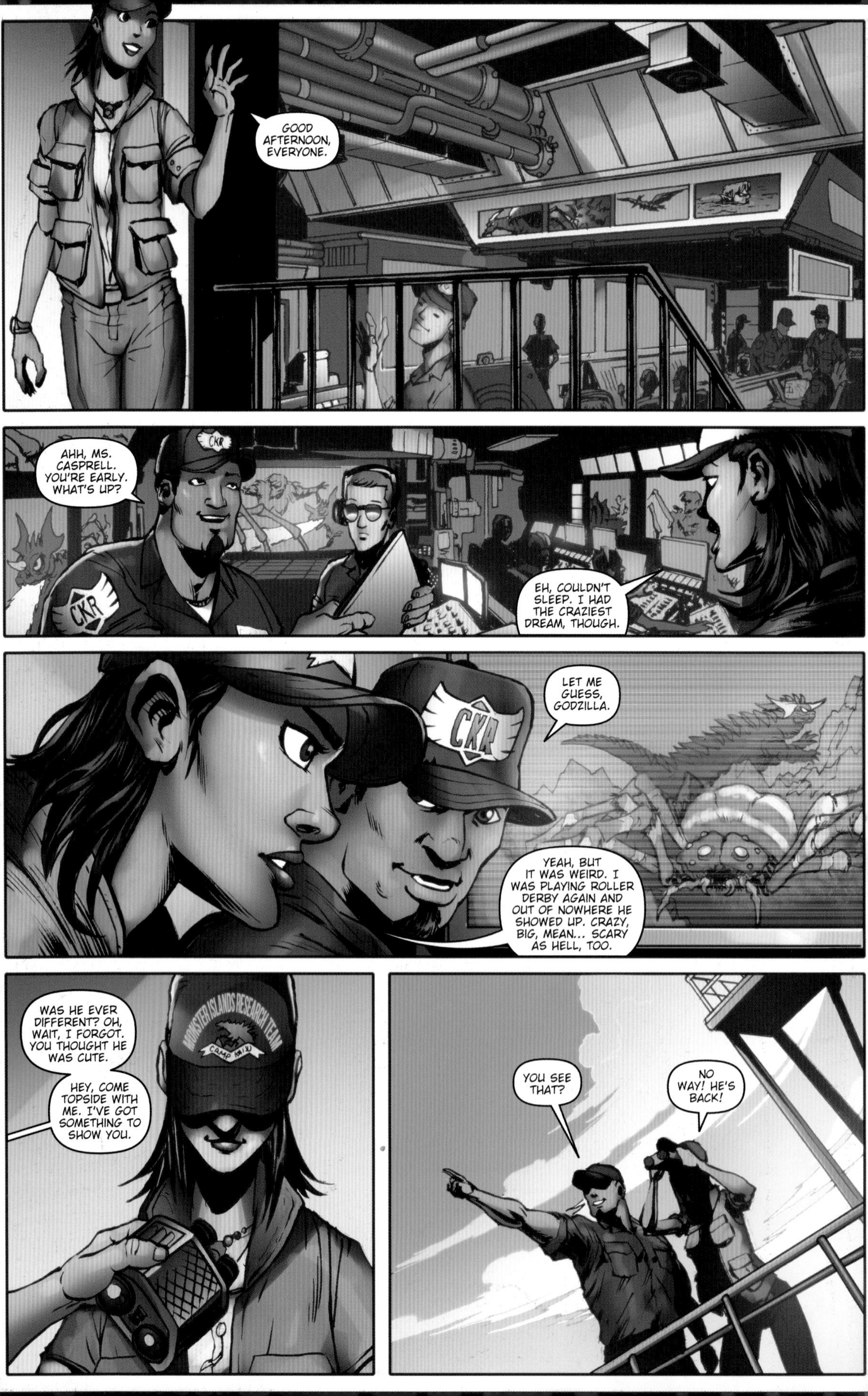

GOOD AFTERNOON, EVERYONE.
AHH, MS. CASPRELL. YOU'RE EARLY. WHAT'S UP?
EH, COULDN'T SLEEP. I HAD THE CRAZIEST DREAM, THOUGH.
LET ME GUESS, GODZILLA.
YEAH, BUT IT WAS WEIRD. I WAS PLAYING ROLLER DERBY AGAIN AND OUT OF NOWHERE HE SHOWED UP. CRAZY, BIG, MEAN... SCARY AS HELL, TOO.
WAS HE EVER DIFFERENT? OH, WAIT, I FORGOT. YOU THOUGHT HE WAS CUTE.
HEY, COME TOPSIDE WITH ME. I'VE GOT SOMETHING TO SHOW YOU.
MONSTER ISLANDS RESEARCH TEAM
YOU SEE THAT?
NO WAY! HE'S BACK!

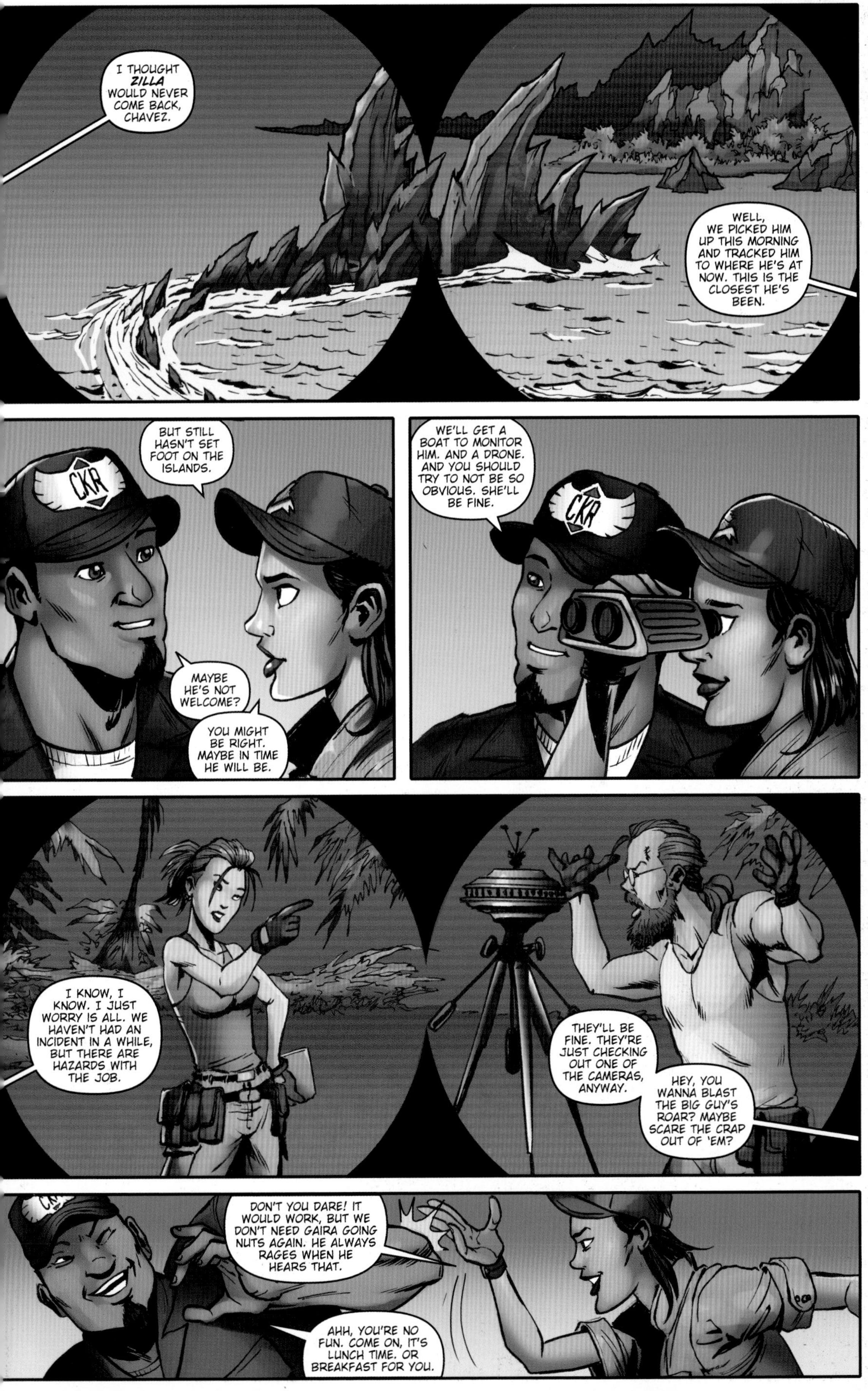
I THOUGHT ZILLA WOULD NEVER COME BACK, CHAVEZ.
WELL, WE PICKED HIM UP THIS MORNING AND TRACKED HIM TO WHERE HE'S AT NOW. THIS IS THE CLOSEST HE'S BEEN.
BUT STILL HASN'T SET FOOT ON THE ISLANDS.
CKR
MAYBE HE'S NOT WELCOME?
YOU MIGHT BE RIGHT. MAYBE IN TIME HE WILL BE.
WE'LL GET A BOAT TO MONITOR HIM. AND A DRONE. AND YOU SHOULD TRY TO NOT BE SO OBVIOUS. SHE'LL BE FINE.
CKR
I KNOW, I KNOW. I JUST WORRY IS ALL. WE HAVEN'T HAD AN INCIDENT IN A WHILE, BUT THERE ARE HAZARDS WITH THE JOB.
THEY'LL BE FINE. THEY'RE JUST CHECKING OUT ONE OF THE CAMERAS, ANYWAY.
HEY, YOU WANNA BLAST THE BIG GUY'S ROAR? MAYBE SCARE THE CRAP OUT OF 'EM?
DON'T YOU DARE! IT WOULD WORK, BUT WE DON'T NEED GAIRA GOING NUTS AGAIN. HE ALWAYS RAGES WHEN HE HEARS THAT.
AHH, YOU'RE NO FUN. COME ON, IT'S LUNCH TIME. OR BREAKFAST FOR YOU.

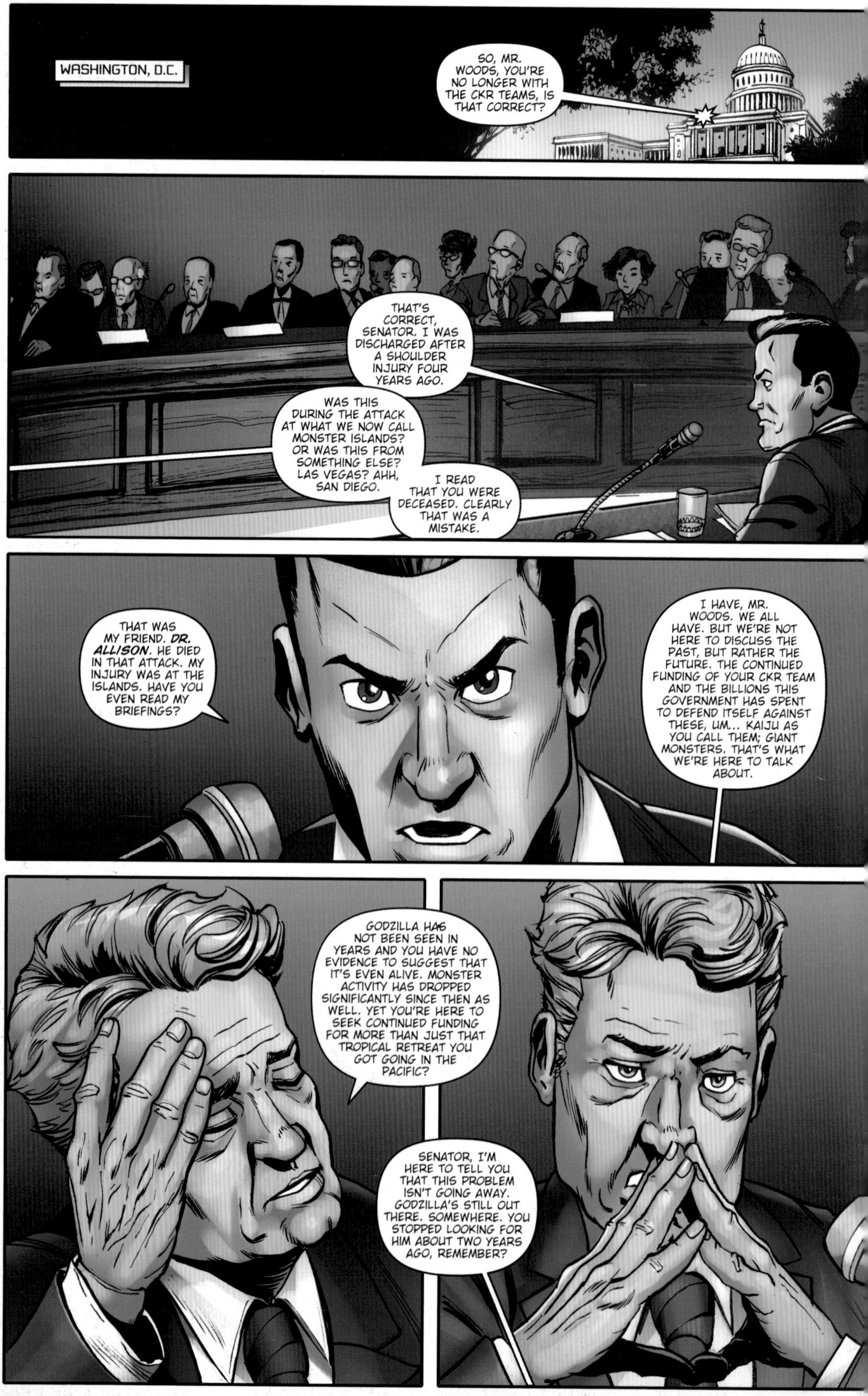
WASHINGTON, D.C.
SO, MR. WOODS, YOU'RE NO LONGER WITH THE CKR TEAMS, IS THAT CORRECT?
THAT'S CORRECT, SENATOR. I WAS DISCHARGED AFTER A SHOULDER INJURY FOUR YEARS AGO.
WAS THIS DURING THE ATTACK AT WHAT WE NOW CALL MONSTER ISLANDS? OR WAS THIS FROM SOMETHING ELSE? LAS VEGAS? AHH, SAN DIEGO.
I READ THAT YOU WERE DECEASED. CLEARLY THAT WAS A MISTAKE.
THAT WAS MY FRIEND. DR. ALLISON. HE DIED IN THAT ATTACK. MY INJURY WAS AT THE ISLANDS. HAVE YOU EVEN READ MY BRIEFINGS?
I HAVE, MR. WOODS. WE ALL HAVE. BUT WE'RE NOT HERE TO DISCUSS THE PAST, BUT RATHER THE FUTURE. THE CONTINUED FUNDING OF YOUR CKR TEAM AND THE BILLIONS THIS GOVERNMENT HAS SPENT TO DEFEND ITSELF AGAINST THESE, UM... KAIJU AS YOU CALL THEM; GIANT MONSTERS. THAT'S WHAT WE'RE HERE TO TALK ABOUT.
GODZILLA HAS NOT BEEN SEEN IN YEARS AND YOU HAVE NO EVIDENCE TO SUGGEST THAT IT'S EVEN ALIVE. MONSTER ACTIVITY HAS DROPPED SIGNIFICANTLY SINCE THEN AS WELL. YET YOU'RE HERE TO SEEK CONTINUED FUNDING FOR MORE THAN JUST THAT TROPICAL RETREAT YOU GOT GOING IN THE PACIFIC?
SENATOR, I'M HERE TO TELL YOU THAT THIS PROBLEM ISN'T GOING AWAY. GODZILLA'S STILL OUT THERE. SOMEWHERE. YOU STOPPED LOOKING FOR HIM ABOUT TWO YEARS AGO, REMEMBER?

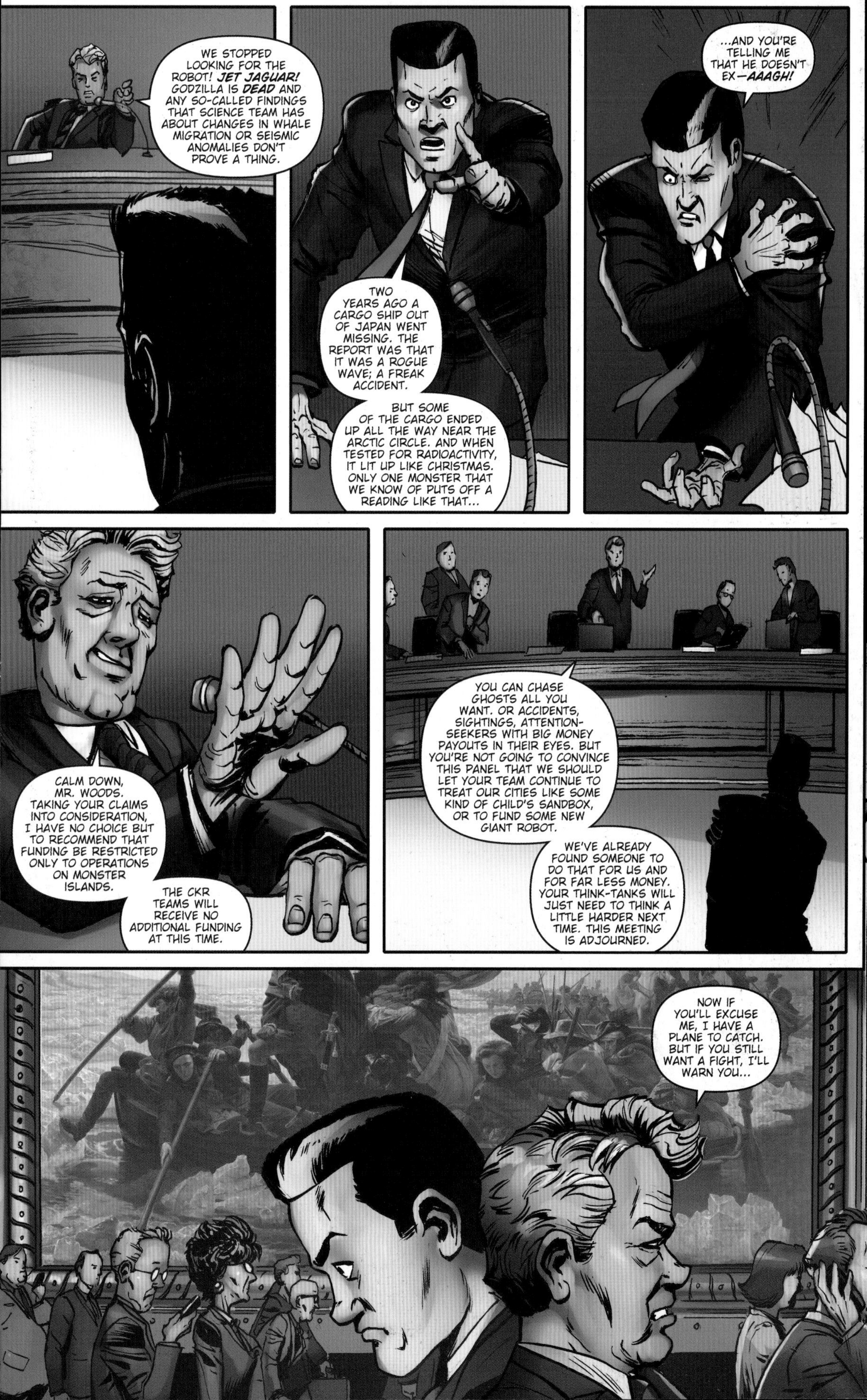
WE STOPPED LOOKING FOR THE ROBOT! JET JAGUAR! GODZILLA IS DEAD AND ANY SO-CALLED FINDINGS THAT SCIENCE TEAM HAS ABOUT CHANGES IN WHALE MIGRATION OR SEISMIC ANOMALIES DON'T PROVE A THING.
TWO YEARS AGO A CARGO SHIP OUT OF JAPAN WENT MISSING. THE REPORT WAS THAT IT WAS A ROGUE WAVE; A FREAK ACCIDENT.
BUT SOME OF THE CARGO ENDED UP ALL THE WAY NEAR THE ARCTIC CIRCLE. AND WHEN TESTED FOR RADIOACTIVITY, IT LIT UP LIKE CHRISTMAS. ONLY ONE MONSTER THAT WE KNOW OF PUTS OFF A READING LIKE THAT...
...AND YOU'RE TELLING ME THAT HE DOESN'T EX—AAAGH!
CALM DOWN, MR. WOODS. TAKING YOUR CLAIMS INTO CONSIDERATION, I HAVE NO CHOICE BUT TO RECOMMEND THAT FUNDING BE RESTRICTED ONLY TO OPERATIONS ON MONSTER ISLANDS.
THE CKR TEAMS WILL RECEIVE NO ADDITIONAL FUNDING AT THIS TIME.
YOU CAN CHASE GHOSTS ALL YOU WANT. OR ACCIDENTS, SIGHTINGS, ATTENTION-SEEKERS WITH BIG MONEY PAYOUTS IN THEIR EYES. BUT YOU'RE NOT GOING TO CONVINCE THIS PANEL THAT WE SHOULD LET YOUR TEAM CONTINUE TO TREAT OUR CITIES LIKE SOME KIND OF CHILD'S SANDBOX, OR TO FUND SOME NEW GIANT ROBOT.
WE'VE ALREADY FOUND SOMEONE TO DO THAT FOR US AND FOR FAR LESS MONEY. YOUR THINK-TANKS WILL JUST NEED TO THINK A LITTLE HARDER NEXT TIME. THIS MEETING IS ADJOURNED.
NOW IF YOU'LL EXCUSE ME, I HAVE A PLANE TO CATCH. BUT IF YOU STILL WANT A FIGHT, I'LL WARN YOU...

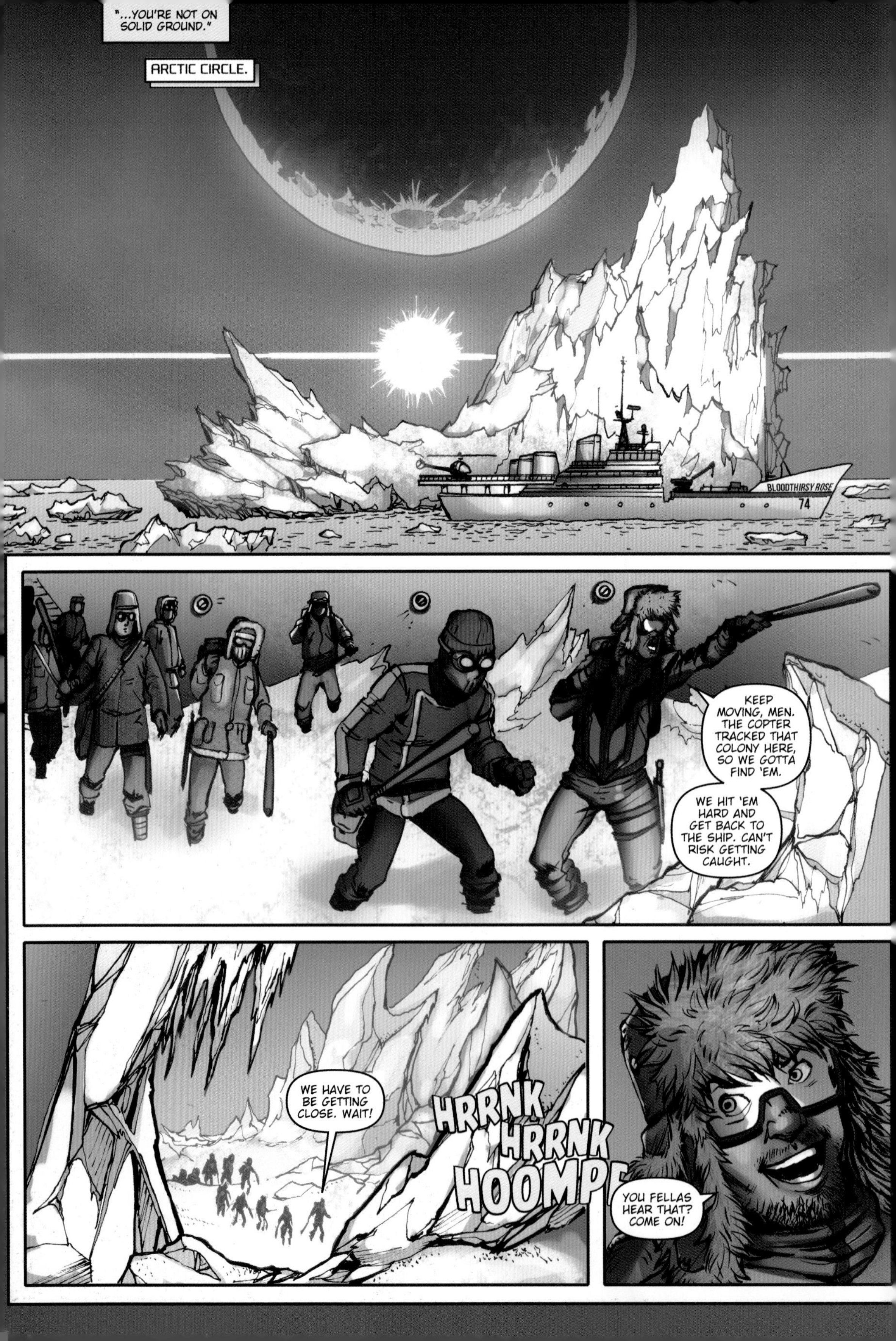
"...YOU'RE NOT ON SOLID GROUND."
ARCTIC CIRCLE.
BLOODTHIRSY ROSE
74
KEEP MOVING, MEN. THE COPTER TRACKED THAT COLONY HERE, SO WE GOTTA FIND 'EM.
WE HIT 'EM HARD AND GET BACK TO THE SHIP. CAN'T RISK GETTING CAUGHT.
WE HAVE TO BE GETTING CLOSE. WAIT!
HRRNK HRRNK HOOMPF
YOU FELLAS HEAR THAT? COME ON!

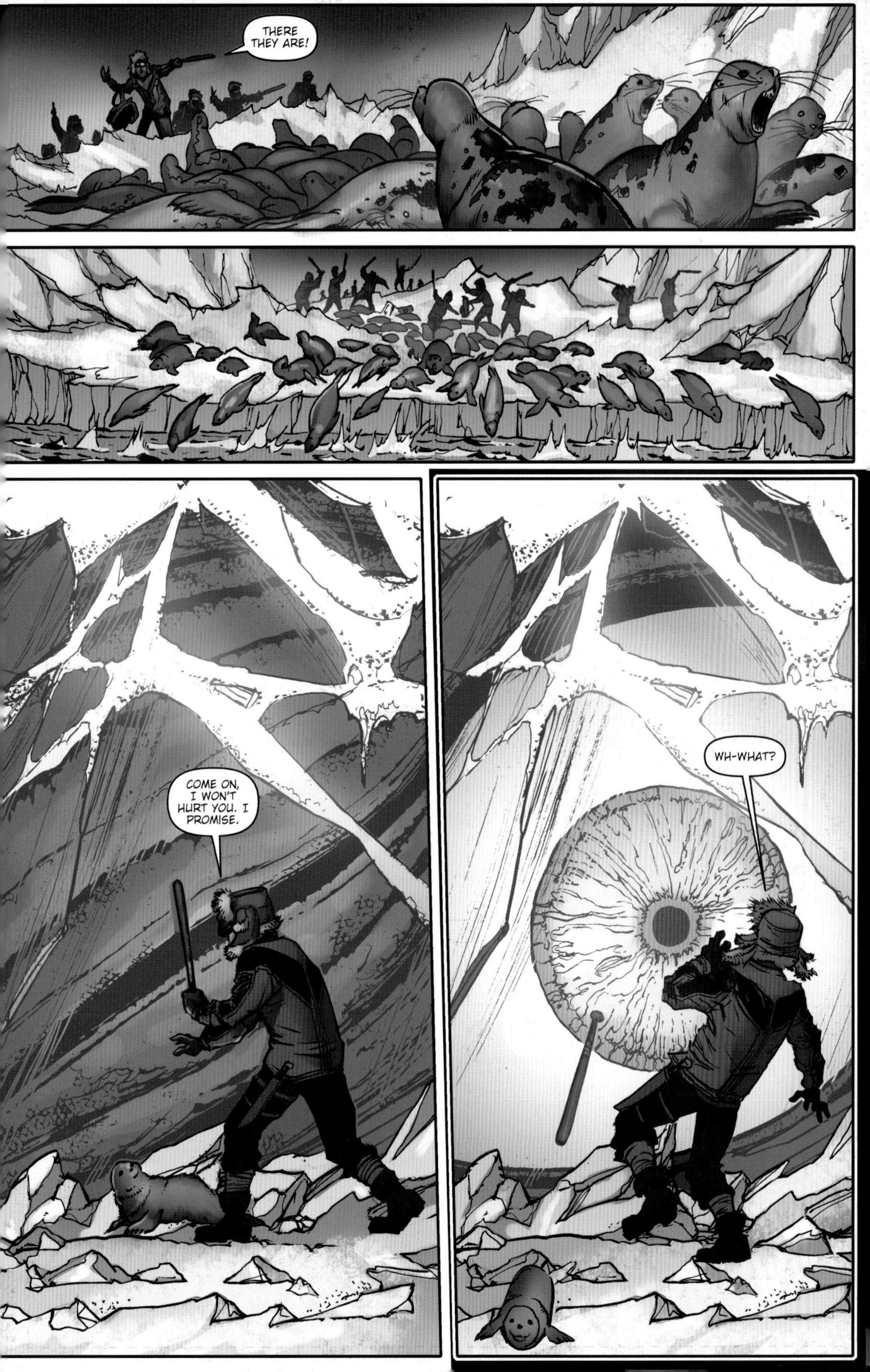
THERE THEY ARE!
COME ON, I WON'T HURT YOU. I PROMISE.
WH-WHAT?

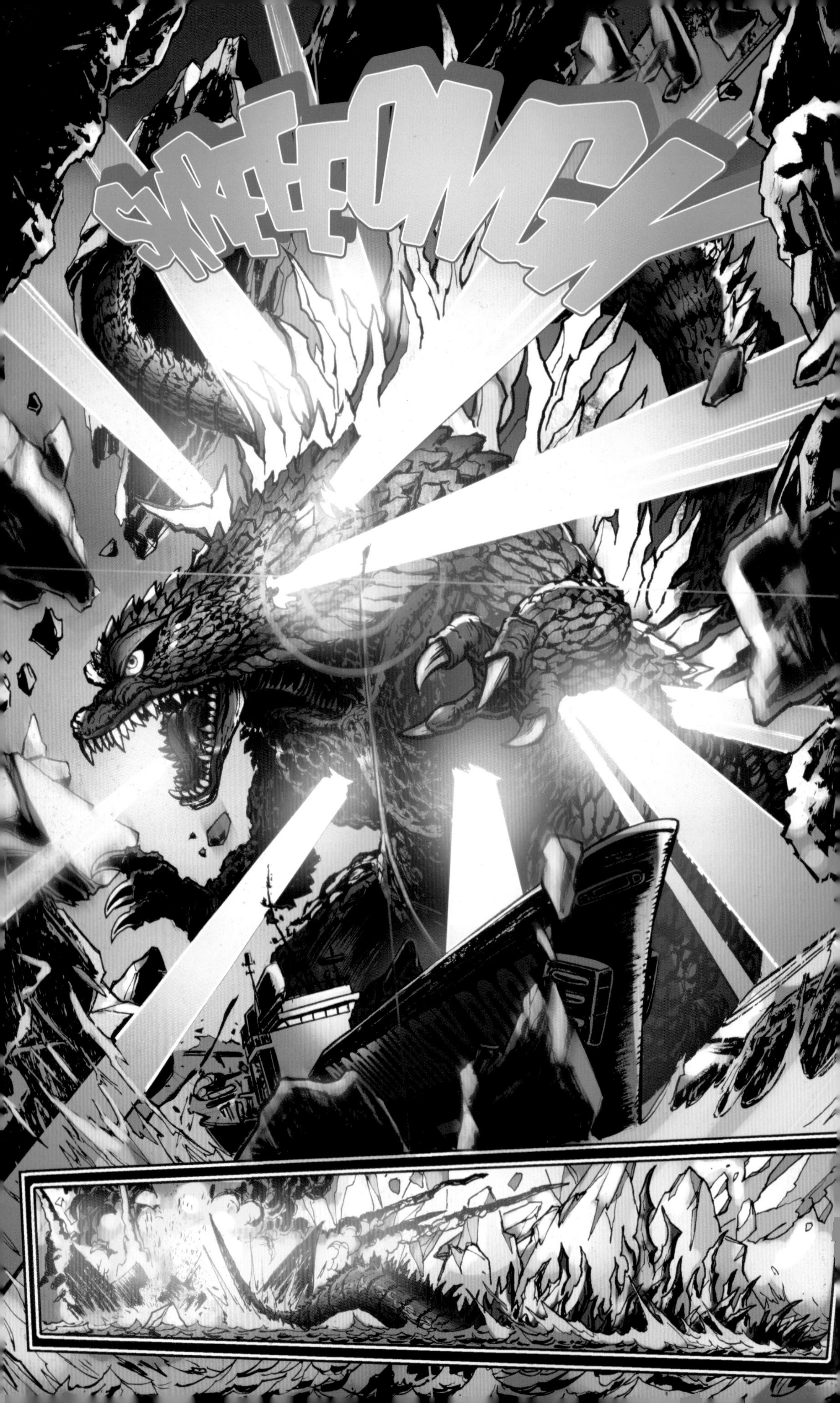
SKREEONGK

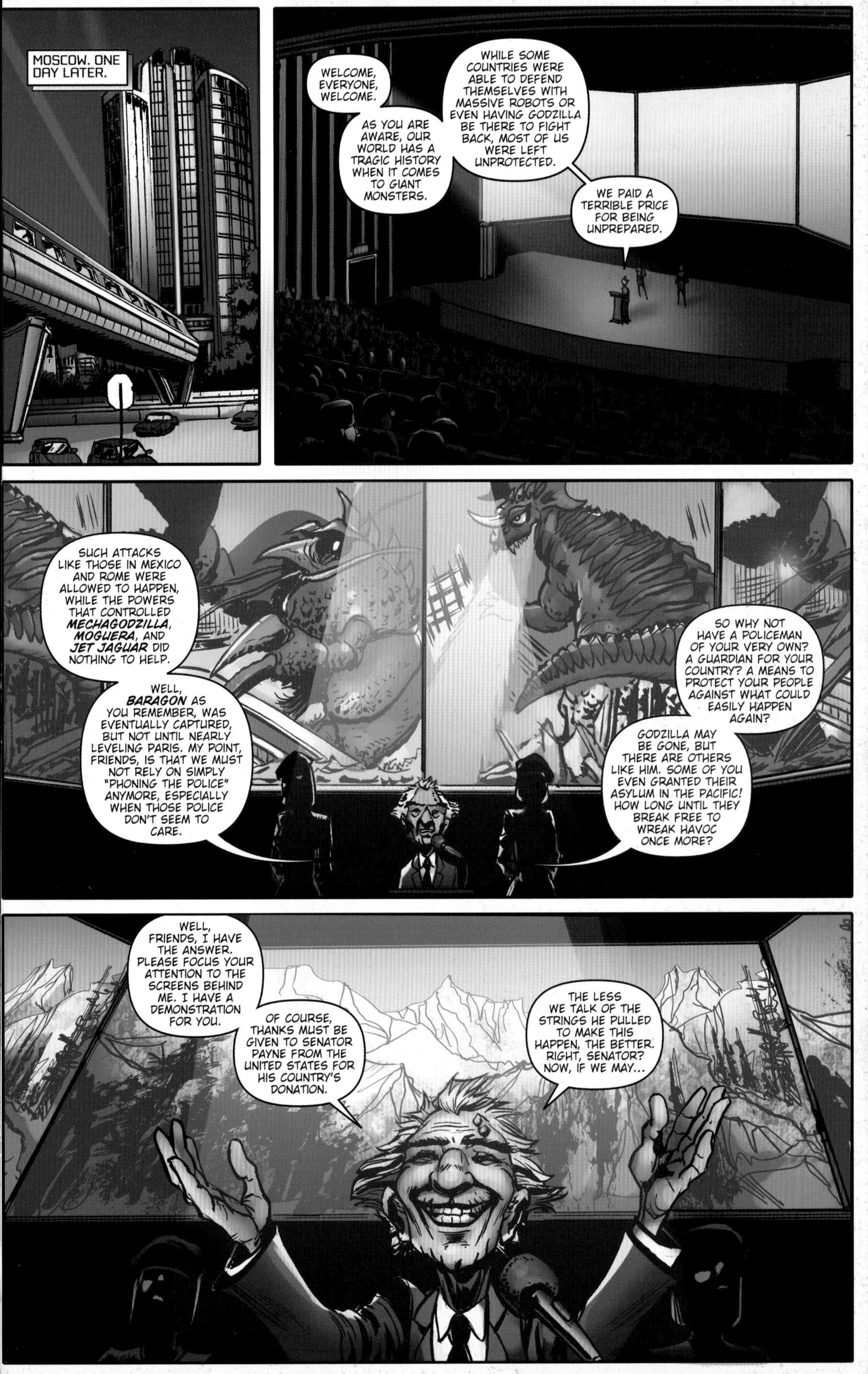
MOSCOW. ONE DAY LATER.
WELCOME, EVERYONE, WELCOME.
AS YOU ARE AWARE, OUR WORLD HAS A TRAGIC HISTORY WHEN IT COMES TO GIANT MONSTERS.
WHILE SOME COUNTRIES WERE ABLE TO DEFEND THEMSELVES WITH MASSIVE ROBOTS OR EVEN HAVING GODZILLA BE THERE TO FIGHT BACK, MOST OF US WERE LEFT UNPROTECTED.
WE PAID A TERRIBLE PRICE FOR BEING UNPREPARED.
SUCH ATTACKS LIKE THOSE IN MEXICO AND ROME WERE ALLOWED TO HAPPEN, WHILE THE POWERS THAT CONTROLLED ***MECHAGODZILLA***, ***MOGUERA***, AND ***JET JAGUAR*** DID NOTHING TO HELP.
WELL, ***BARAGON*** AS YOU REMEMBER, WAS EVENTUALLY CAPTURED, BUT NOT UNTIL NEARLY LEVELING PARIS. MY POINT, FRIENDS, IS THAT WE MUST NOT RELY ON SIMPLY "PHONING THE POLICE" ANYMORE, ESPECIALLY WHEN THOSE POLICE DON'T SEEM TO CARE.
SO WHY NOT HAVE A POLICEMAN OF YOUR VERY OWN? A GUARDIAN FOR YOUR COUNTRY? A MEANS TO PROTECT YOUR PEOPLE AGAINST WHAT COULD EASILY HAPPEN AGAIN?
GODZILLA MAY BE GONE, BUT THERE ARE OTHERS LIKE HIM. SOME OF YOU EVEN GRANTED THEIR ASYLUM IN THE PACIFIC! HOW LONG UNTIL THEY BREAK FREE TO WREAK HAVOC ONCE MORE?
WELL, FRIENDS, I HAVE THE ANSWER. PLEASE FOCUS YOUR ATTENTION TO THE SCREENS BEHIND ME. I HAVE A DEMONSTRATION FOR YOU.
OF COURSE, THANKS MUST BE GIVEN TO SENATOR PAYNE FROM THE UNITED STATES FOR HIS COUNTRY'S DONATION.
THE LESS WE TALK OF THE STRINGS HE PULLED TO MAKE THIS HAPPEN, THE BETTER. RIGHT, SENATOR? NOW, IF WE MAY...

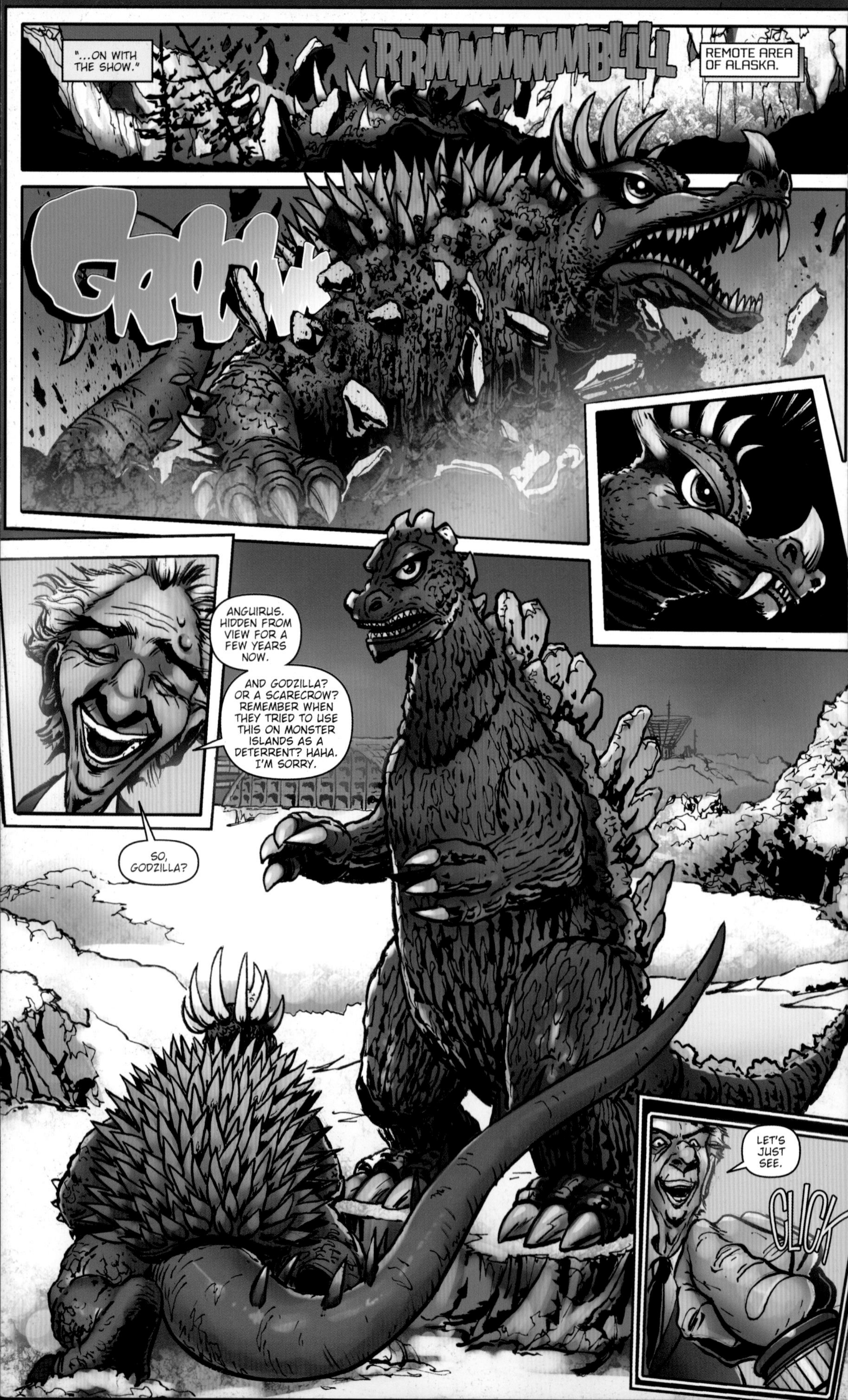
"...ON WITH THE SHOW."
RRRMMMMMMMBLLL
REMOTE AREA OF ALASKA.
GROOOW
ANGUIRUS. HIDDEN FROM VIEW FOR A FEW YEARS NOW.
AND GODZILLA? OR A SCARECROW? REMEMBER WHEN THEY TRIED TO USE THIS ON MONSTER ISLANDS AS A DETERRENT? HAHA. I'M SORRY.
SO, GODZILLA?
LET'S JUST SEE.
CLICK

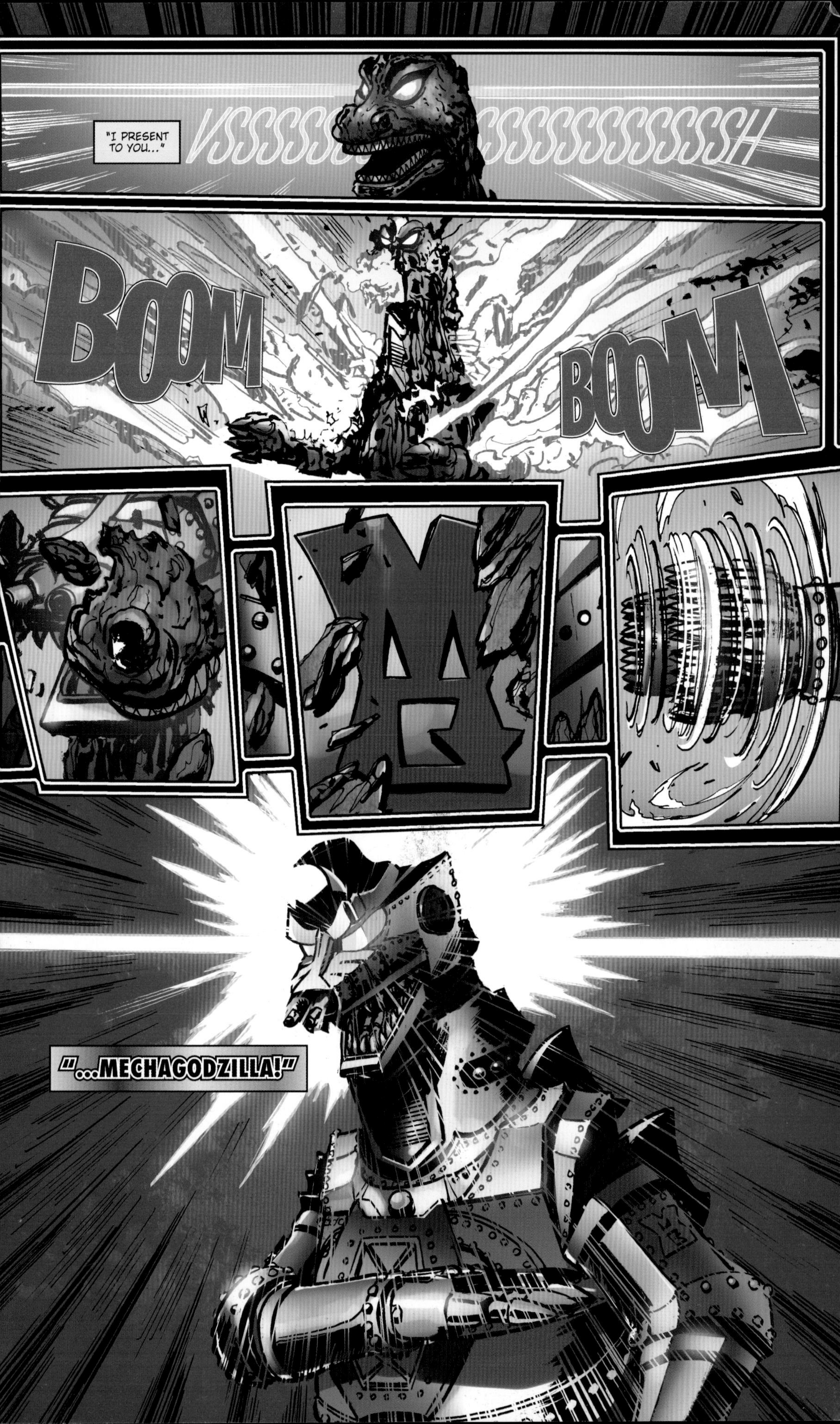
"I PRESENT TO YOU..."
VSSSSSS SSSSSSSSSSSH
BOOM
BOOM
"...MECHAGODZILLA!"

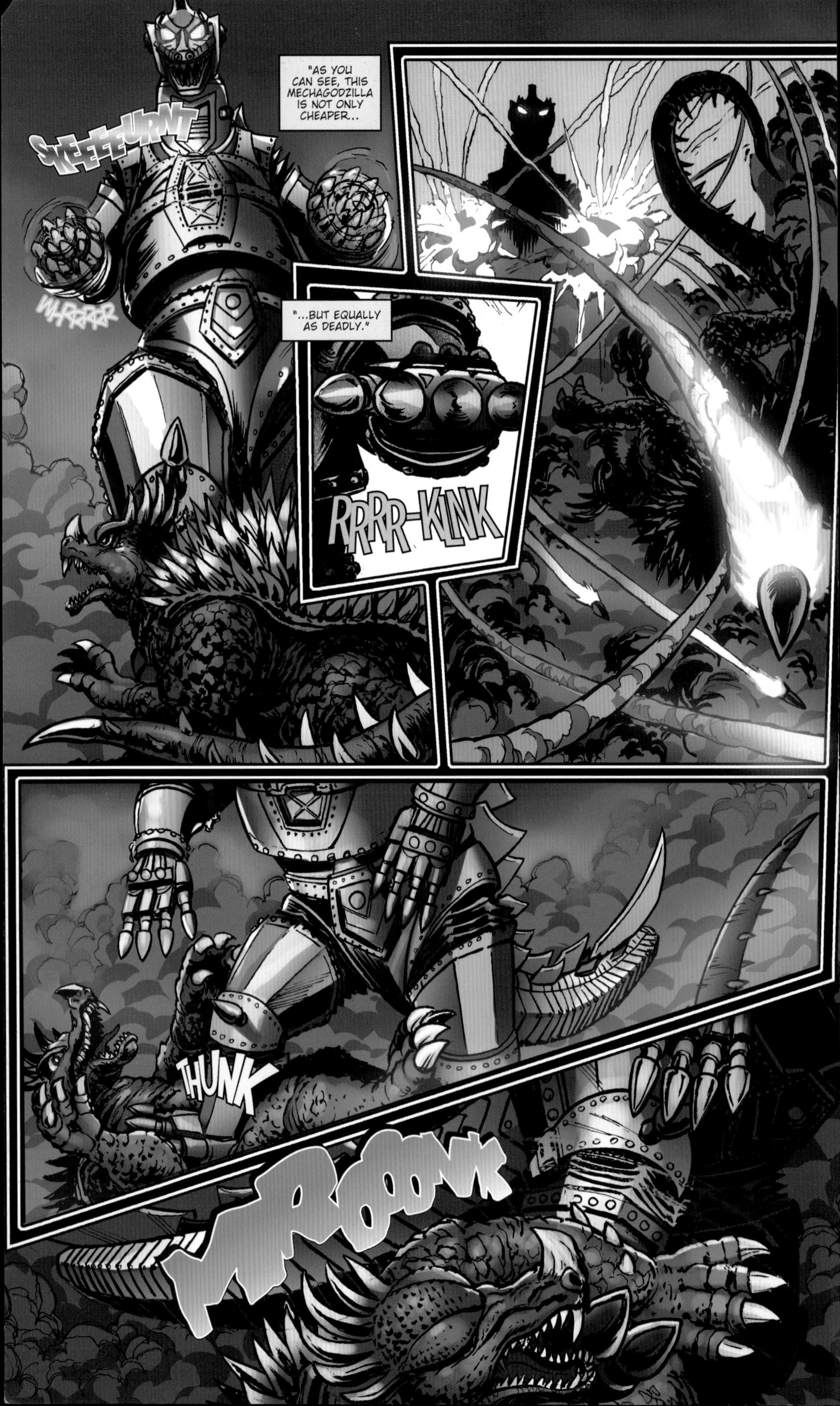
"AS YOU CAN SEE, THIS MECHAGODZILLA IS NOT ONLY CHEAPER...
SKEEEEURNT
WHRRRR
"...BUT EQUALLY AS DEADLY."
RRRR-KLINK
THUNK
WRROOONK

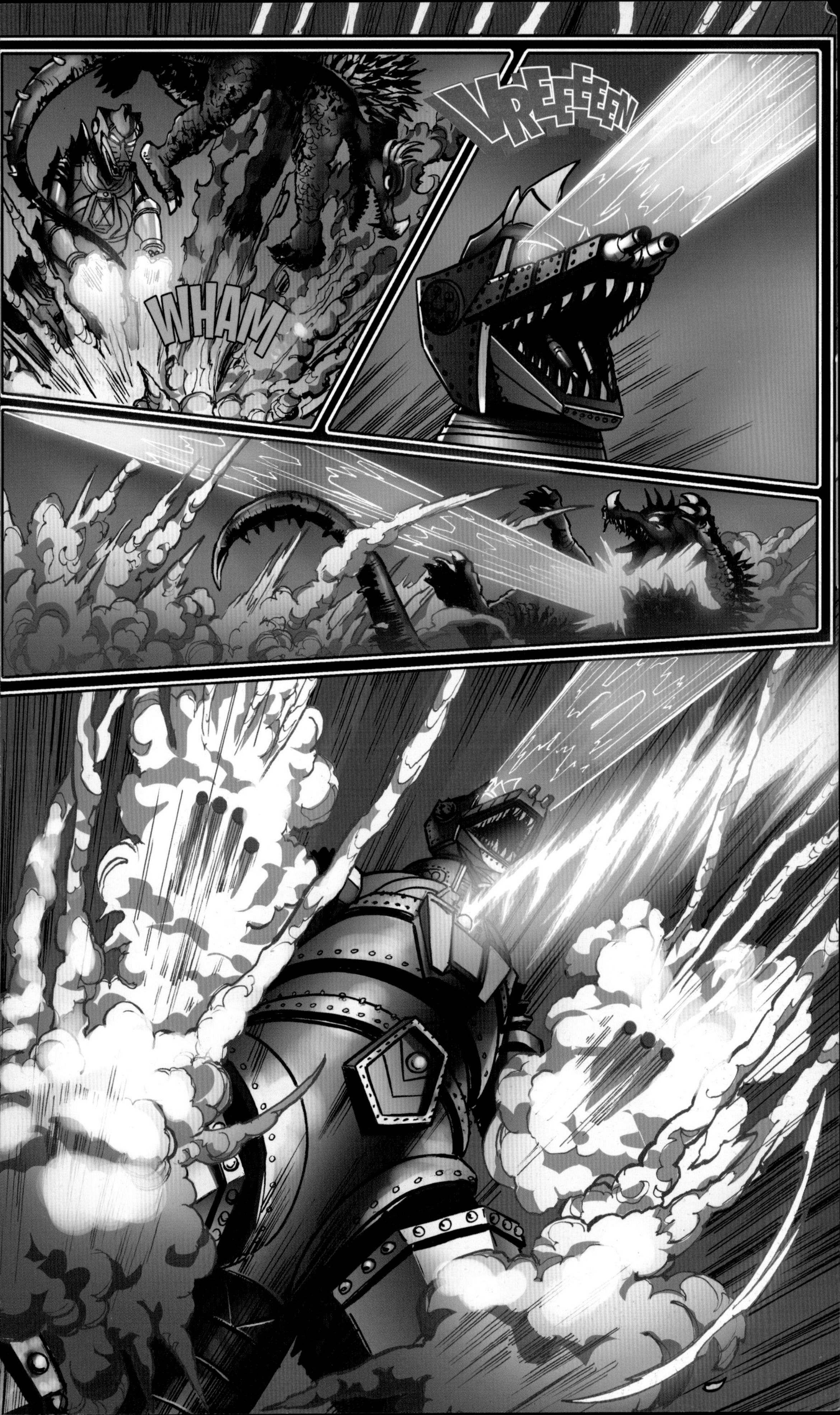
WHAM
VREEEEEN

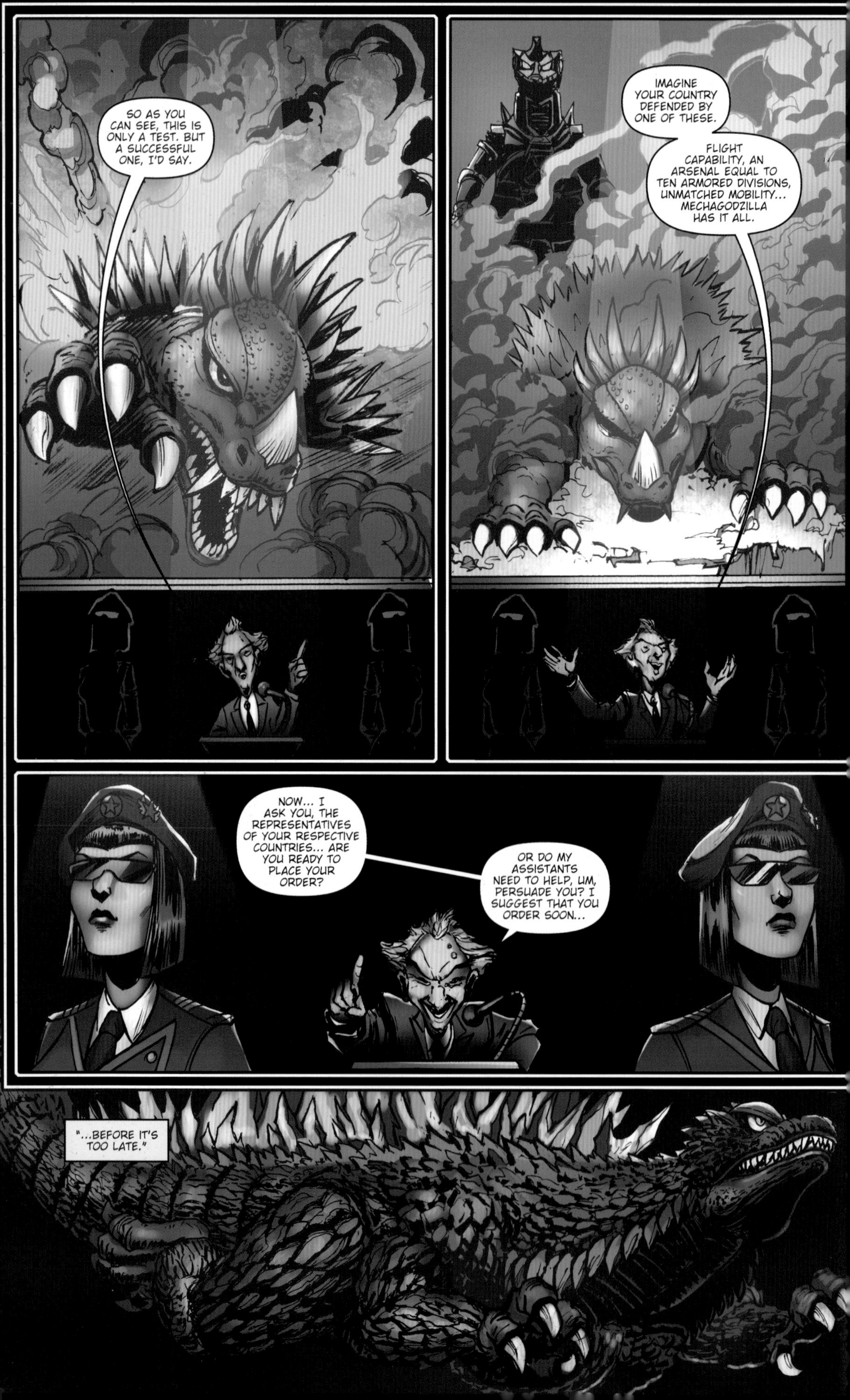
SO AS YOU CAN SEE, THIS IS ONLY A TEST. BUT A SUCCESSFUL ONE, I'D SAY.
IMAGINE YOUR COUNTRY DEFENDED BY ONE OF THESE.
FLIGHT CAPABILITY, AN ARSENAL EQUAL TO TEN ARMORED DIVISIONS, UNMATCHED MOBILITY... MECHAGODZILLA HAS IT ALL.
NOW... I ASK YOU, THE REPRESENTATIVES OF YOUR RESPECTIVE COUNTRIES... ARE YOU READY TO PLACE YOUR ORDER?
OR DO MY ASSISTANTS NEED TO HELP, UM, PERSUADE YOU? I SUGGEST THAT YOU ORDER SOON...
"...BEFORE IT'S TOO LATE."

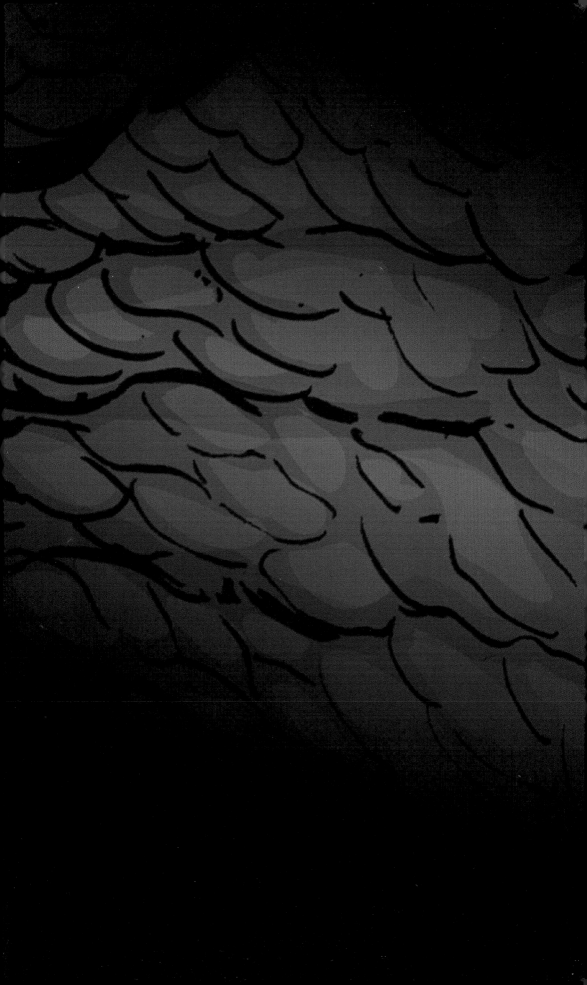

CHAPTER TWO:
STRANGERS

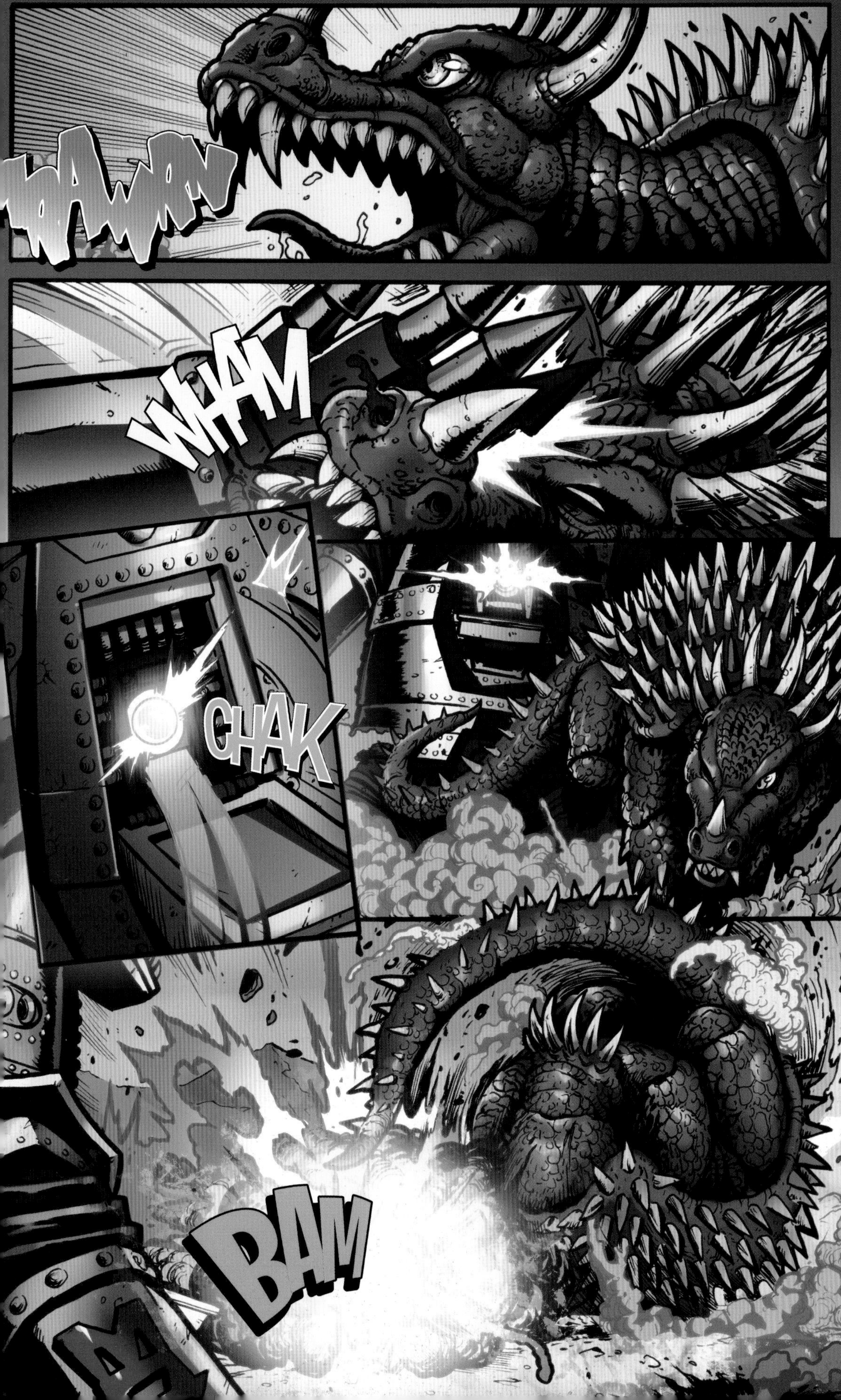

HRAWRR
WHAM
CHAK
BAM

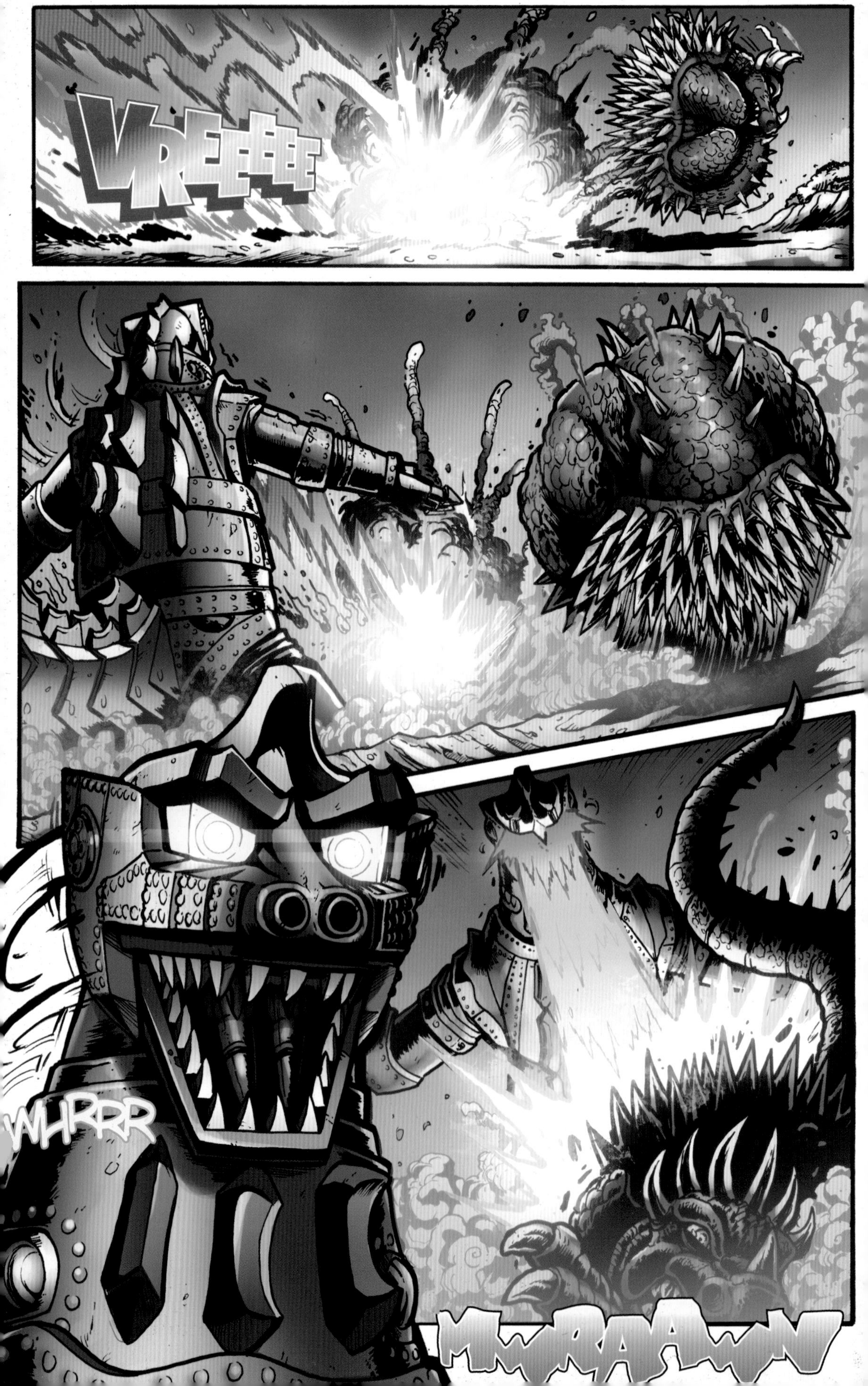
VREEEEE
WHRRR
MWRAAWN

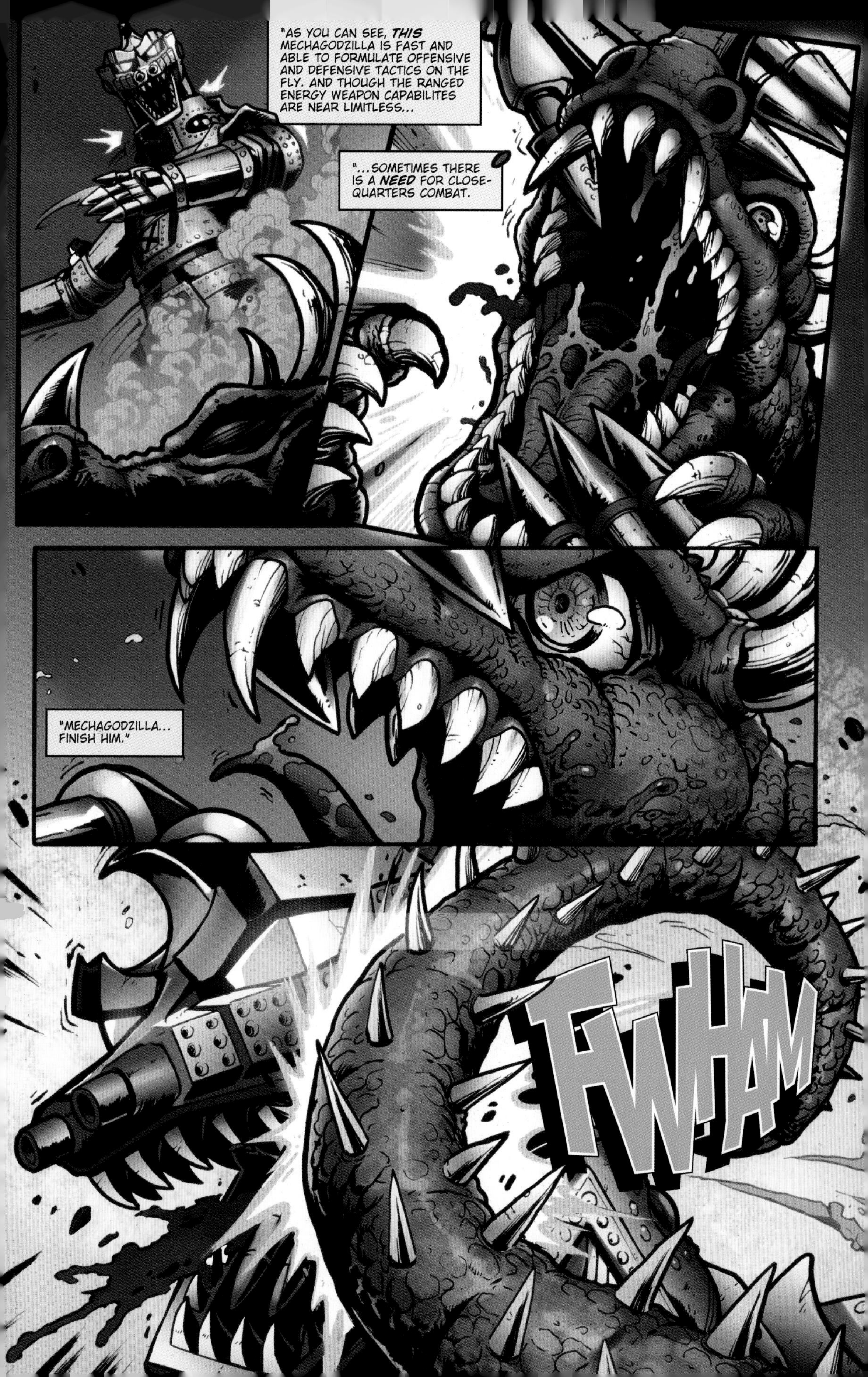
"AS YOU CAN SEE, THIS MECHAGODZILLA IS FAST AND ABLE TO FORMULATE OFFENSIVE AND DEFENSIVE TACTICS ON THE FLY. AND THOUGH THE RANGED ENERGY WEAPON CAPABILITES ARE NEAR LIMITLESS...
"...SOMETIMES THERE IS A NEED FOR CLOSE-QUARTERS COMBAT.
"MECHAGODZILLA... FINISH HIM."
FWHAM

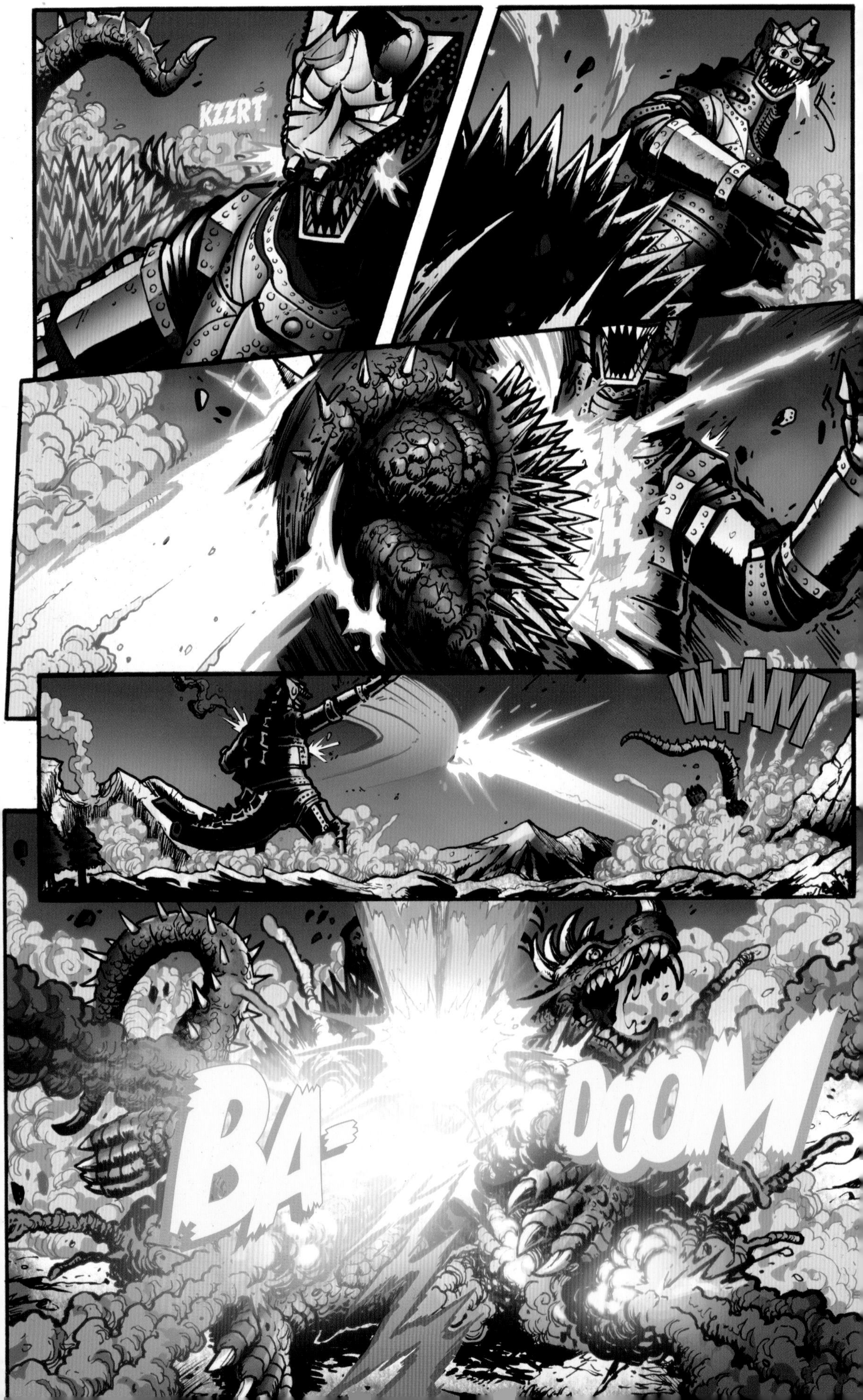
KZZRT
WHAM
BA-
DOOM

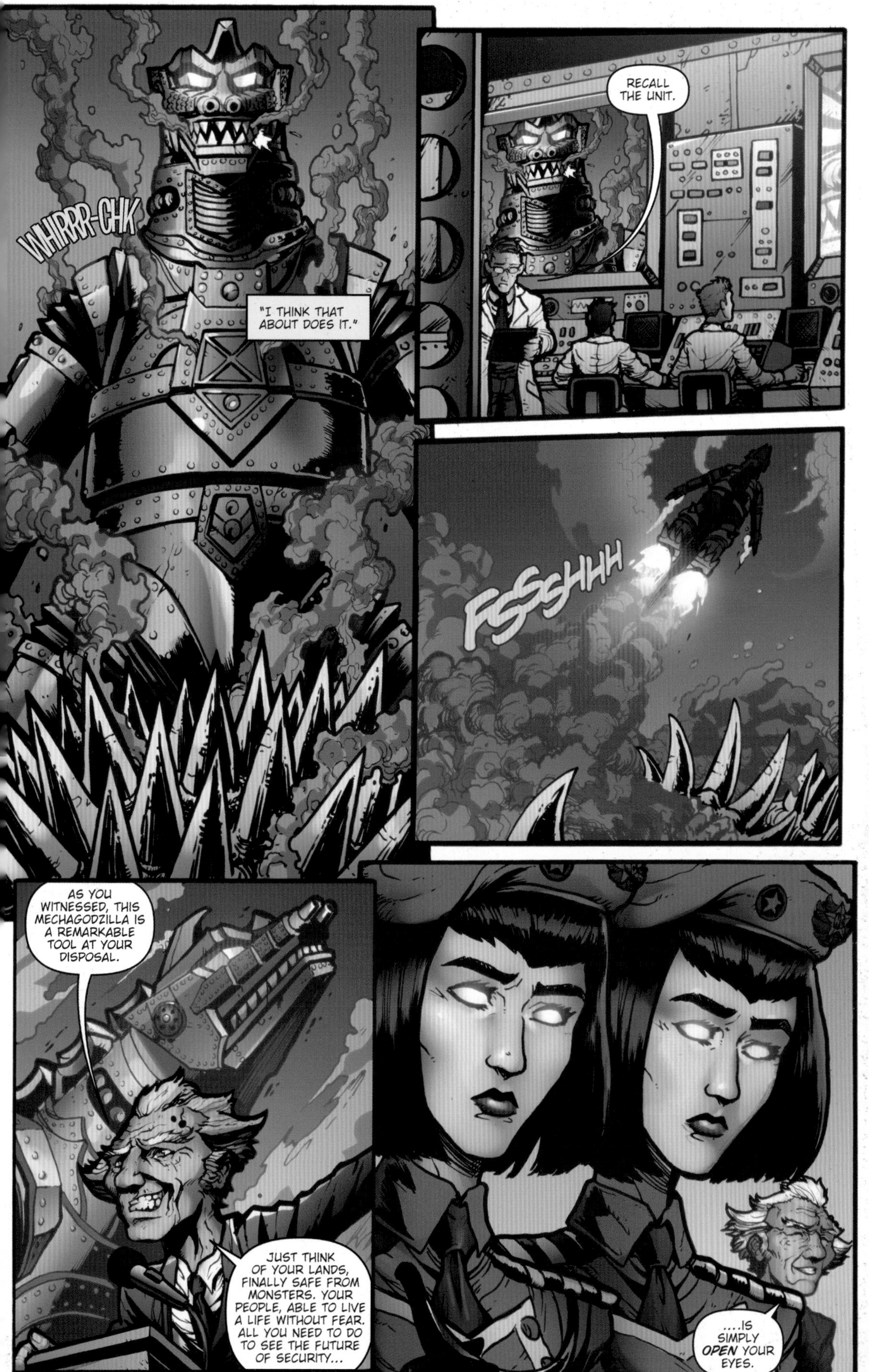
WHIRRR-CHK
"I THINK THAT ABOUT DOES IT."
RECALL THE UNIT.
FSSSHHH
AS YOU WITNESSED, THIS MECHAGODZILLA IS A REMARKABLE TOOL AT YOUR DISPOSAL.
JUST THINK OF YOUR LANDS, FINALLY SAFE FROM MONSTERS. YOUR PEOPLE, ABLE TO LIVE A LIFE WITHOUT FEAR. ALL YOU NEED TO DO TO SEE THE FUTURE OF SECURITY...
....IS SIMPLY *OPEN* YOUR EYES.

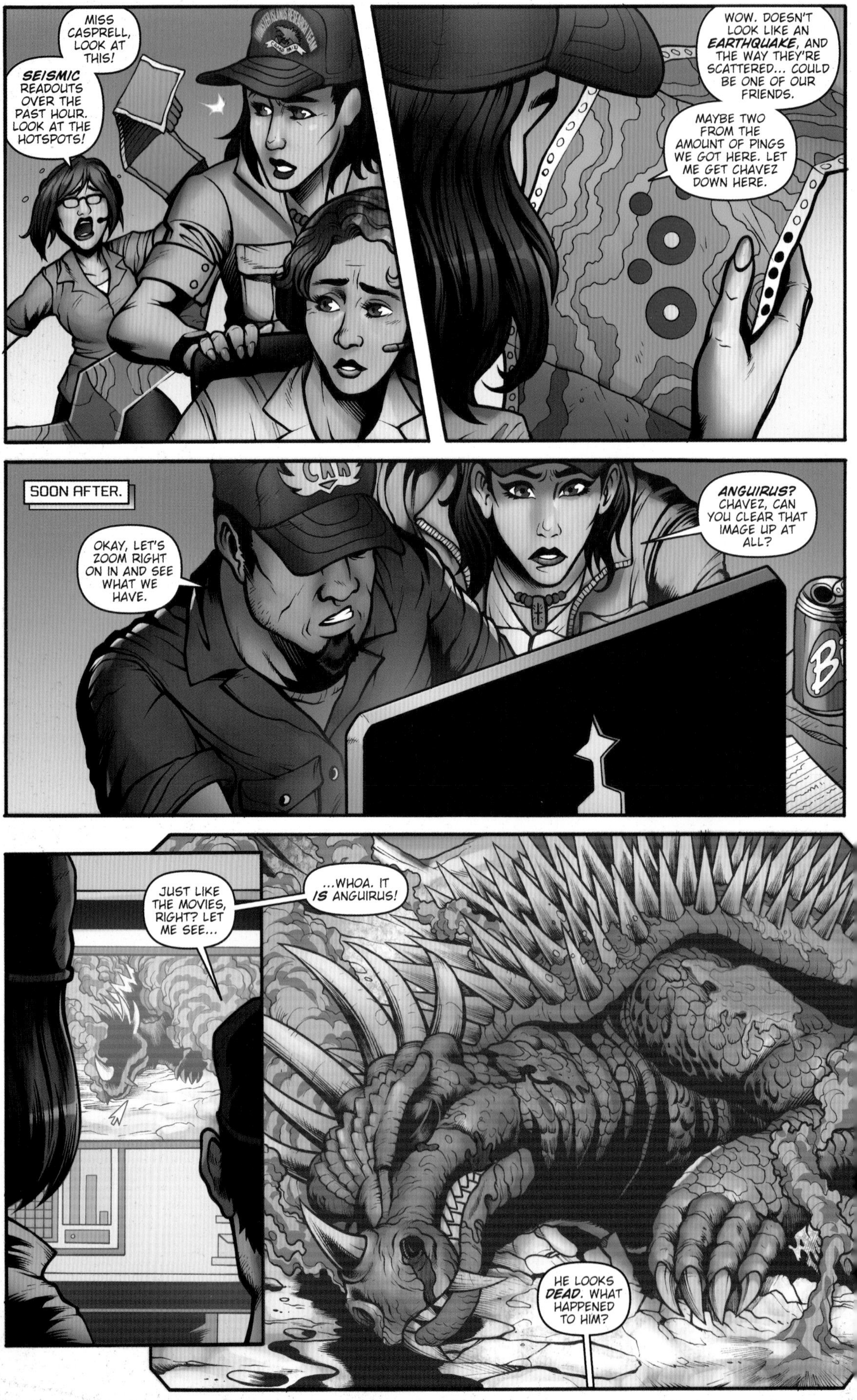
MISS CASPRELL, LOOK AT THIS!
SEISMIC READOUTS OVER THE PAST HOUR. LOOK AT THE HOTSPOTS!
WOW. DOESN'T LOOK LIKE AN EARTHQUAKE, AND THE WAY THEY'RE SCATTERED... COULD BE ONE OF OUR FRIENDS.
MAYBE TWO FROM THE AMOUNT OF PINGS WE GOT HERE. LET ME GET CHAVEZ DOWN HERE.
SOON AFTER.
OKAY, LET'S ZOOM RIGHT ON IN AND SEE WHAT WE HAVE.
ANGUIRUS? CHAVEZ, CAN YOU CLEAR THAT IMAGE UP AT ALL?
JUST LIKE THE MOVIES, RIGHT? LET ME SEE...
...WHOA. IT IS ANGUIRUS!
HE LOOKS DEAD. WHAT HAPPENED TO HIM?

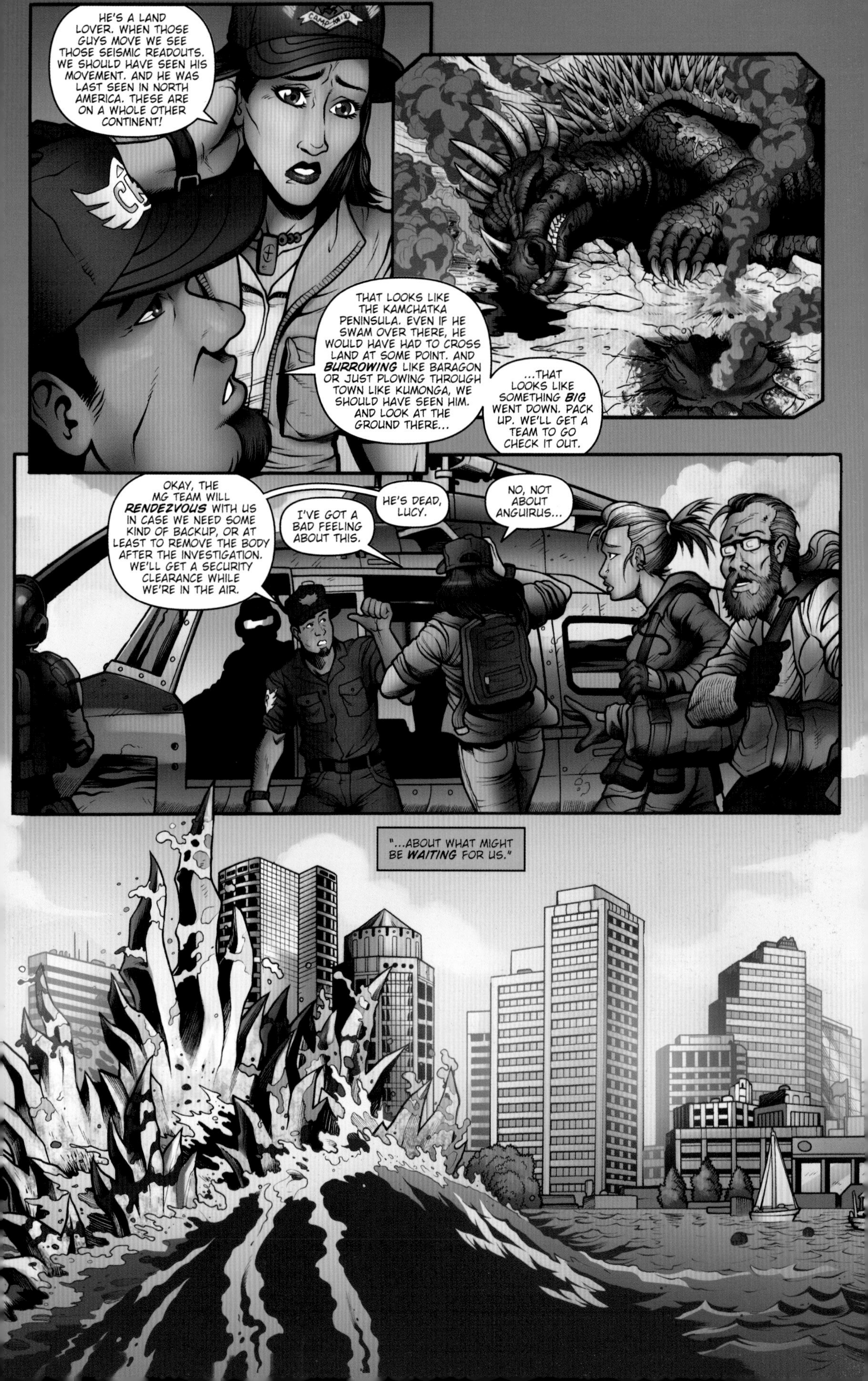
HE'S A LAND LOVER. WHEN THOSE GUYS MOVE WE SEE THOSE SEISMIC READOUTS. WE SHOULD HAVE SEEN HIS MOVEMENT. AND HE WAS LAST SEEN IN NORTH AMERICA. THESE ARE ON A WHOLE OTHER CONTINENT!
THAT LOOKS LIKE THE KAMCHATKA PENINSULA. EVEN IF HE SWAM OVER THERE, HE WOULD HAVE HAD TO CROSS LAND AT SOME POINT. AND BURROWING LIKE BARAGON OR JUST PLOWING THROUGH TOWN LIKE KUMONGA, WE SHOULD HAVE SEEN HIM. AND LOOK AT THE GROUND THERE...
...THAT LOOKS LIKE SOMETHING BIG WENT DOWN. PACK UP. WE'LL GET A TEAM TO GO CHECK IT OUT.
OKAY, THE MG TEAM WILL RENDEZVOUS WITH US IN CASE WE NEED SOME KIND OF BACKUP, OR AT LEAST TO REMOVE THE BODY AFTER THE INVESTIGATION. WE'LL GET A SECURITY CLEARANCE WHILE WE'RE IN THE AIR.
I'VE GOT A BAD FEELING ABOUT THIS.
HE'S DEAD, LUCY.
NO, NOT ABOUT ANGUIRUS...
"...ABOUT WHAT MIGHT BE WAITING FOR US."

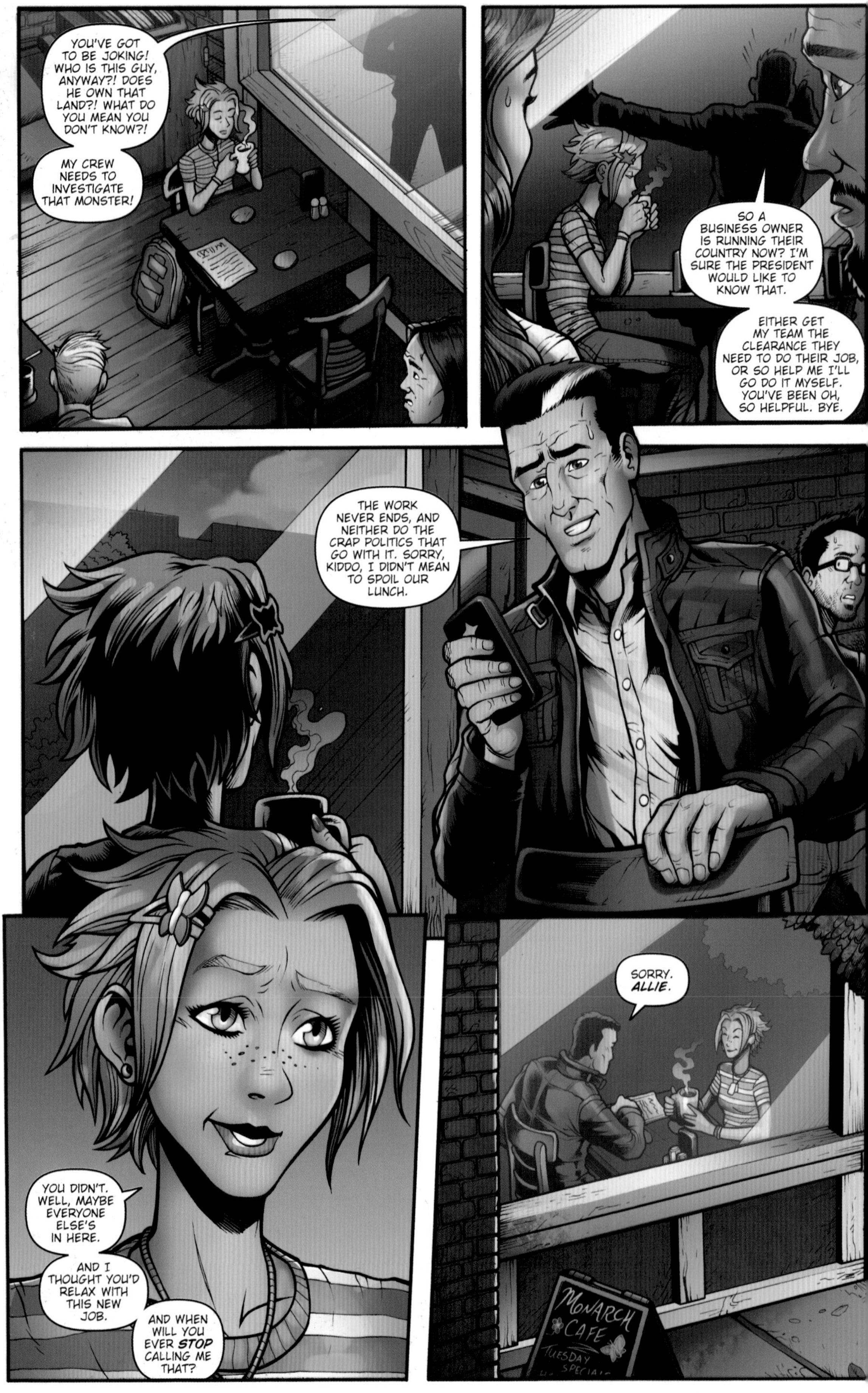

YOU'VE GOT TO BE JOKING! WHO IS THIS GUY, ANYWAY?! DOES HE OWN THAT LAND?! WHAT DO YOU MEAN YOU DON'T KNOW?!
MY CREW NEEDS TO INVESTIGATE THAT MONSTER!
SO A BUSINESS OWNER IS RUNNING THEIR COUNTRY NOW? I'M SURE THE PRESIDENT WOULD LIKE TO KNOW THAT.
EITHER GET MY TEAM THE CLEARANCE THEY NEED TO DO THEIR JOB, OR SO HELP ME I'LL GO DO IT MYSELF. YOU'VE BEEN OH, SO HELPFUL. BYE.
THE WORK NEVER ENDS, AND NEITHER DO THE CRAP POLITICS THAT GO WITH IT. SORRY, KIDDO, I DIDN'T MEAN TO SPOIL OUR LUNCH.
YOU DIDN'T. WELL, MAYBE EVERYONE ELSE'S IN HERE.
AND I THOUGHT YOU'D RELAX WITH THIS NEW JOB.
AND WHEN WILL YOU EVER **STOP** CALLING ME THAT?
SORRY. ***ALLIE.***
MONARCH CAFE
TUESDAY

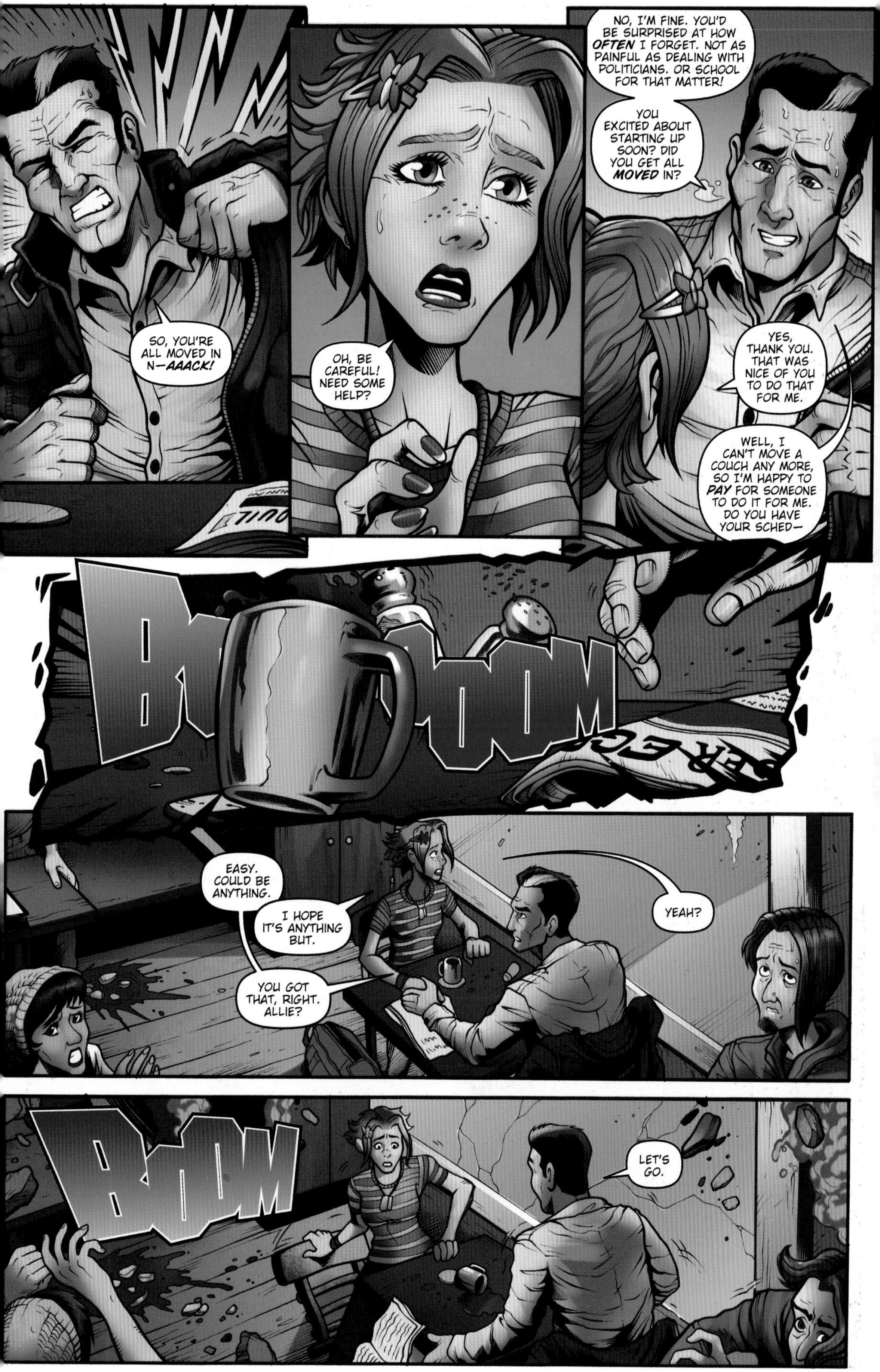
SO, YOU'RE ALL MOVED IN N—AAACK!
OH, BE CAREFUL! NEED SOME HELP?
NO, I'M FINE. YOU'D BE SURPRISED AT HOW OFTEN I FORGET. NOT AS PAINFUL AS DEALING WITH POLITICIANS. OR SCHOOL FOR THAT MATTER!
YOU EXCITED ABOUT STARTING UP SOON? DID YOU GET ALL MOVED IN?
YES, THANK YOU. THAT WAS NICE OF YOU TO DO THAT FOR ME.
WELL, I CAN'T MOVE A COUCH ANY MORE, SO I'M HAPPY TO PAY FOR SOMEONE TO DO IT FOR ME. DO YOU HAVE YOUR SCHED—
EASY. COULD BE ANYTHING.
I HOPE IT'S ANYTHING BUT.
YOU GOT THAT, RIGHT. ALLIE?
YEAH?
BOOM
LET'S GO.

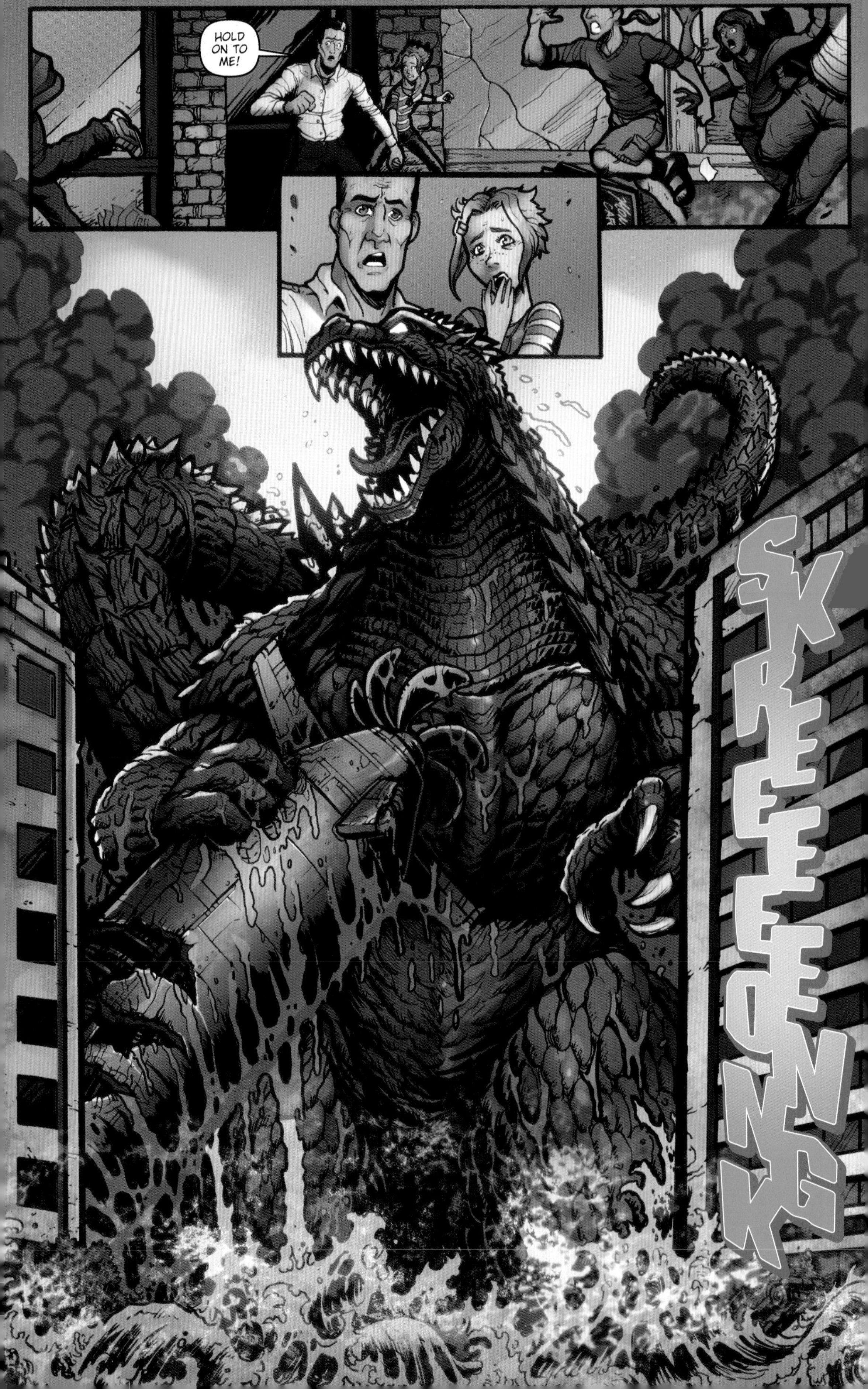

HOLD ON TO ME!
SKREEEONNGK

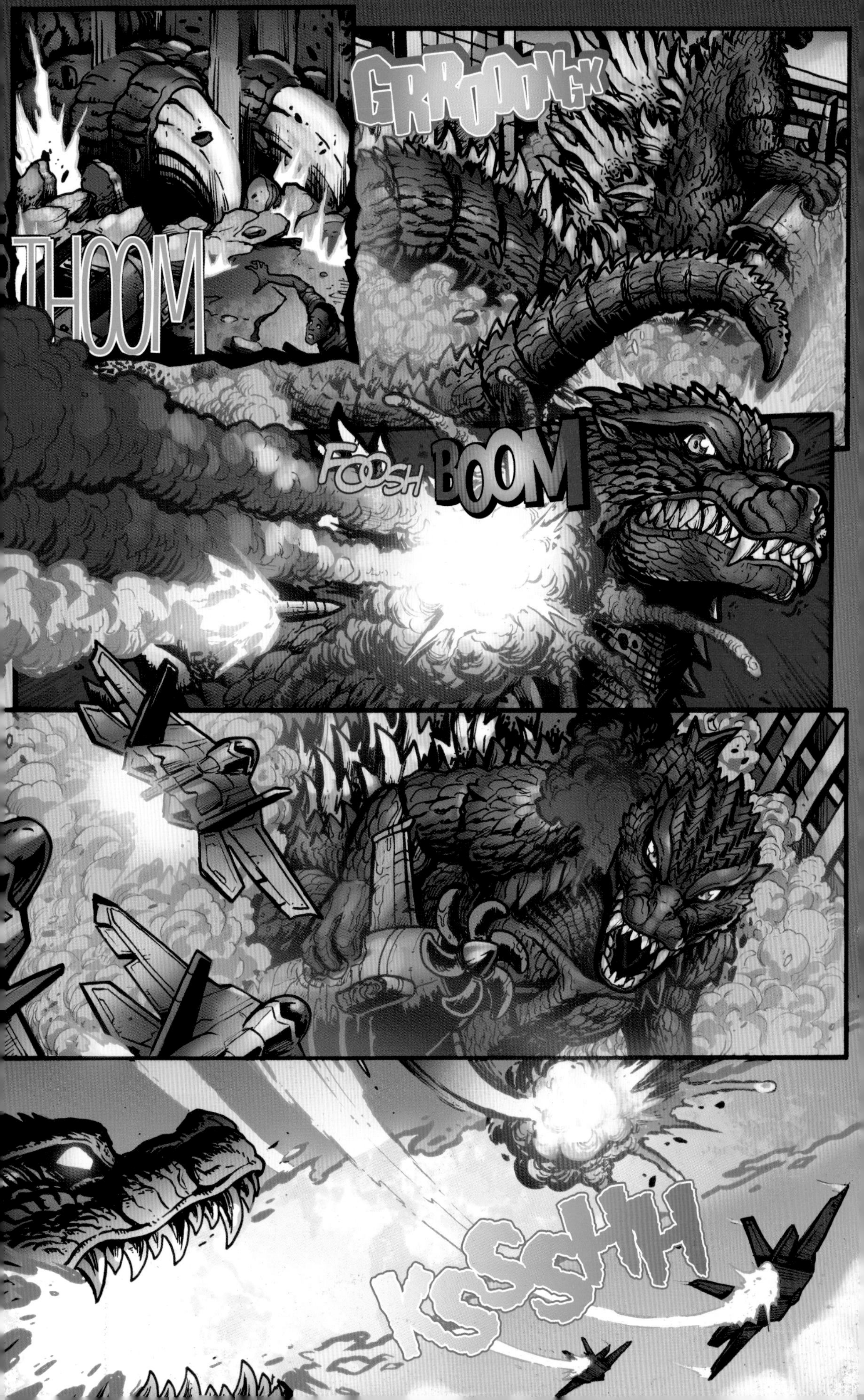
THOOM
GRROOONGK
FOOSH
BOOM
KSSHH

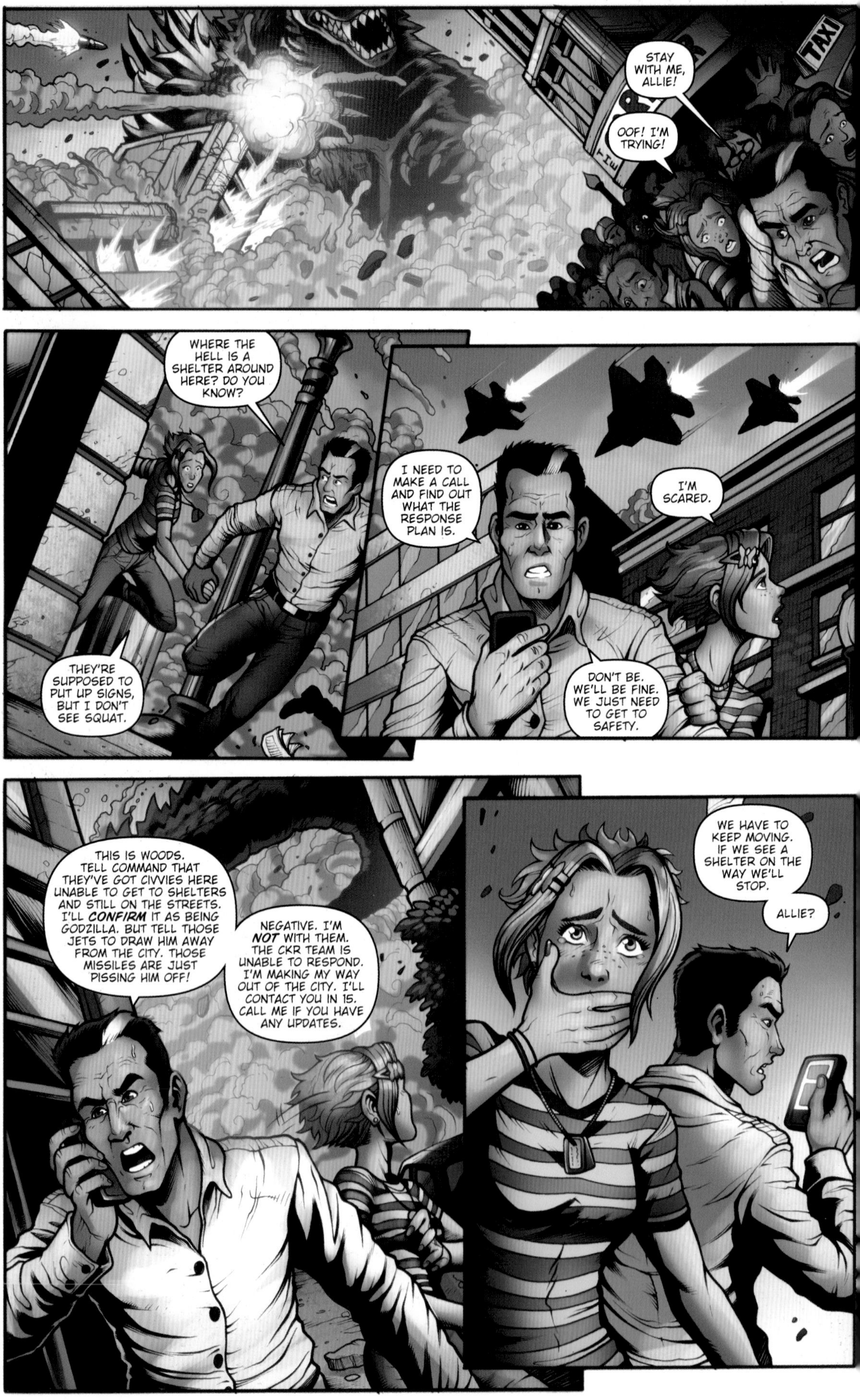
STAY WITH ME, ALLIE!
OOF! I'M TRYING!
WHERE THE HELL IS A SHELTER AROUND HERE? DO YOU KNOW?
THEY'RE SUPPOSED TO PUT UP SIGNS, BUT I DON'T SEE SQUAT.
I NEED TO MAKE A CALL AND FIND OUT WHAT THE RESPONSE PLAN IS.
I'M SCARED.
DON'T BE. WE'LL BE FINE. WE JUST NEED TO GET TO SAFETY.
THIS IS WOODS. TELL COMMAND THAT THEY'VE GOT CIVVIES HERE UNABLE TO GET TO SHELTERS AND STILL ON THE STREETS. I'LL CONFIRM IT AS BEING GODZILLA. BUT TELL THOSE JETS TO DRAW HIM AWAY FROM THE CITY. THOSE MISSILES ARE JUST PISSING HIM OFF!
NEGATIVE. I'M NOT WITH THEM. THE CKR TEAM IS UNABLE TO RESPOND. I'M MAKING MY WAY OUT OF THE CITY. I'LL CONTACT YOU IN 15. CALL ME IF YOU HAVE ANY UPDATES.
WE HAVE TO KEEP MOVING. IF WE SEE A SHELTER ON THE WAY WE'LL STOP.
ALLIE?

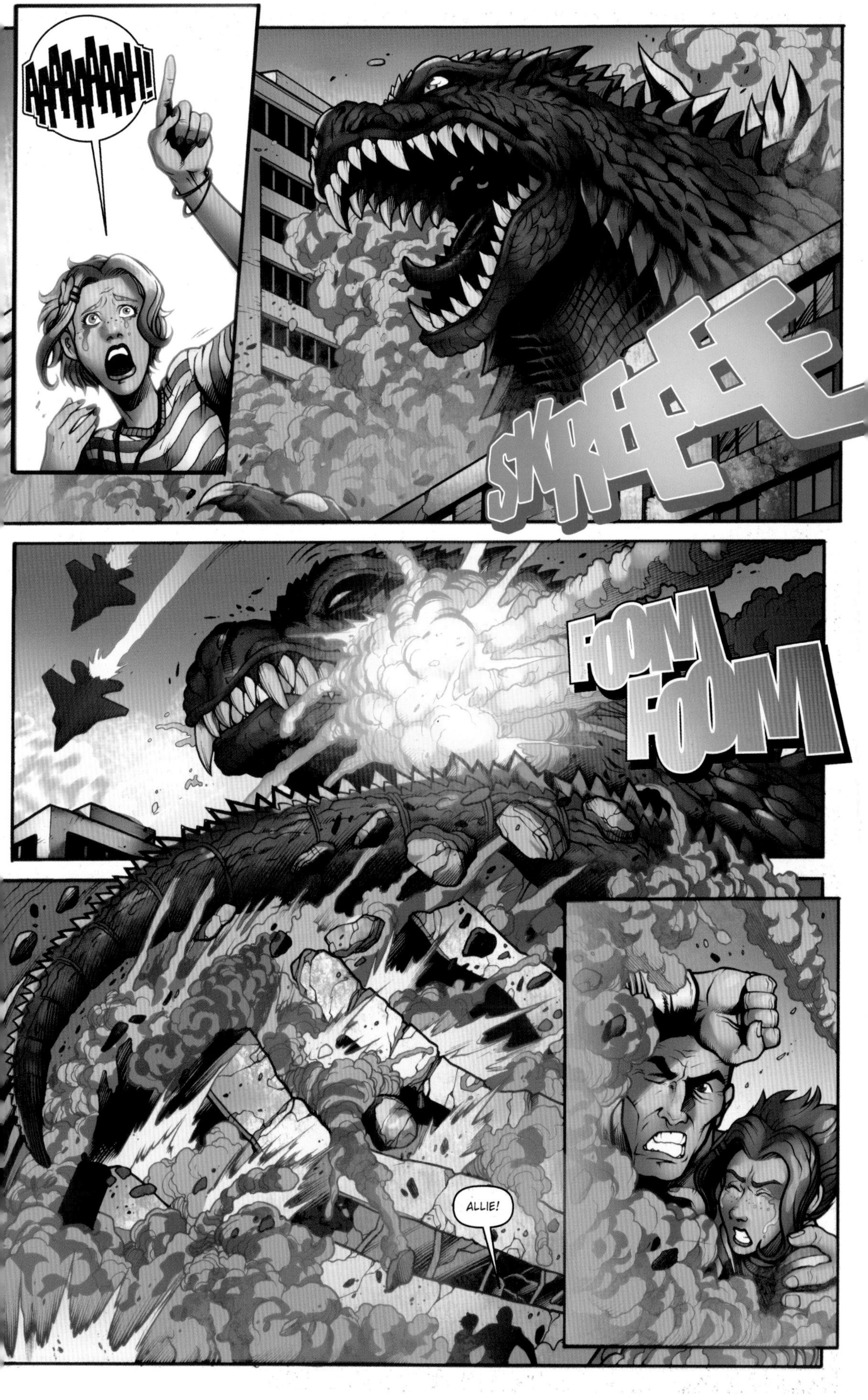
AAAAAAAH!
SKREEEE
FOOM
FOOM
ALLIE!

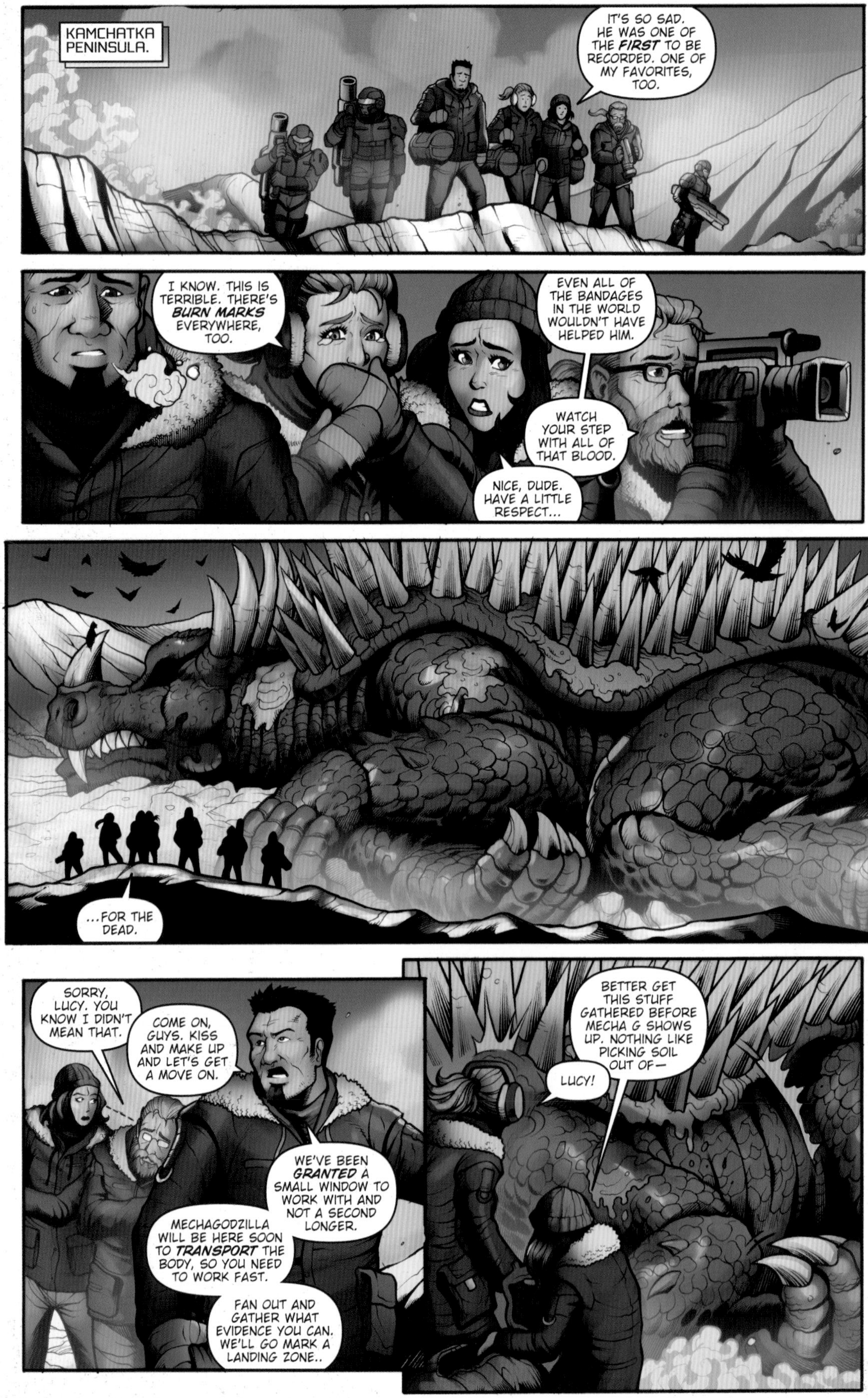
KAMCHATKA PENINSULA.
IT'S SO SAD. HE WAS ONE OF THE FIRST TO BE RECORDED. ONE OF MY FAVORITES, TOO.
I KNOW. THIS IS TERRIBLE. THERE'S BURN MARKS EVERYWHERE, TOO.
EVEN ALL OF THE BANDAGES IN THE WORLD WOULDN'T HAVE HELPED HIM.
WATCH YOUR STEP WITH ALL OF THAT BLOOD.
NICE, DUDE. HAVE A LITTLE RESPECT...
...FOR THE DEAD.
SORRY, LUCY. YOU KNOW I DIDN'T MEAN THAT.
COME ON, GUYS. KISS AND MAKE UP AND LET'S GET A MOVE ON.
WE'VE BEEN GRANTED A SMALL WINDOW TO WORK WITH AND NOT A SECOND LONGER.
MECHAGODZILLA WILL BE HERE SOON TO TRANSPORT THE BODY, SO YOU NEED TO WORK FAST.
FAN OUT AND GATHER WHAT EVIDENCE YOU CAN. WE'LL GO MARK A LANDING ZONE..
BETTER GET THIS STUFF GATHERED BEFORE MECHA G SHOWS UP. NOTHING LIKE PICKING SOIL OUT OF—
LUCY!

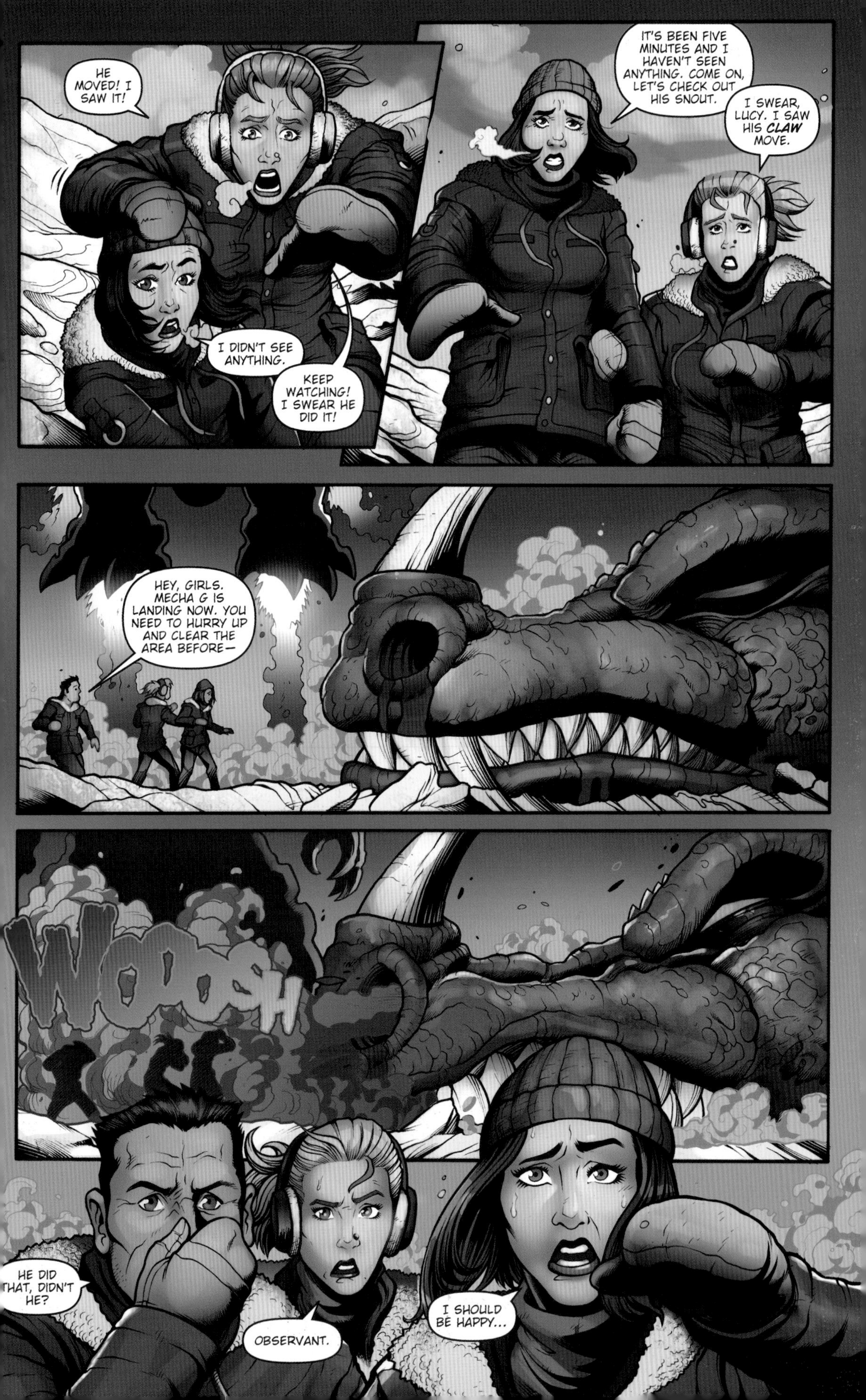
HE MOVED! I SAW IT!
I DIDN'T SEE ANYTHING.
KEEP WATCHING! I SWEAR HE DID IT!
IT'S BEEN FIVE MINUTES AND I HAVEN'T SEEN ANYTHING. COME ON, LET'S CHECK OUT HIS SNOUT.
I SWEAR, LUCY. I SAW HIS CLAW MOVE.
HEY, GIRLS. MECHA G IS LANDING NOW. YOU NEED TO HURRY UP AND CLEAR THE AREA BEFORE—
WOOSH
HE DID THAT, DIDN'T HE?
OBSERVANT.
I SHOULD BE HAPPY...

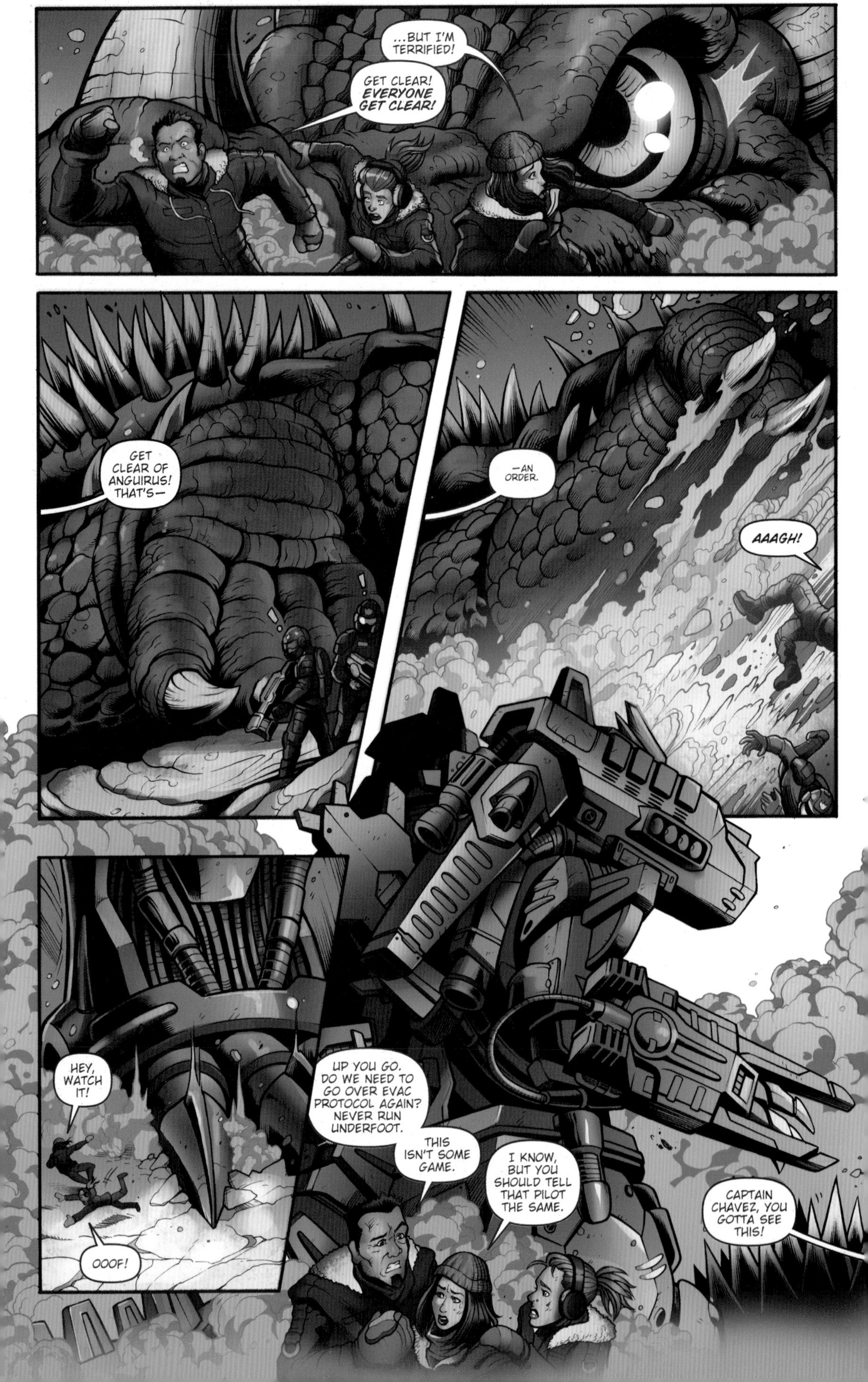

...BUT I'M TERRIFIED!
GET CLEAR! EVERYONE GET CLEAR!
GET CLEAR OF ANGUIRUS! THAT'S—
—AN ORDER.
AAAGH!
HEY, WATCH IT!
OOOF!
UP YOU GO. DO WE NEED TO GO OVER EVAC PROTOCOL AGAIN? NEVER RUN UNDERFOOT.
THIS ISN'T SOME GAME.
I KNOW, BUT YOU SHOULD TELL THAT PILOT THE SAME.
CAPTAIN CHAVEZ, YOU GOTTA SEE THIS!

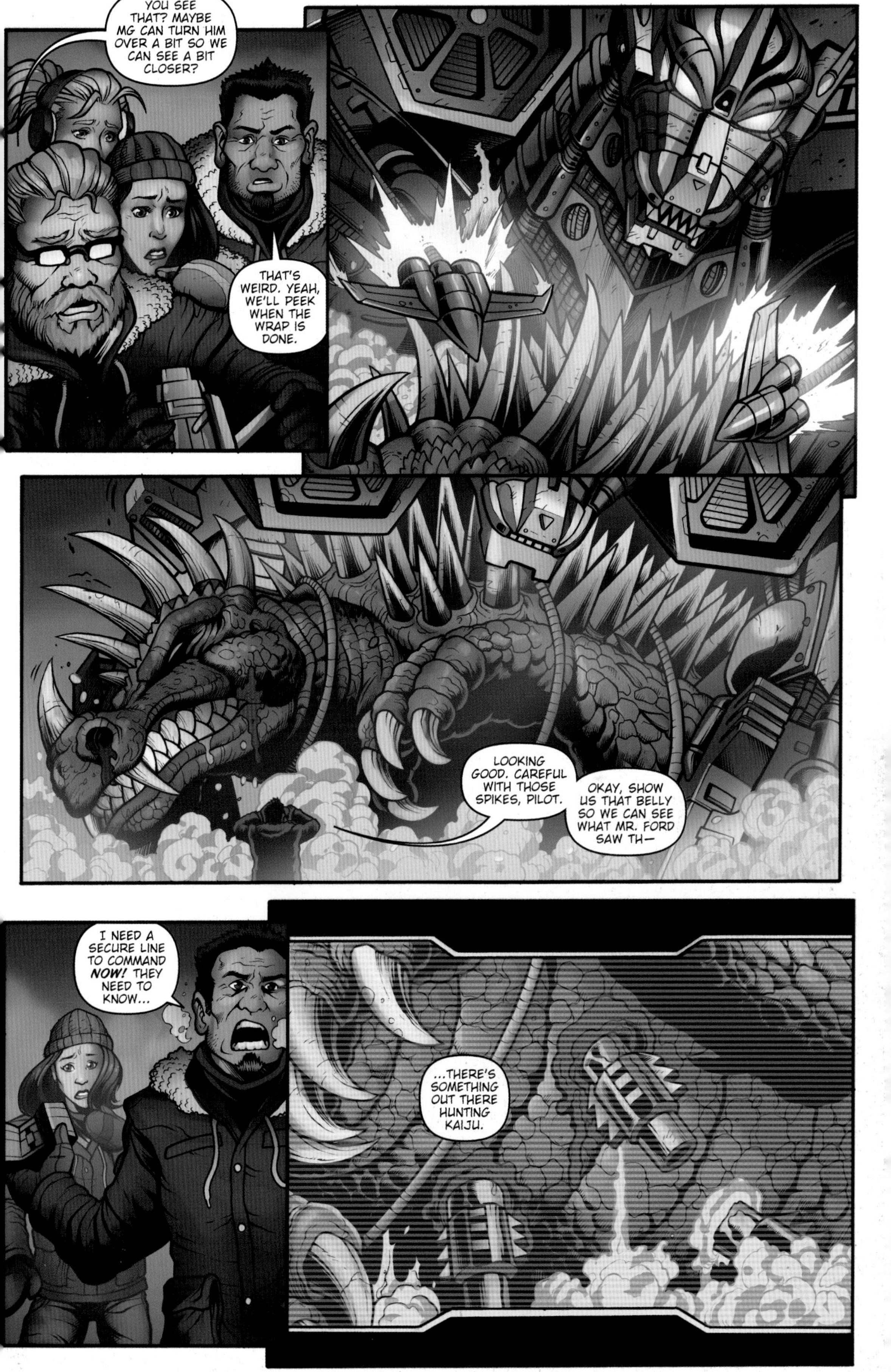
YOU SEE THAT? MAYBE MG CAN TURN HIM OVER A BIT SO WE CAN SEE A BIT CLOSER?
THAT'S WEIRD. YEAH, WE'LL PEEK WHEN THE WRAP IS DONE.
LOOKING GOOD. CAREFUL WITH THOSE SPIKES, PILOT.
OKAY, SHOW US THAT BELLY SO WE CAN SEE WHAT MR. FORD SAW TH—
I NEED A SECURE LINE TO COMMAND ***NOW!*** THEY NEED TO KNOW...
...THERE'S SOMETHING OUT THERE HUNTING KAIJU.

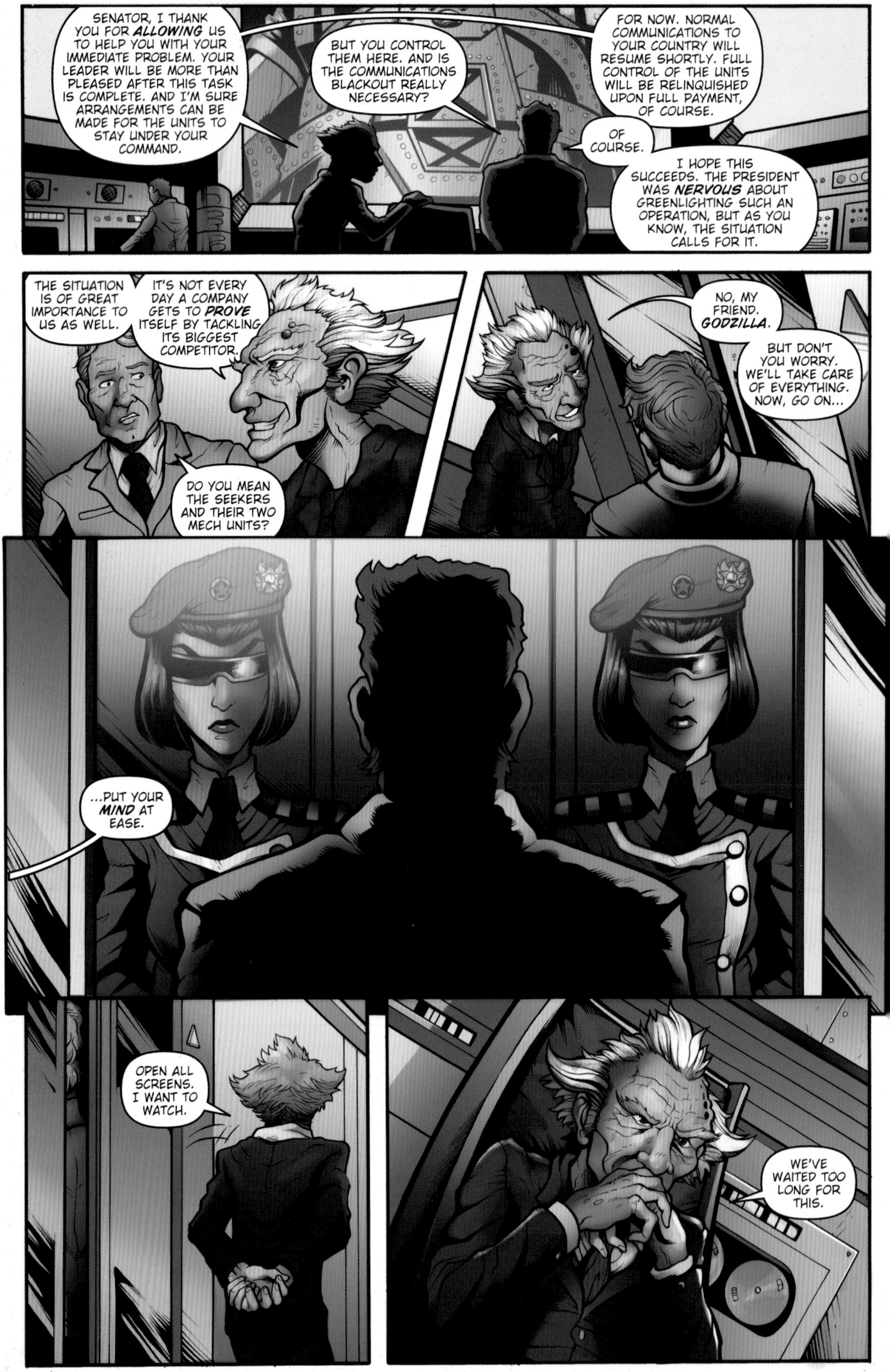

SENATOR, I THANK YOU FOR ALLOWING US TO HELP YOU WITH YOUR IMMEDIATE PROBLEM. YOUR LEADER WILL BE MORE THAN PLEASED AFTER THIS TASK IS COMPLETE. AND I'M SURE ARRANGEMENTS CAN BE MADE FOR THE UNITS TO STAY UNDER YOUR COMMAND.
BUT YOU CONTROL THEM HERE. AND IS THE COMMUNICATIONS BLACKOUT REALLY NECESSARY?
FOR NOW. NORMAL COMMUNICATIONS TO YOUR COUNTRY WILL RESUME SHORTLY. FULL CONTROL OF THE UNITS WILL BE RELINQUISHED UPON FULL PAYMENT, OF COURSE.
OF COURSE.
I HOPE THIS SUCCEEDS. THE PRESIDENT WAS NERVOUS ABOUT GREENLIGHTING SUCH AN OPERATION, BUT AS YOU KNOW, THE SITUATION CALLS FOR IT.
THE SITUATION IS OF GREAT IMPORTANCE TO US AS WELL.
IT'S NOT EVERY DAY A COMPANY GETS TO PROVE ITSELF BY TACKLING ITS BIGGEST COMPETITOR.
DO YOU MEAN THE SEEKERS AND THEIR TWO MECH UNITS?
NO, MY FRIEND. GODZILLA.
BUT DON'T YOU WORRY. WE'LL TAKE CARE OF EVERYTHING. NOW, GO ON...
...PUT YOUR MIND AT EASE.
OPEN ALL SCREENS. I WANT TO WATCH.
WE'VE WAITED TOO LONG FOR THIS.

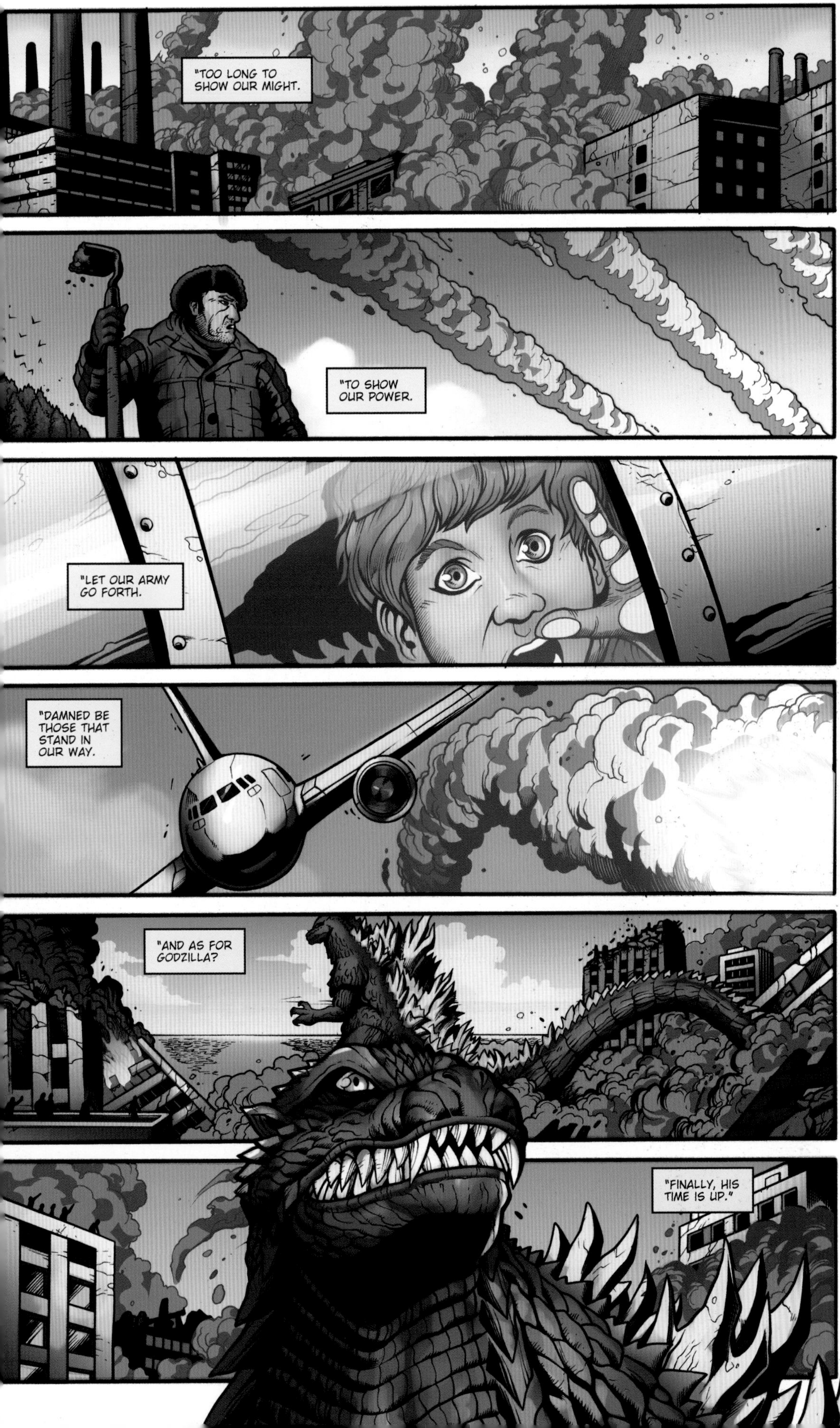
"TOO LONG TO SHOW OUR MIGHT.
"TO SHOW OUR POWER.
"LET OUR ARMY GO FORTH.
"DAMNED BE THOSE THAT STAND IN OUR WAY.
"AND AS FOR GODZILLA?
"FINALLY, HIS TIME IS UP."

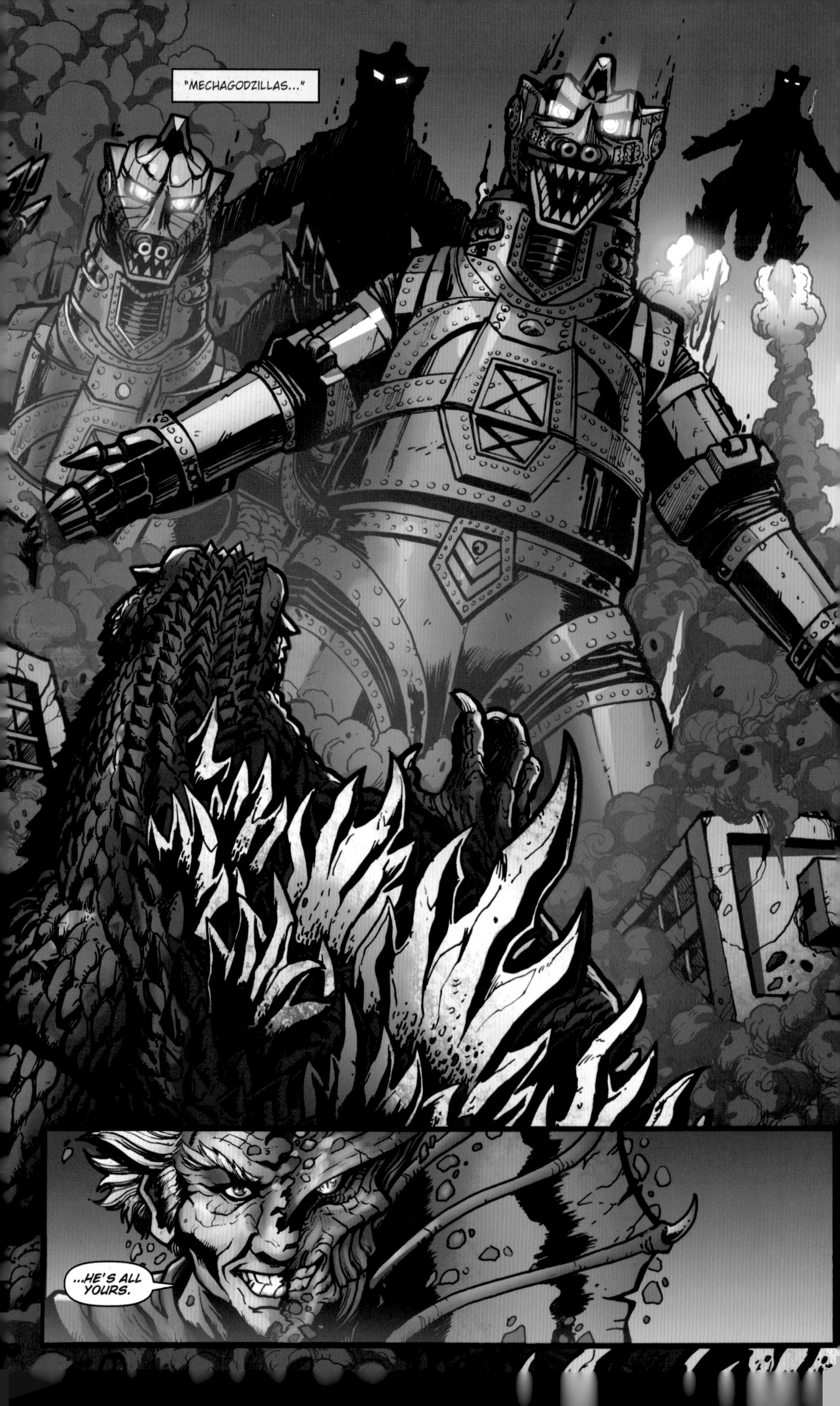
"MECHAGODZILLAS..."
...HE'S ALL YOURS.

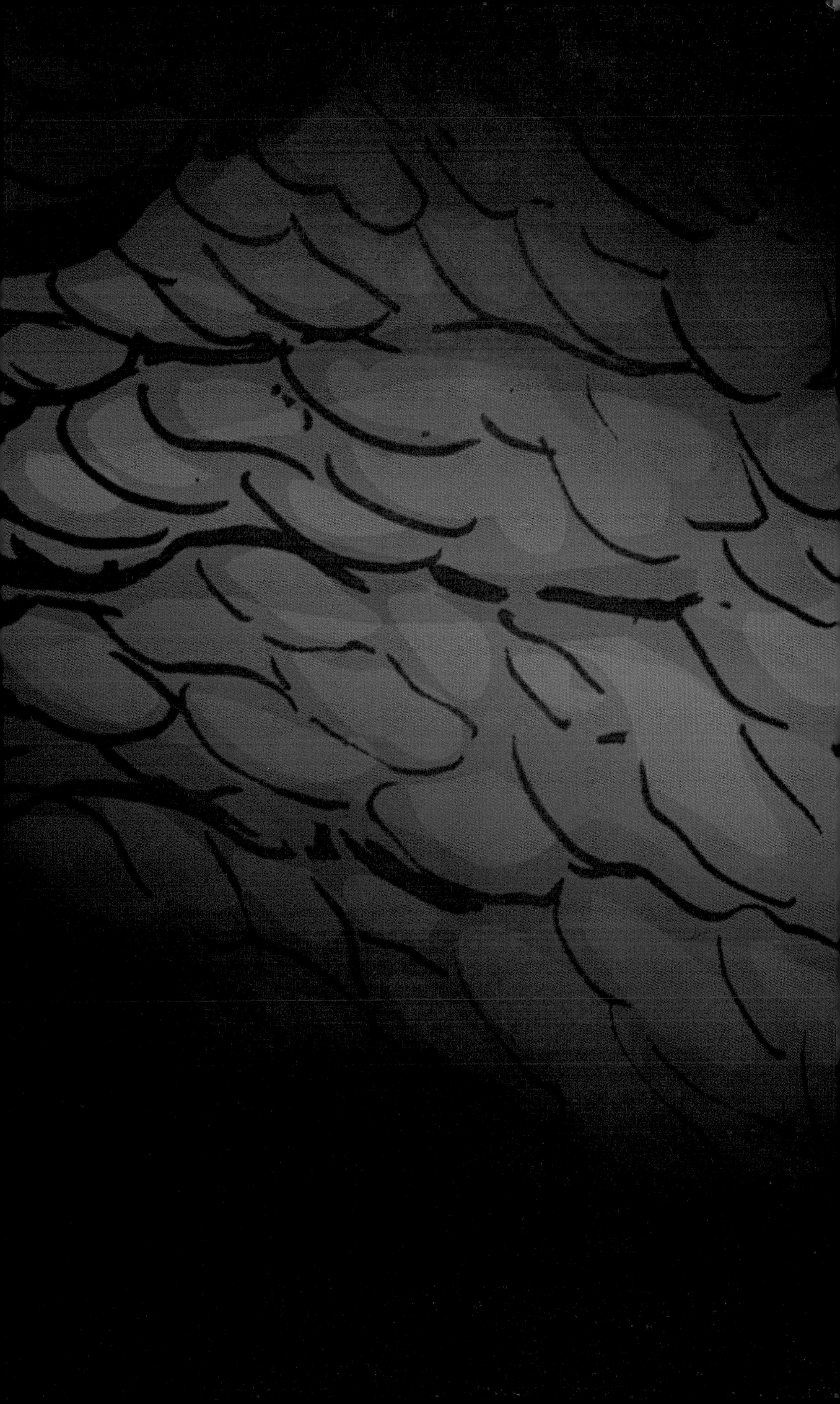

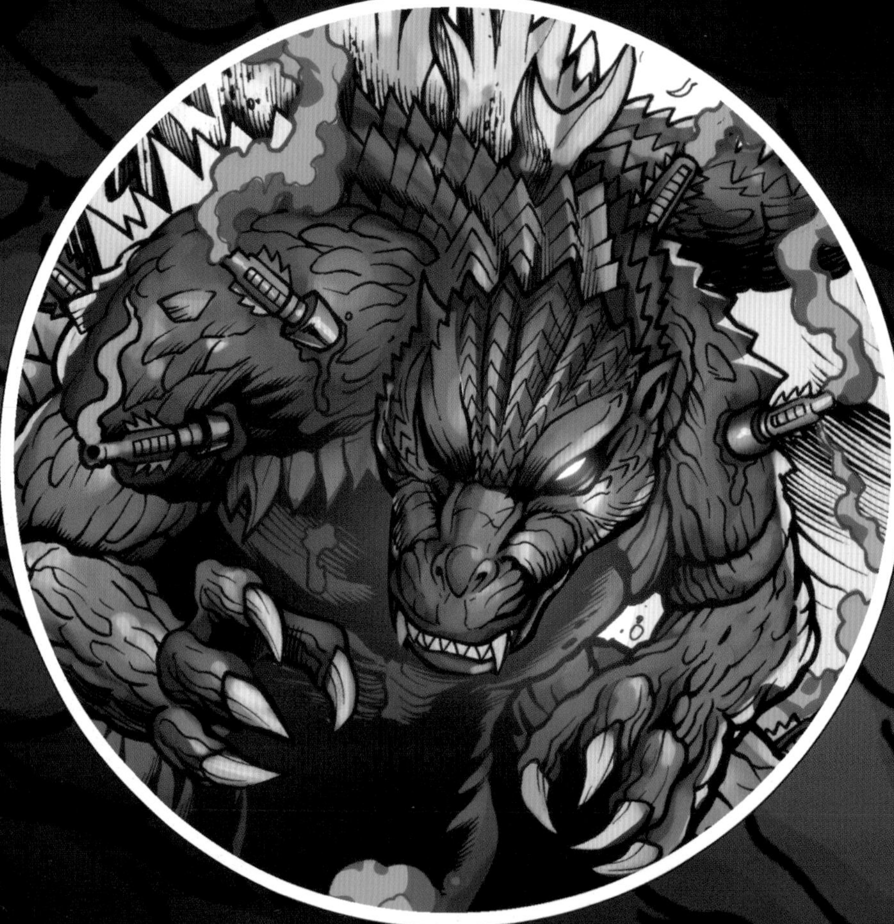

CHAPTER THREE:
HUNTING PARTY

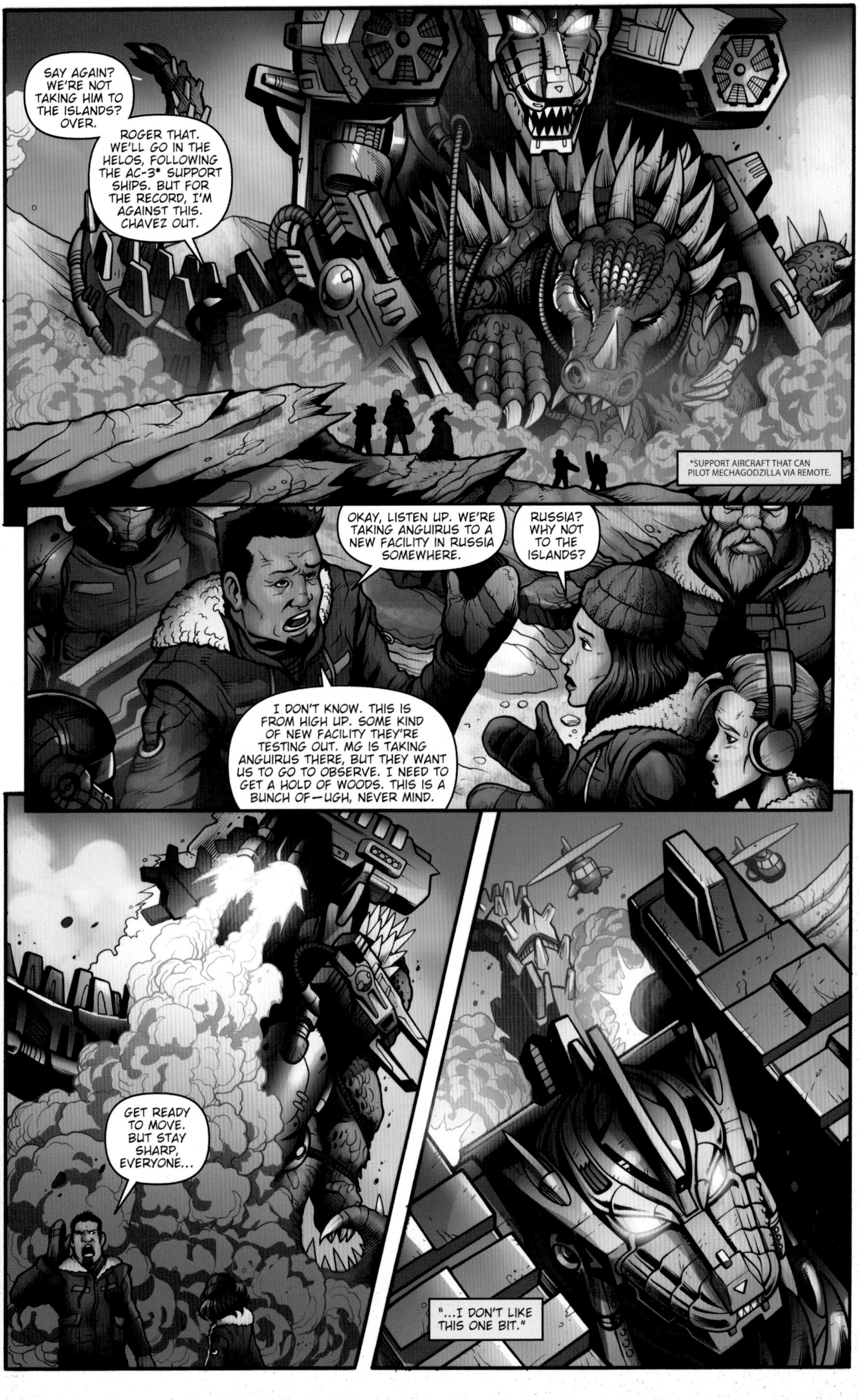

SAY AGAIN? WE'RE NOT TAKING HIM TO THE ISLANDS? OVER.
ROGER THAT. WE'LL GO IN THE HELOS, FOLLOWING THE AC-3* SUPPORT SHIPS. BUT FOR THE RECORD, I'M AGAINST THIS. CHAVEZ OUT.
*SUPPORT AIRCRAFT THAT CAN PILOT MECHAGODZILLA VIA REMOTE.
OKAY, LISTEN UP. WE'RE TAKING ANGUIRUS TO A NEW FACILITY IN RUSSIA SOMEWHERE.
RUSSIA? WHY NOT TO THE ISLANDS?
I DON'T KNOW. THIS IS FROM HIGH UP. SOME KIND OF NEW FACILITY THEY'RE TESTING OUT. MG IS TAKING ANGUIRUS THERE, BUT THEY WANT US TO GO TO OBSERVE. I NEED TO GET A HOLD OF WOODS. THIS IS A BUNCH OF—UGH, NEVER MIND.
GET READY TO MOVE. BUT STAY SHARP, EVERYONE...
"...I DON'T LIKE THIS ONE BIT."

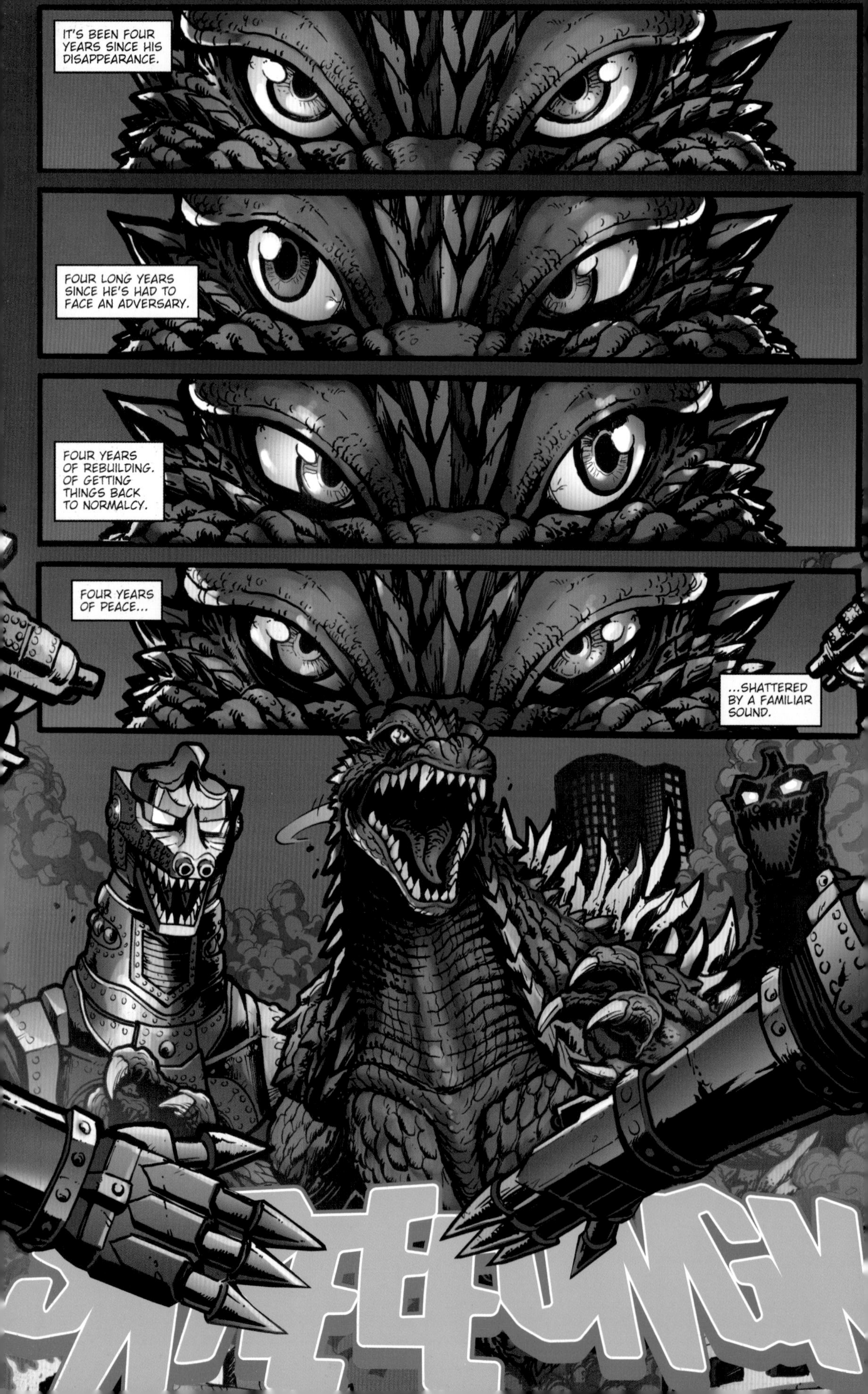
IT'S BEEN FOUR YEARS SINCE HIS DISAPPEARANCE.
FOUR LONG YEARS SINCE HE'S HAD TO FACE AN ADVERSARY.
FOUR YEARS OF REBUILDING. OF GETTING THINGS BACK TO NORMALCY.
FOUR YEARS OF PEACE...
...SHATTERED BY A FAMILIAR SOUND.

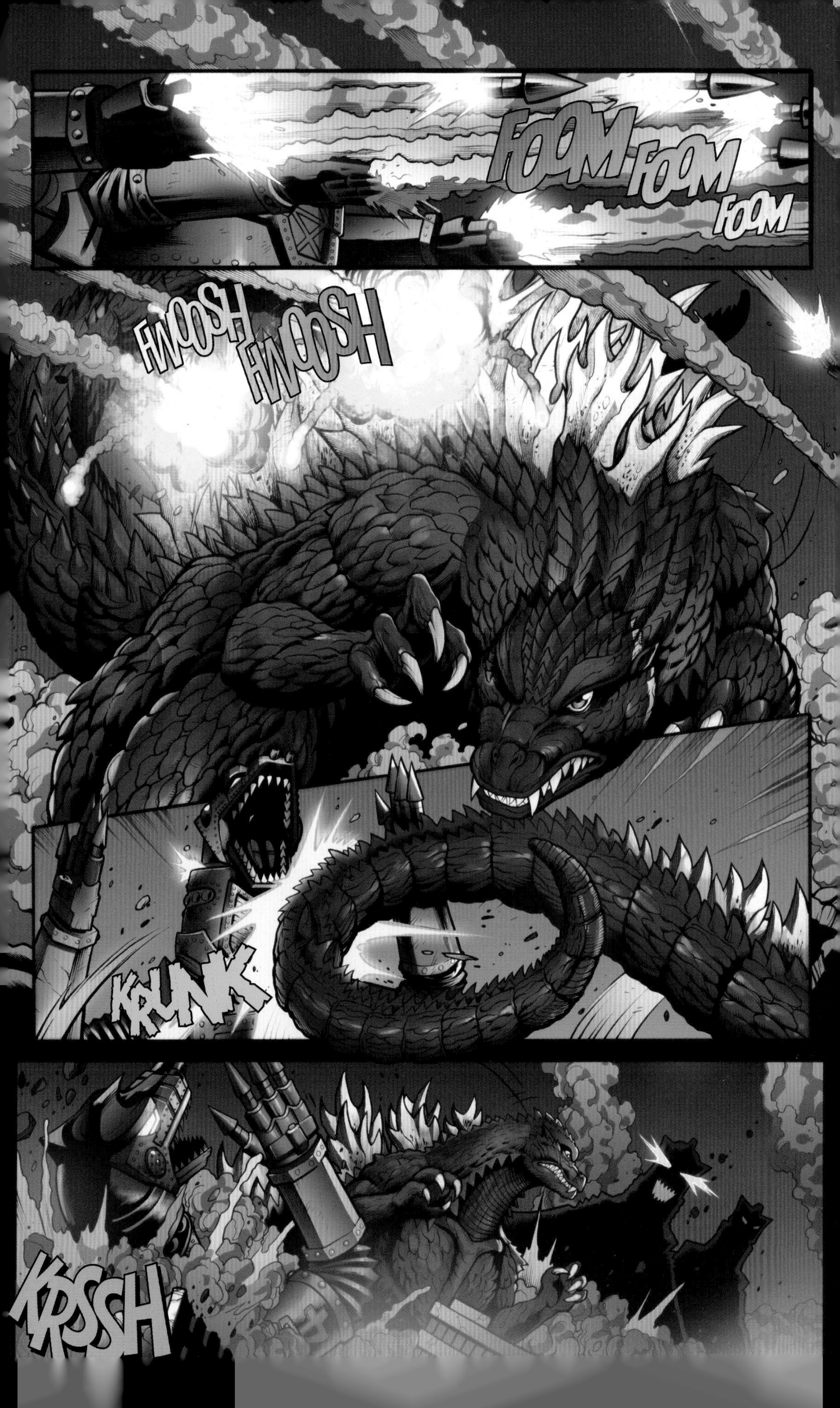
FOOM FOOM FOOM
FWOOSH FWOOSH
KRUNK
KRSSH

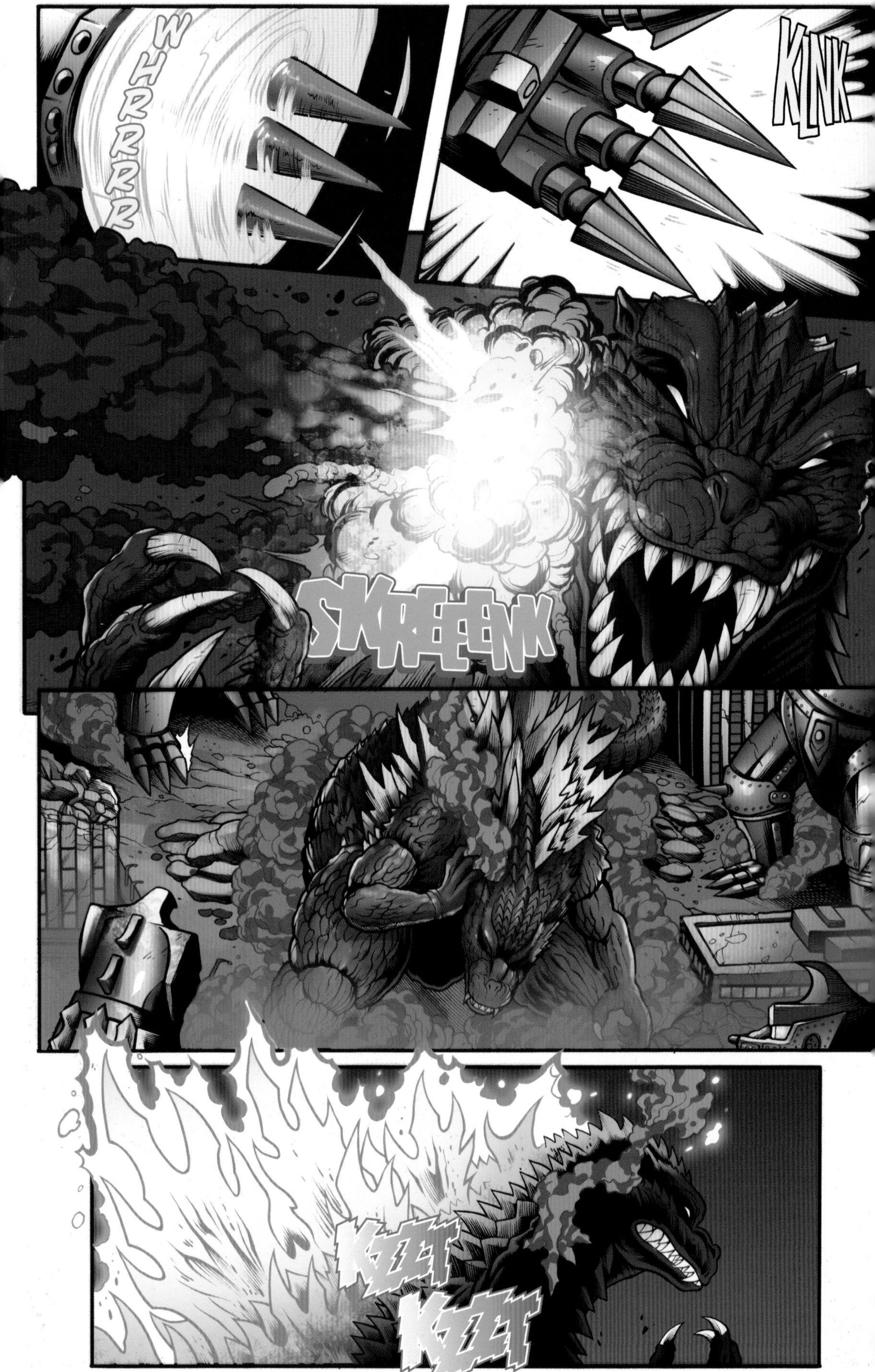
WHRRRRR
KLINK
SKREEENK
KZZT
KZZT

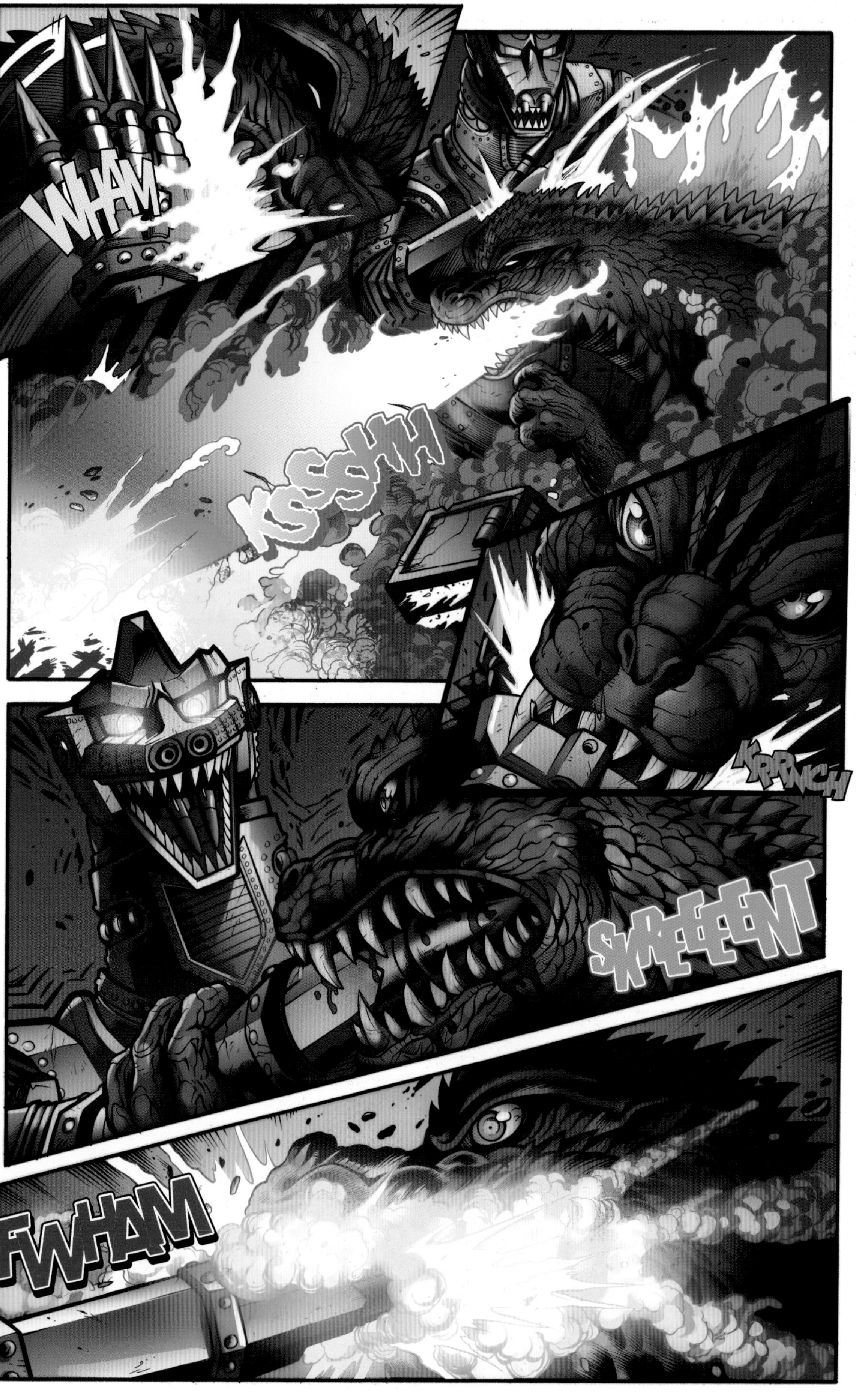

WHAM
KSSSHH
KRRNCH
SKREEEENT
FWHAM

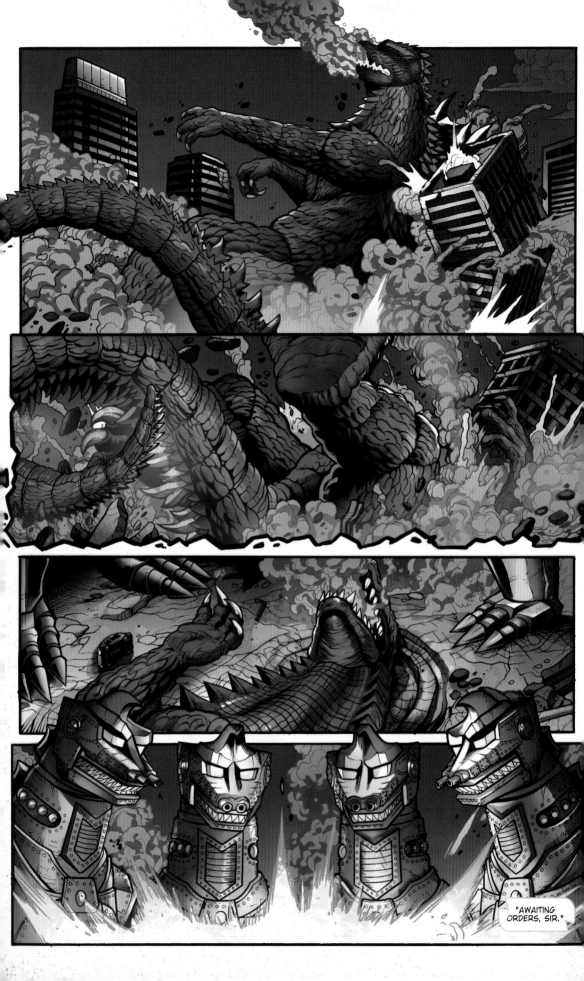

"AWAITING
ORDERS, SIR."

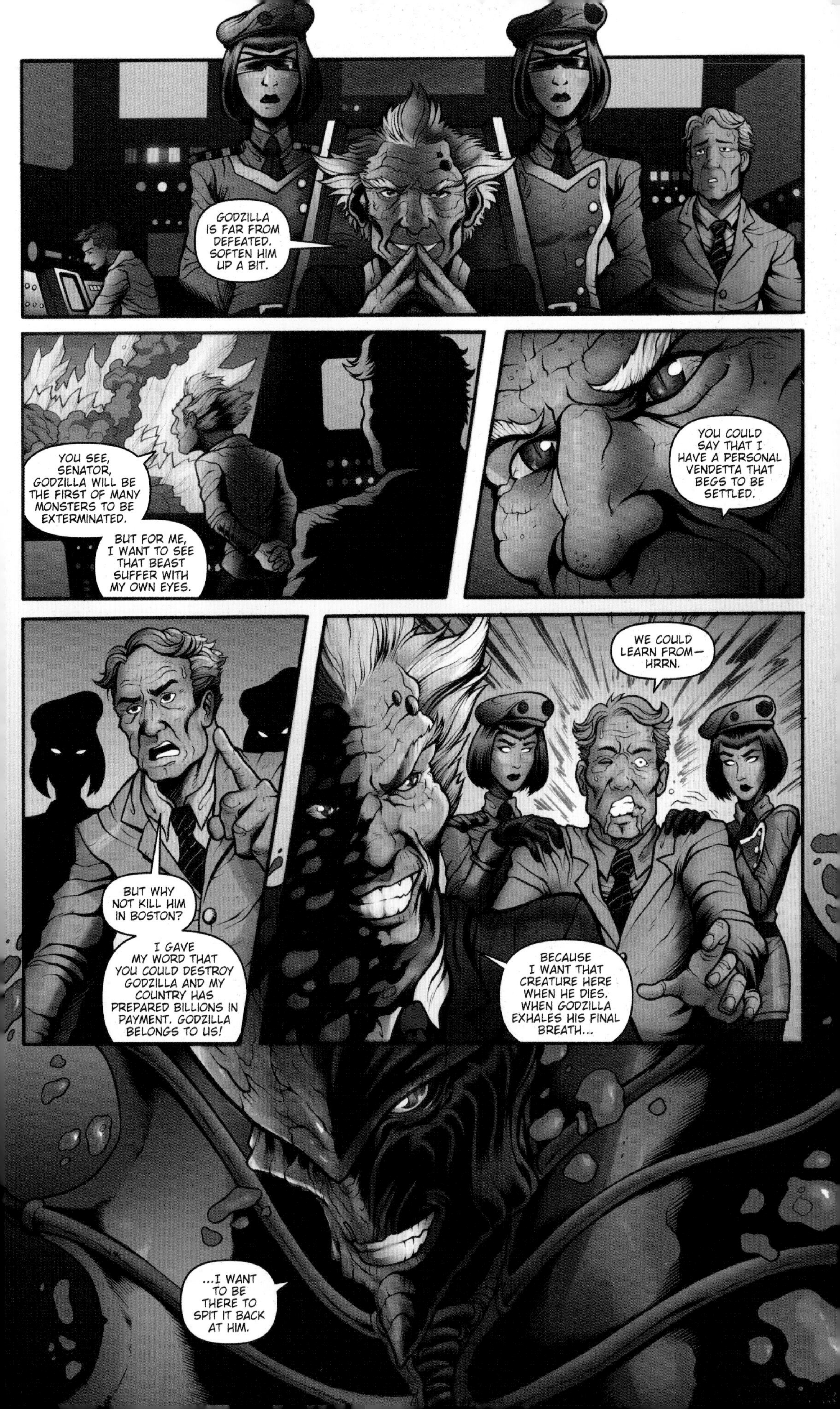
GODZILLA IS FAR FROM DEFEATED. SOFTEN HIM UP A BIT.
YOU SEE, SENATOR, GODZILLA WILL BE THE FIRST OF MANY MONSTERS TO BE EXTERMINATED.
BUT FOR ME, I WANT TO SEE THAT BEAST SUFFER WITH MY OWN EYES.
YOU COULD SAY THAT I HAVE A PERSONAL VENDETTA THAT BEGS TO BE SETTLED.
BUT WHY NOT KILL HIM IN BOSTON?
I GAVE MY WORD THAT YOU COULD DESTROY GODZILLA AND MY COUNTRY HAS PREPARED BILLIONS IN PAYMENT. GODZILLA BELONGS TO US!
WE COULD LEARN FROM— HRRN.
BECAUSE I WANT THAT CREATURE HERE WHEN HE DIES. WHEN GODZILLA EXHALES HIS FINAL BREATH...
...I WANT TO BE THERE TO SPIT IT BACK AT HIM.

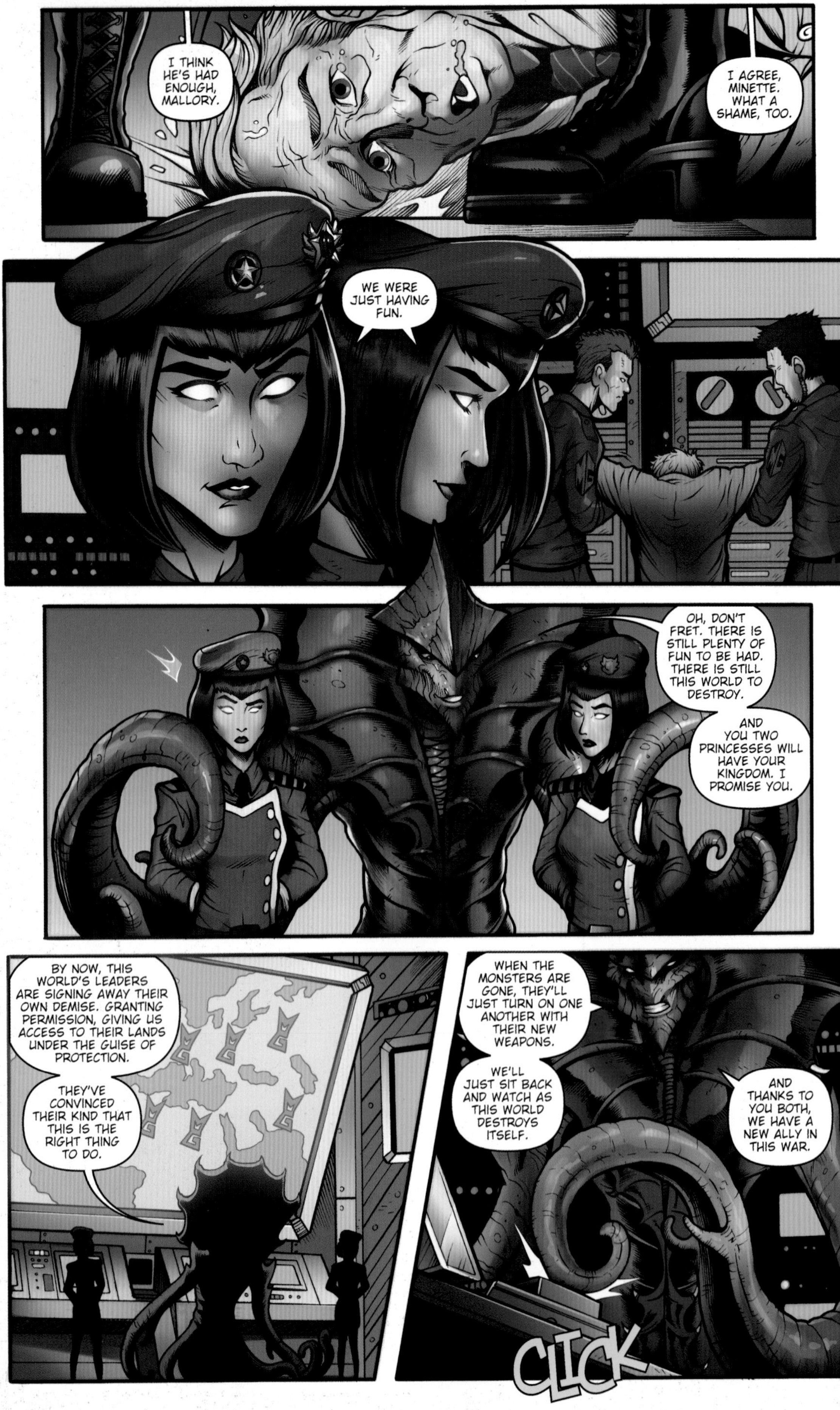
I THINK HE'S HAD ENOUGH, MALLORY.
I AGREE, MINETTE. WHAT A SHAME, TOO.
WE WERE JUST HAVING FUN.
OH, DON'T FRET. THERE IS STILL PLENTY OF FUN TO BE HAD. THERE IS STILL THIS WORLD TO DESTROY.
AND YOU TWO PRINCESSES WILL HAVE YOUR KINGDOM. I PROMISE YOU.
BY NOW, THIS WORLD'S LEADERS ARE SIGNING AWAY THEIR OWN DEMISE. GRANTING PERMISSION, GIVING US ACCESS TO THEIR LANDS UNDER THE GUISE OF PROTECTION.
THEY'VE CONVINCED THEIR KIND THAT THIS IS THE RIGHT THING TO DO.
WHEN THE MONSTERS ARE GONE, THEY'LL JUST TURN ON ONE ANOTHER WITH THEIR NEW WEAPONS.
WE'LL JUST SIT BACK AND WATCH AS THIS WORLD DESTROYS ITSELF.
AND THANKS TO YOU BOTH, WE HAVE A NEW ALLY IN THIS WAR.
CLICK

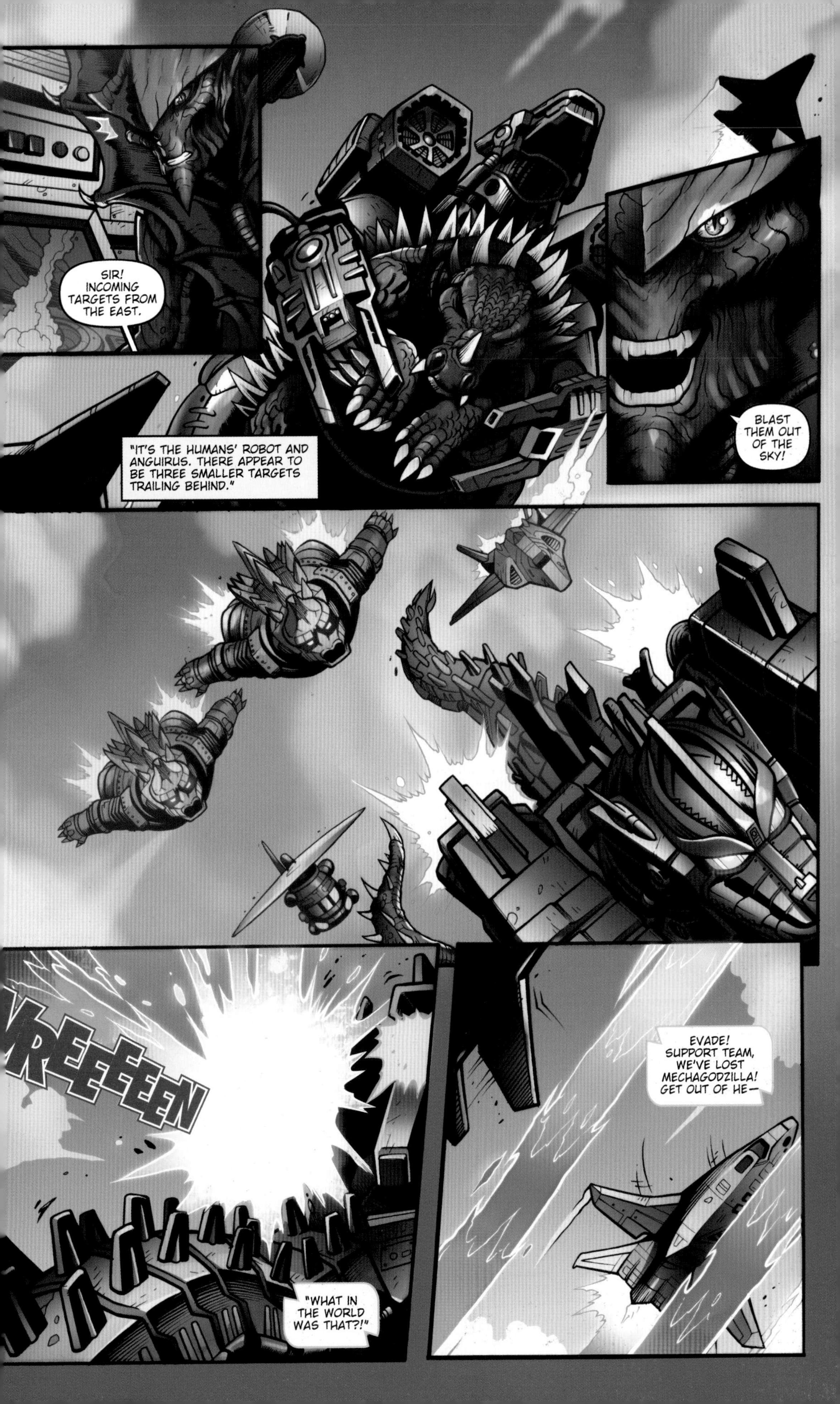

SIR! INCOMING TARGETS FROM THE EAST.
"IT'S THE HUMANS' ROBOT AND ANGUIRUS. THERE APPEAR TO BE THREE SMALLER TARGETS TRAILING BEHIND."
BLAST THEM OUT OF THE SKY!
REEEEEN
"WHAT IN THE WORLD WAS THAT?!"
EVADE! SUPPORT TEAM, WE'VE LOST MECHAGODZILLA! GET OUT OF HE—

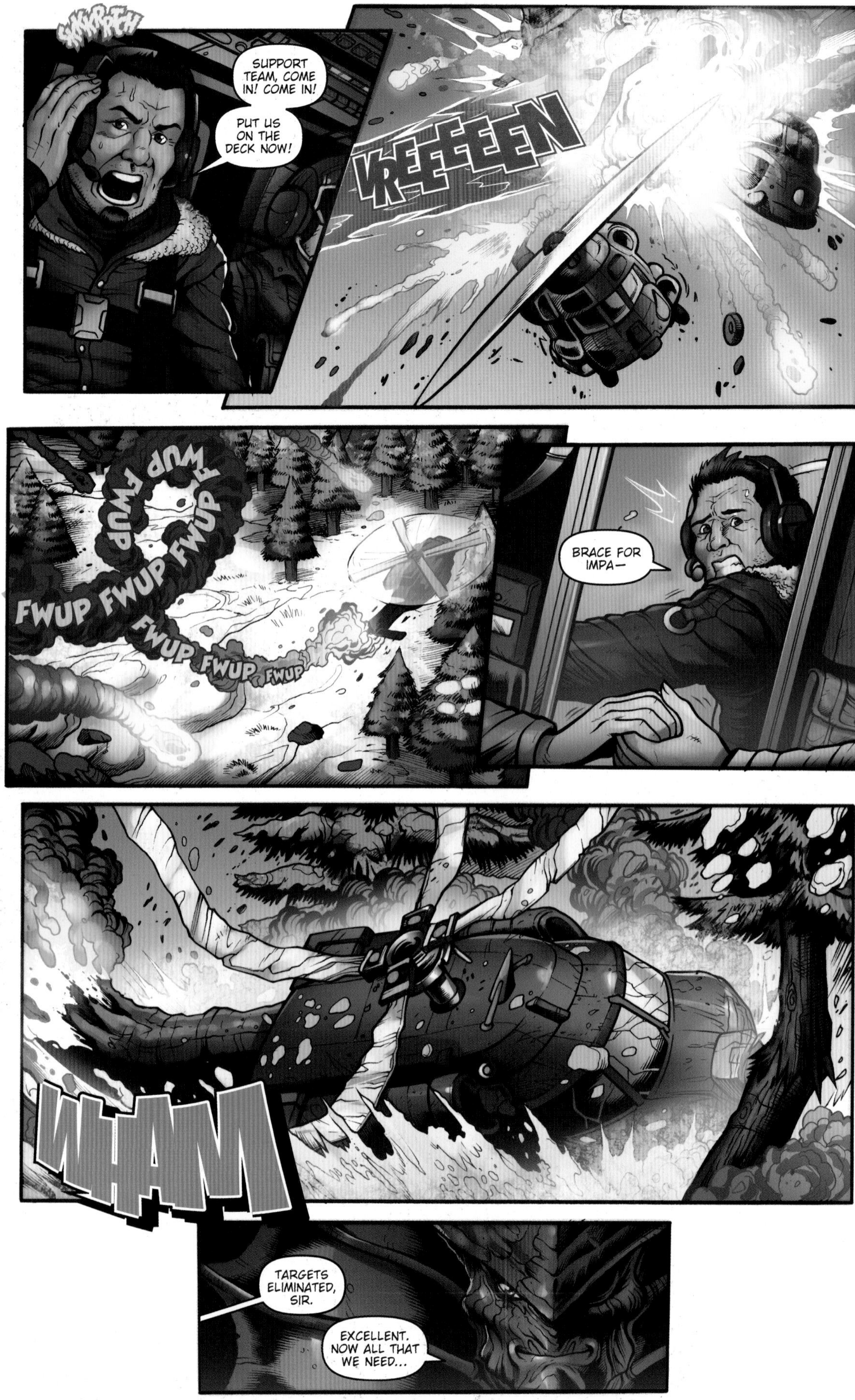
SKKRRTCH
SUPPORT TEAM, COME IN! COME IN!
PUT US ON THE DECK NOW!
VREEEEEN
FWUP FWUP FWUP FWUP FWUP FWUP FWUP FWUP FWUP
BRACE FOR IMPA—
WHAM
TARGETS ELIMINATED, SIR.
EXCELLENT. NOW ALL THAT WE NEED...

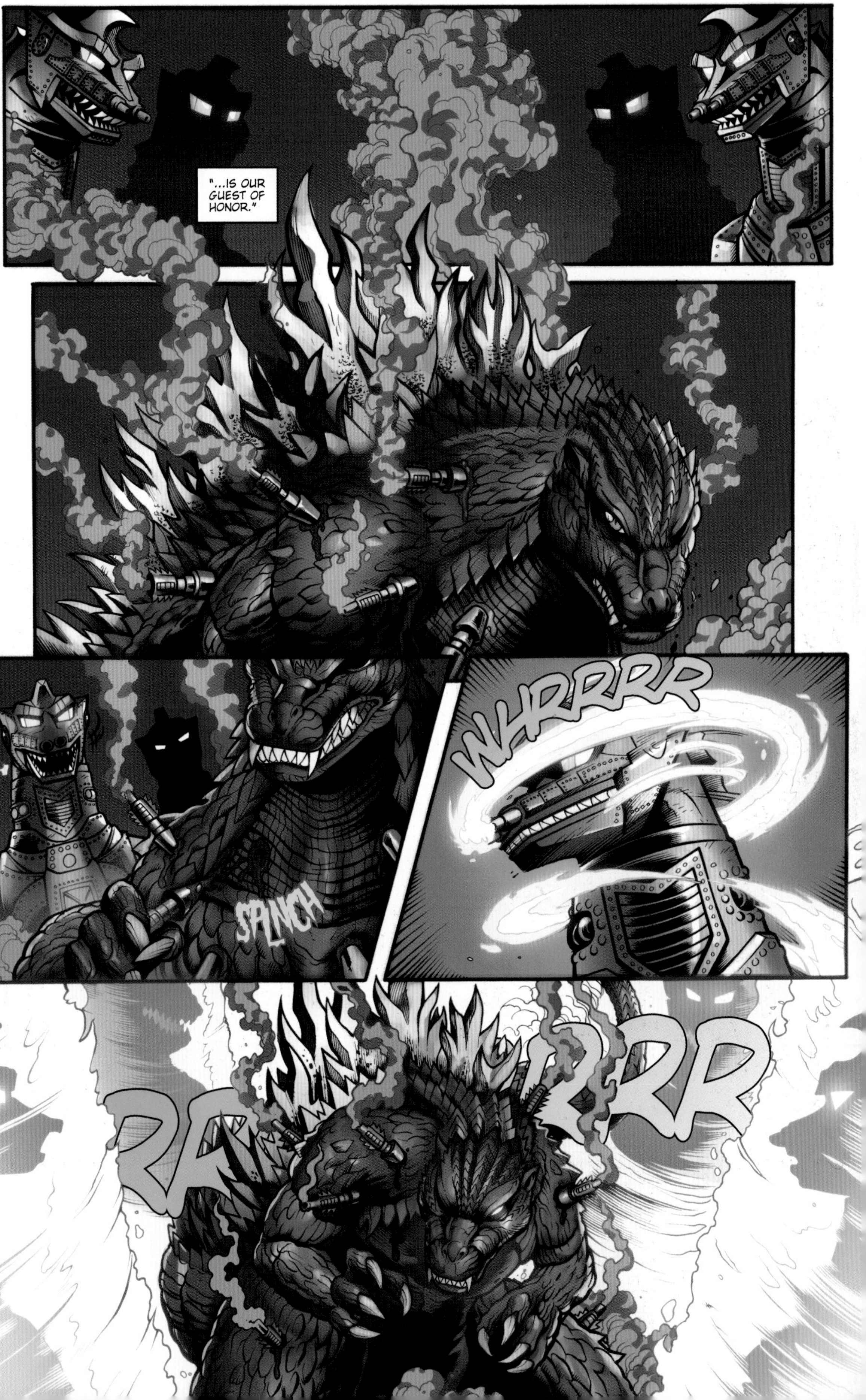
"...IS OUR GUEST OF HONOR."
SPLNCH
WHRRRR
RRRRR

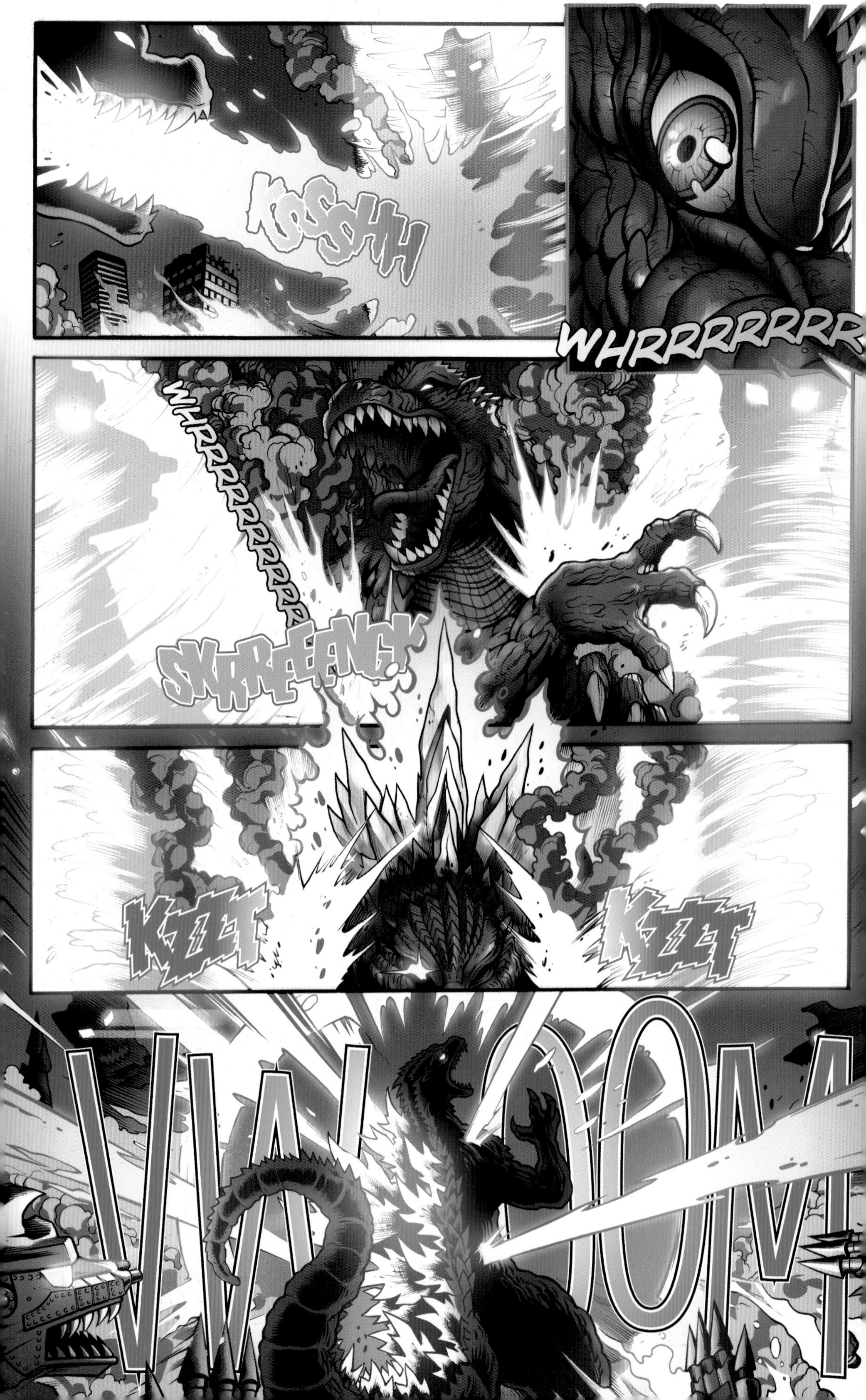
KSSSHHH
WHRRRRRRRR
WHRRRRRRRRRRR
SKRREEENCK
KZZT
KZZT
VWAMOOOM

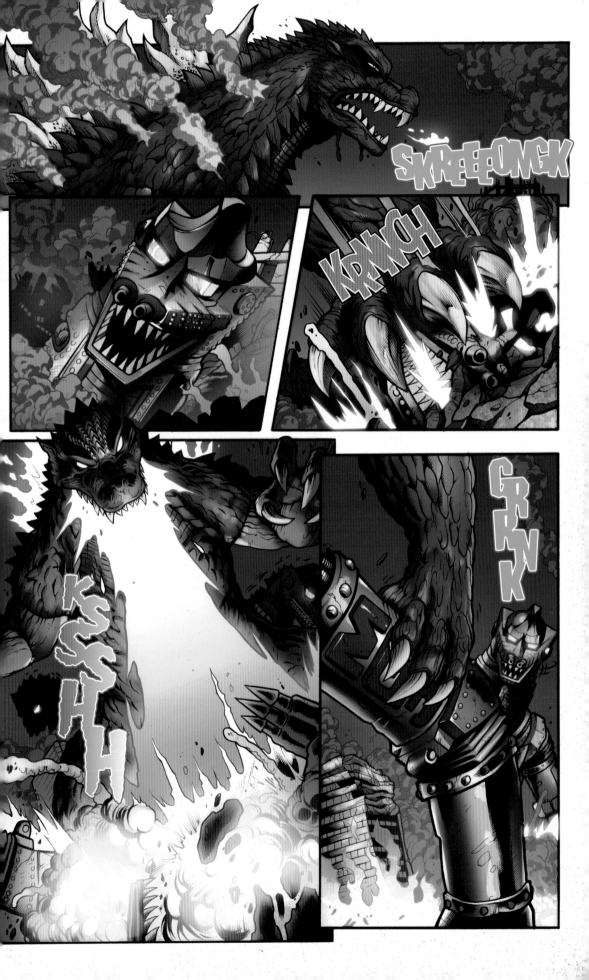

SKREEEONGK

KRNNCH

GRRNK

KSSSH

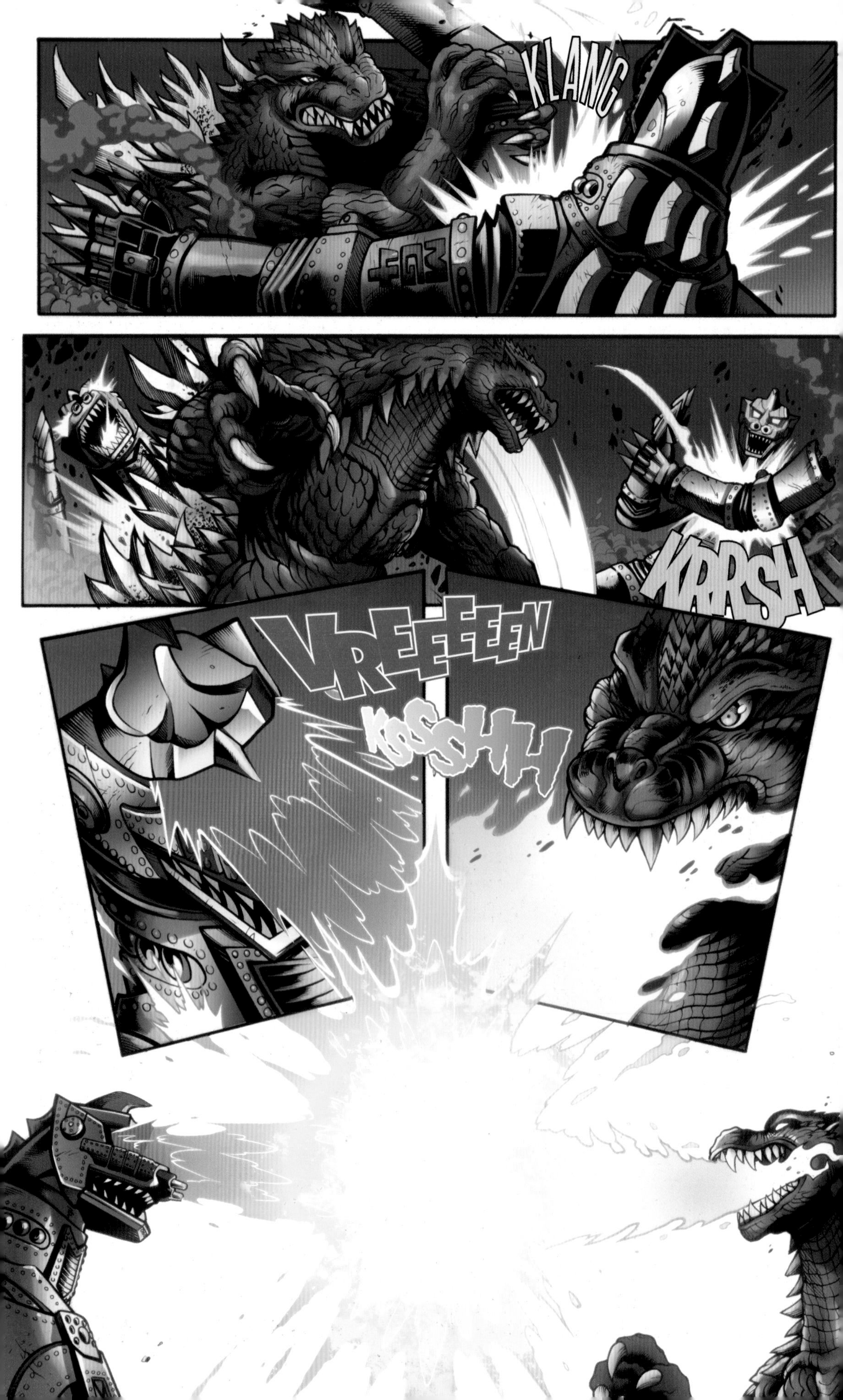
KLANG
KRRSH
VREEEEEN
KSSSHH

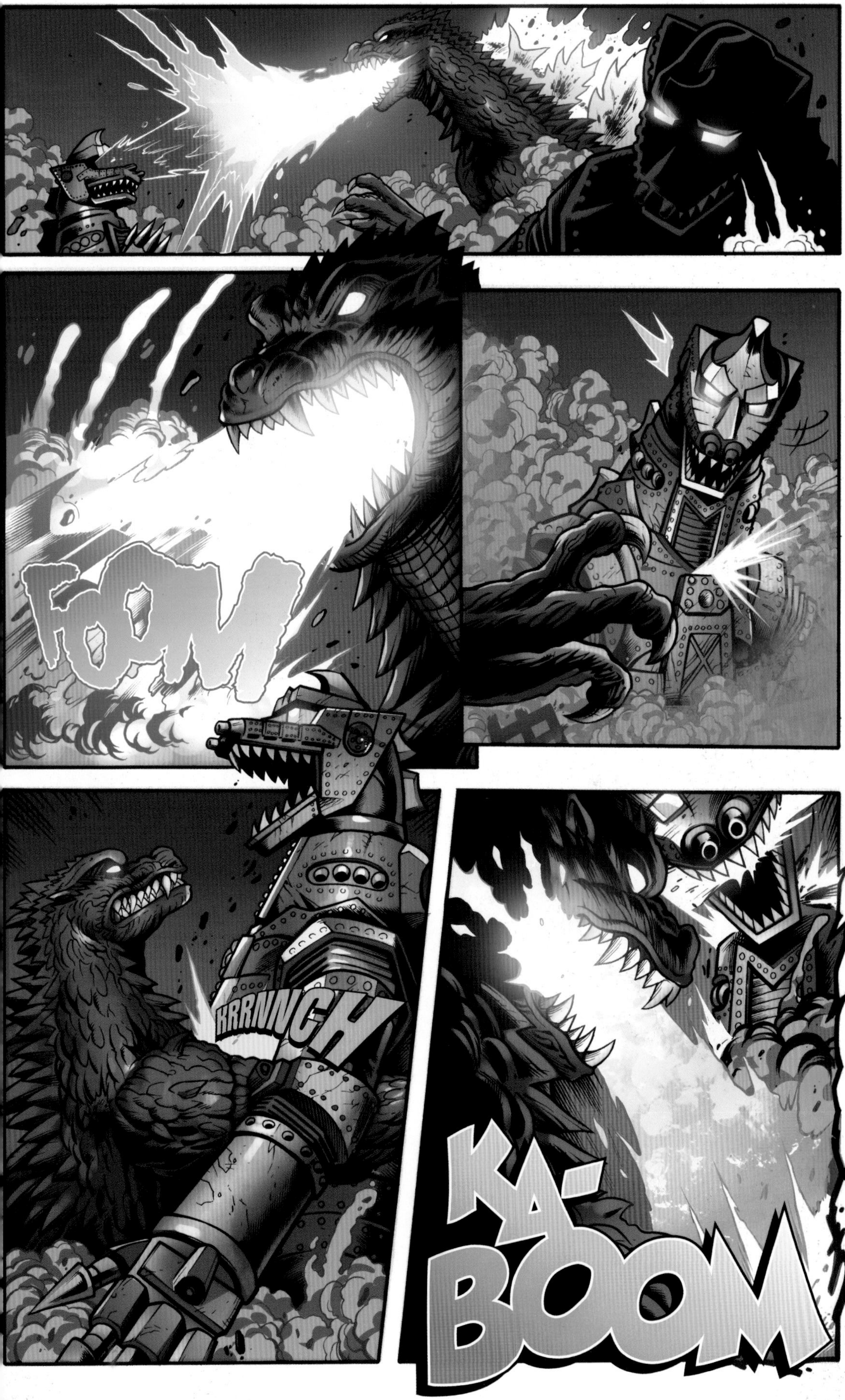
FOOM
KRRNNCH
KA-BOOM

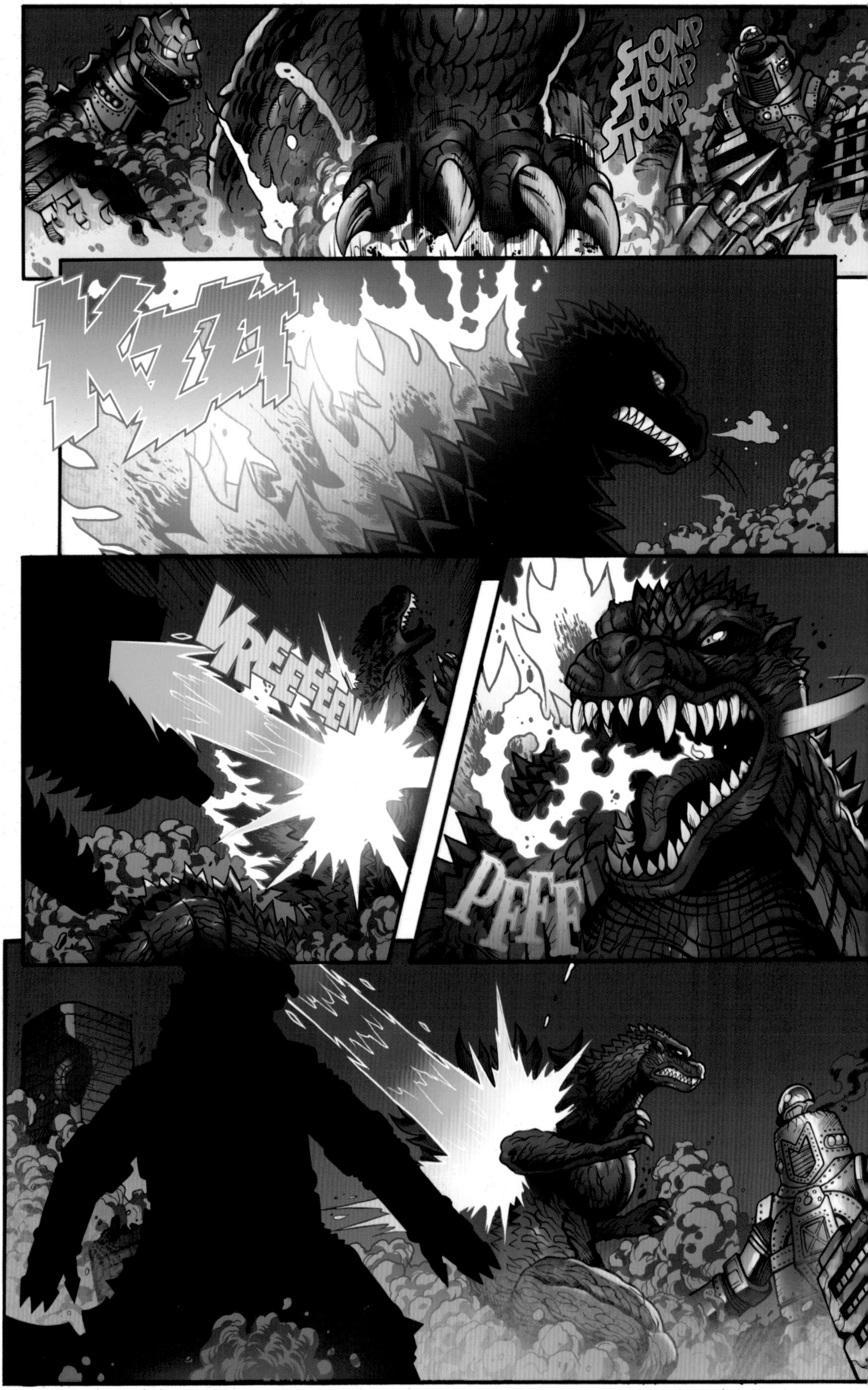
STOMP STOMP STOMP
KZZT
VREEEEEN
PFFF

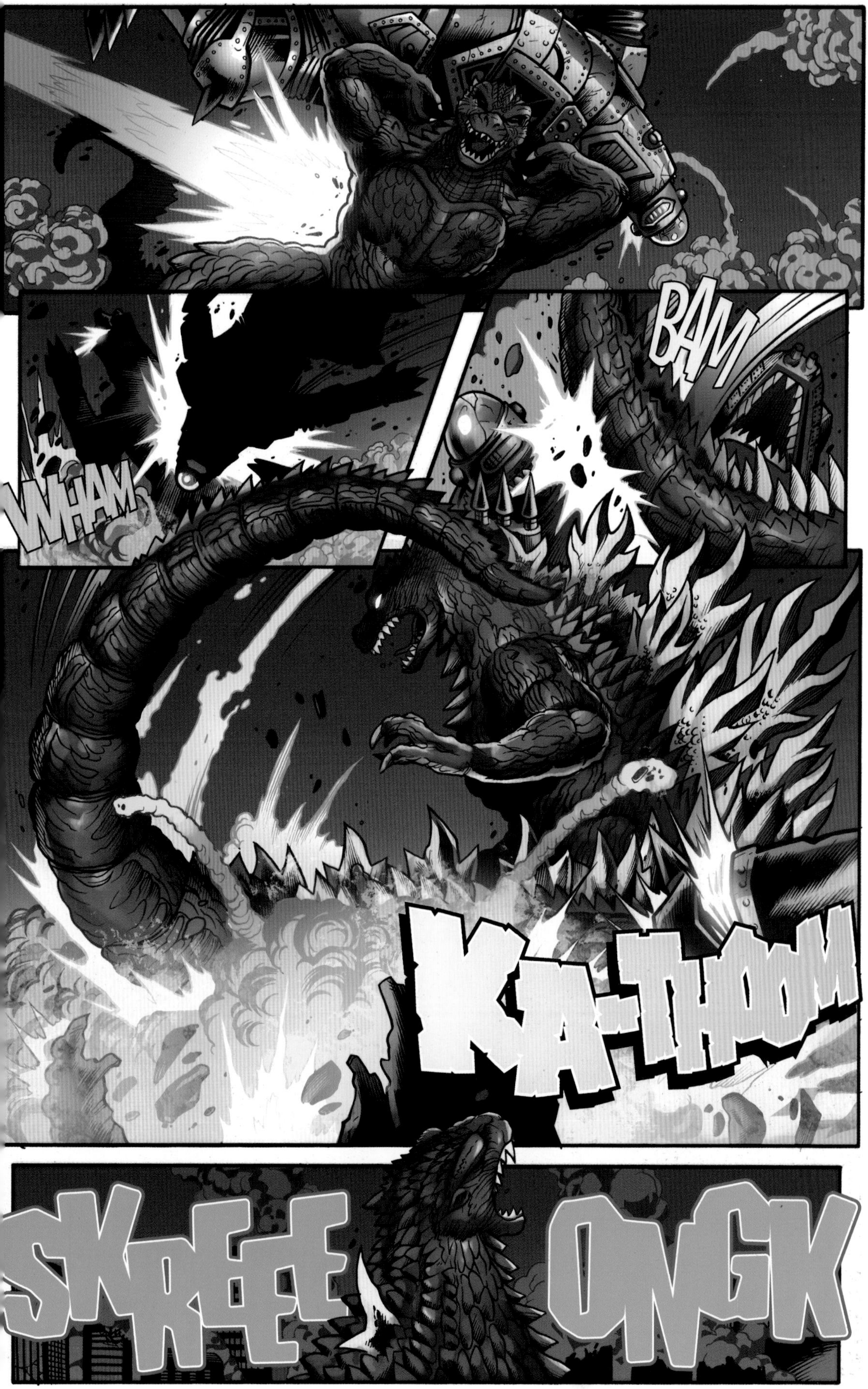
WHAM
BAM
KA-THOOM
SKREEE
ONGK

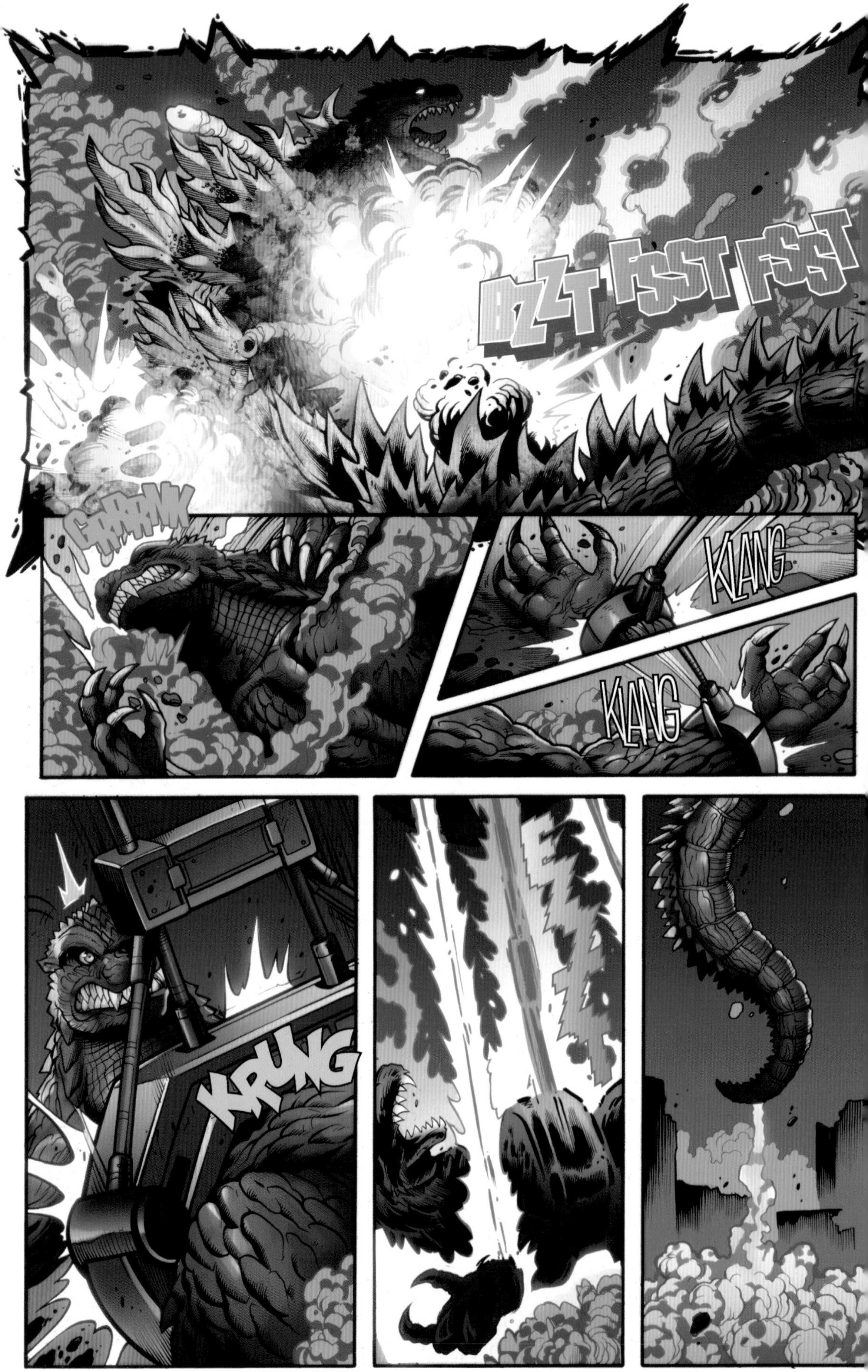
BZZT FSST FSST
GRRRNK
KLANG
KLANG
KRUNG

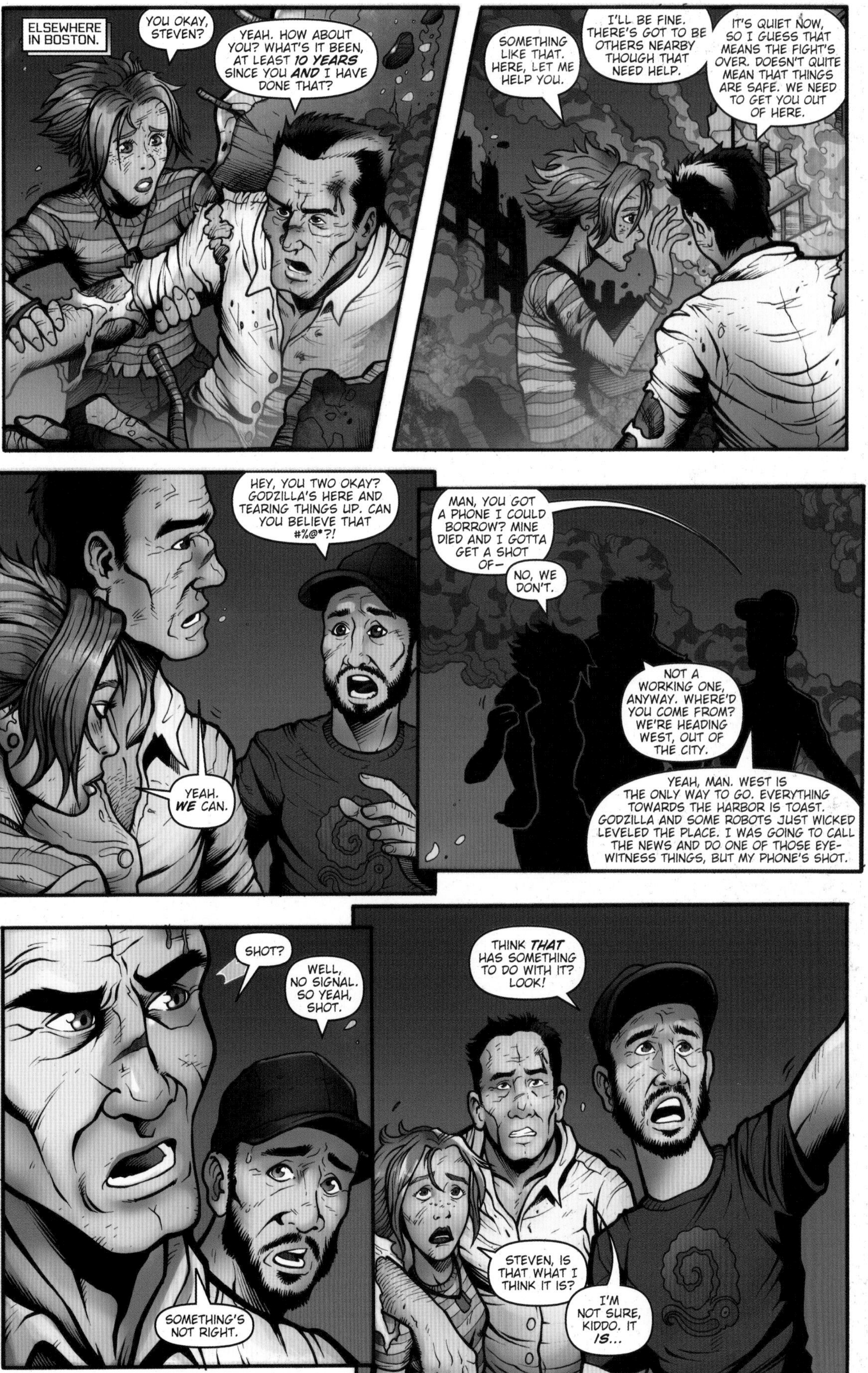
ELSEWHERE IN BOSTON.
YOU OKAY, STEVEN?
YEAH. HOW ABOUT YOU? WHAT'S IT BEEN, AT LEAST 10 YEARS SINCE YOU AND I HAVE DONE THAT?
SOMETHING LIKE THAT. HERE, LET ME HELP YOU.
I'LL BE FINE. THERE'S GOT TO BE OTHERS NEARBY THOUGH THAT NEED HELP.
IT'S QUIET NOW, SO I GUESS THAT MEANS THE FIGHT'S OVER. DOESN'T QUITE MEAN THAT THINGS ARE SAFE. WE NEED TO GET YOU OUT OF HERE.
HEY, YOU TWO OKAY? GODZILLA'S HERE AND TEARING THINGS UP. CAN YOU BELIEVE THAT #%@*?!
YEAH. WE CAN.
MAN, YOU GOT A PHONE I COULD BORROW? MINE DIED AND I GOTTA GET A SHOT OF—
NO, WE DON'T.
NOT A WORKING ONE, ANYWAY. WHERE'D YOU COME FROM? WE'RE HEADING WEST, OUT OF THE CITY.
YEAH, MAN. WEST IS THE ONLY WAY TO GO. EVERYTHING TOWARDS THE HARBOR IS TOAST. GODZILLA AND SOME ROBOTS JUST WICKED LEVELED THE PLACE. I WAS GOING TO CALL THE NEWS AND DO ONE OF THOSE EYE-WITNESS THINGS, BUT MY PHONE'S SHOT.
SHOT?
WELL, NO SIGNAL. SO YEAH, SHOT.
SOMETHING'S NOT RIGHT.
THINK THAT HAS SOMETHING TO DO WITH IT? LOOK!
STEVEN, IS THAT WHAT I THINK IT IS?
I'M NOT SURE, KIDDO. IT IS...

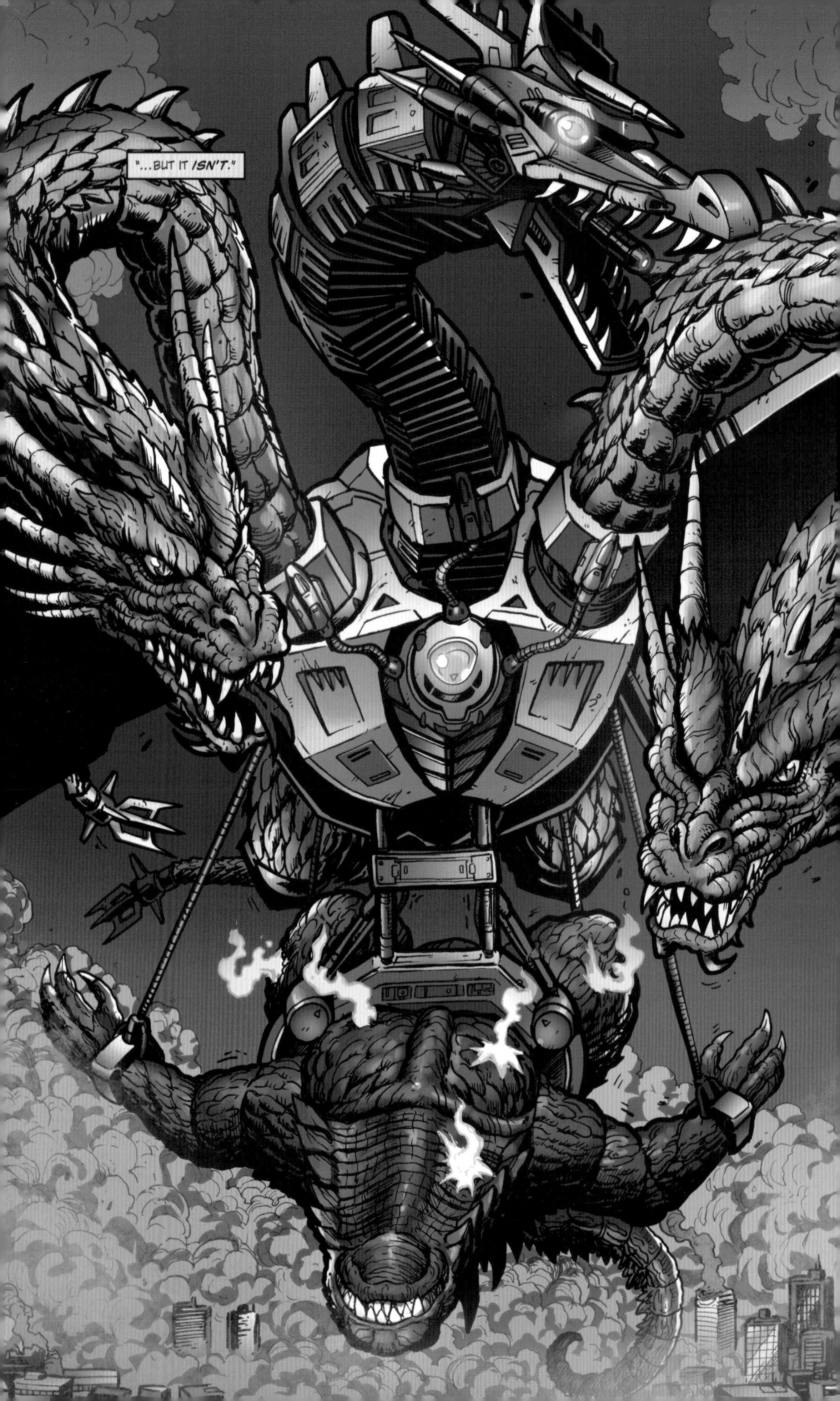
"...BUT IT ISN'T."

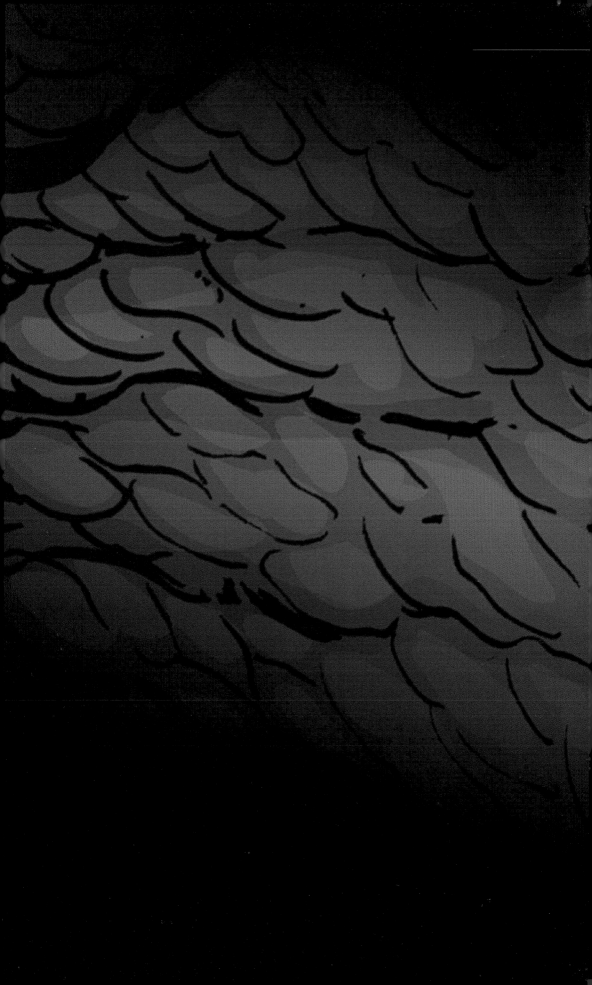

CHAPTER FOUR:
KING FOR A DAY

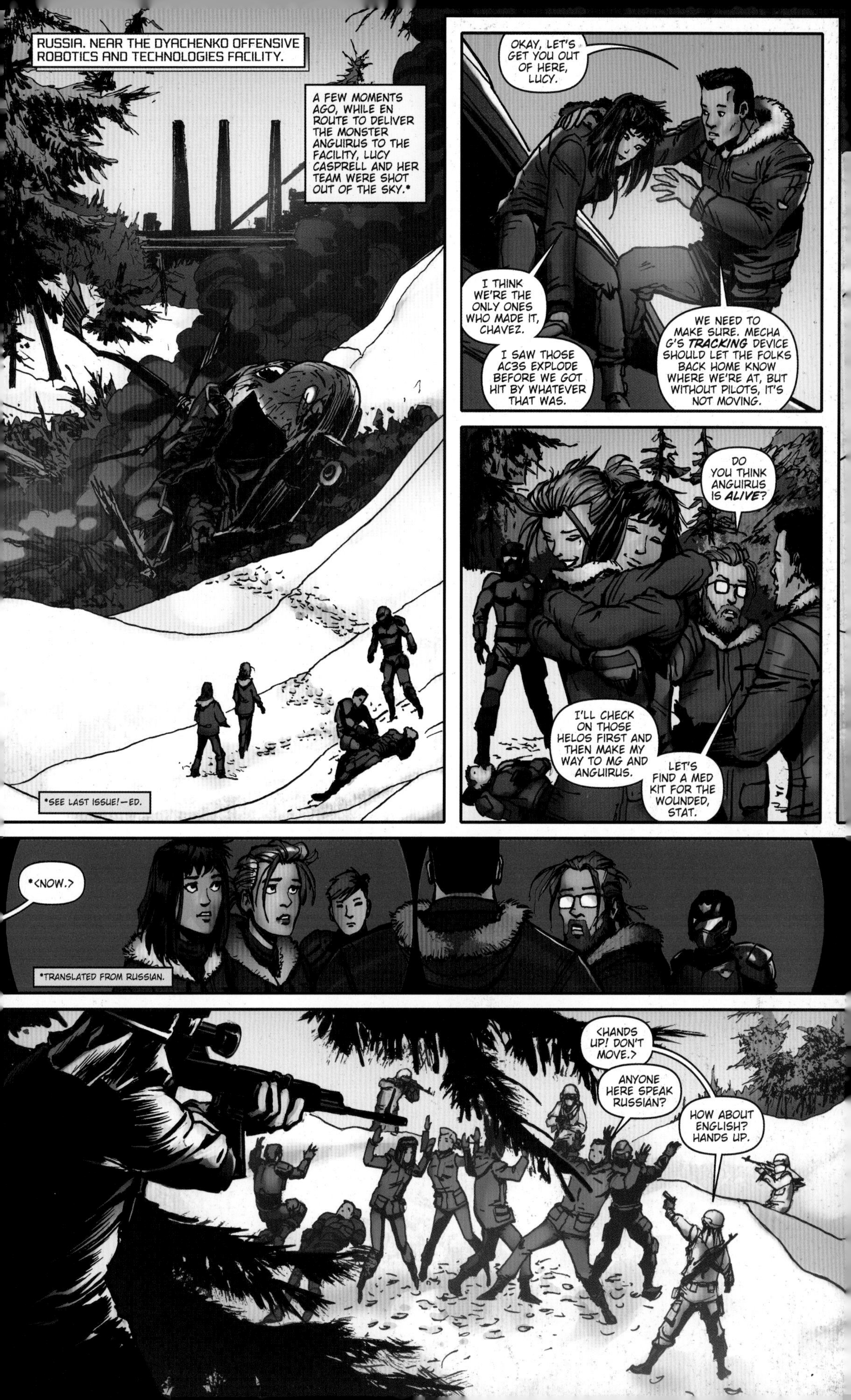
RUSSIA. NEAR THE DYACHENKO OFFENSIVE ROBOTICS AND TECHNOLOGIES FACILITY.
A FEW MOMENTS AGO, WHILE EN ROUTE TO DELIVER THE MONSTER ANGUIRUS TO THE FACILITY, LUCY CASPRELL AND HER TEAM WERE SHOT OUT OF THE SKY.*
*SEE LAST ISSUE! —ED.
OKAY, LET'S GET YOU OUT OF HERE, LUCY.
I THINK WE'RE THE ONLY ONES WHO MADE IT, CHAVEZ.
I SAW THOSE AC3S EXPLODE BEFORE WE GOT HIT BY WHATEVER THAT WAS.
WE NEED TO MAKE SURE. MECHA G'S TRACKING DEVICE SHOULD LET THE FOLKS BACK HOME KNOW WHERE WE'RE AT, BUT WITHOUT PILOTS, IT'S NOT MOVING.
DO YOU THINK ANGUIRUS IS ALIVE?
I'LL CHECK ON THOSE HELOS FIRST AND THEN MAKE MY WAY TO MG AND ANGUIRUS.
LET'S FIND A MED KIT FOR THE WOUNDED, STAT.
*<NOW.>
*TRANSLATED FROM RUSSIAN.
<HANDS UP! DON'T MOVE.>
ANYONE HERE SPEAK RUSSIAN?
HOW ABOUT ENGLISH? HANDS UP.

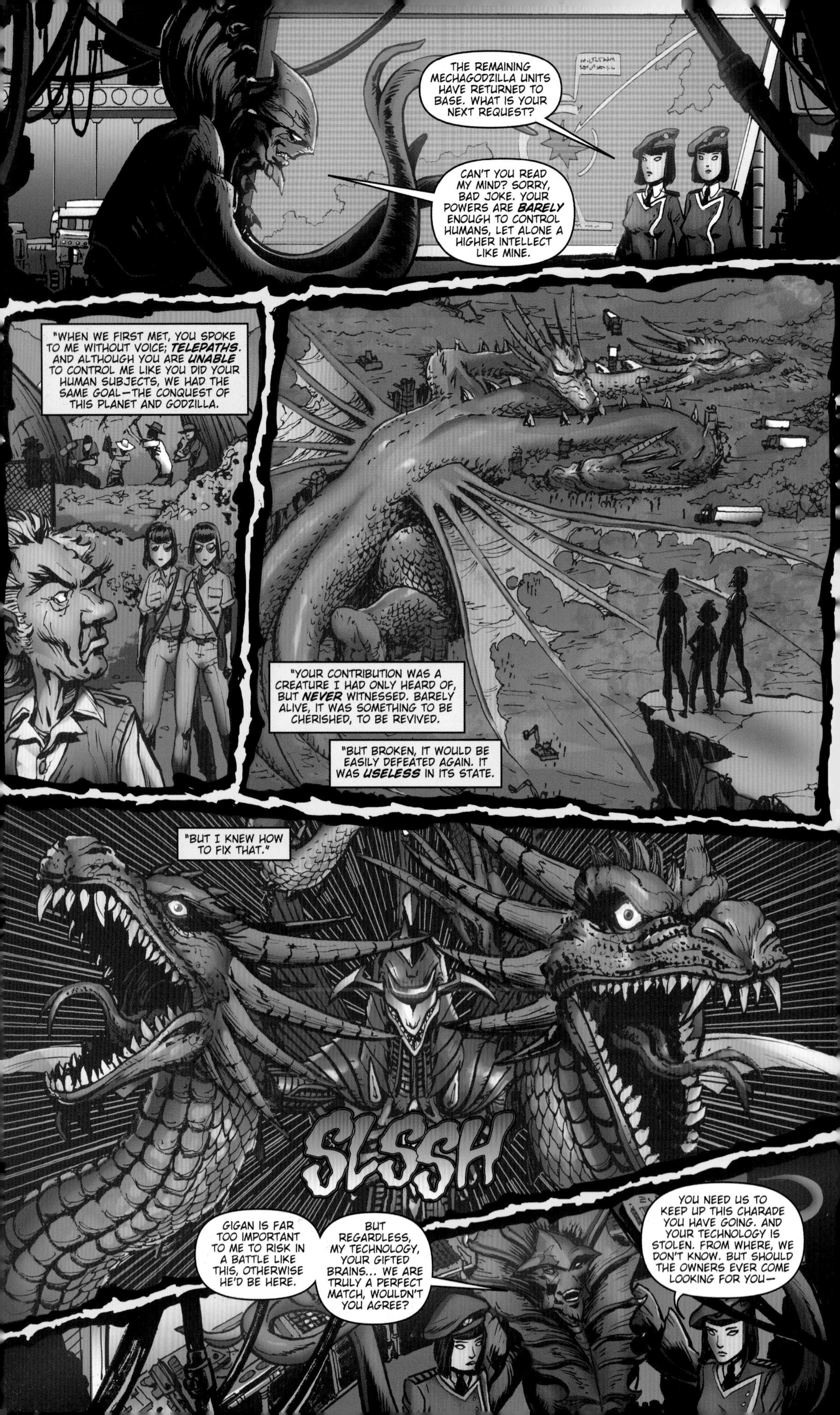
THE REMAINING MECHAGODZILLA UNITS HAVE RETURNED TO BASE. WHAT IS YOUR NEXT REQUEST?
CAN'T YOU READ MY MIND? SORRY, BAD JOKE. YOUR POWERS ARE BARELY ENOUGH TO CONTROL HUMANS, LET ALONE A HIGHER INTELLECT LIKE MINE.
"WHEN WE FIRST MET, YOU SPOKE TO ME WITHOUT VOICE; TELEPATHS. AND ALTHOUGH YOU ARE UNABLE TO CONTROL ME LIKE YOU DID YOUR HUMAN SUBJECTS, WE HAD THE SAME GOAL—THE CONQUEST OF THIS PLANET AND GODZILLA.
"YOUR CONTRIBUTION WAS A CREATURE I HAD ONLY HEARD OF, BUT NEVER WITNESSED. BARELY ALIVE, IT WAS SOMETHING TO BE CHERISHED, TO BE REVIVED.
"BUT BROKEN, IT WOULD BE EASILY DEFEATED AGAIN. IT WAS USELESS IN ITS STATE.
"BUT I KNEW HOW TO FIX THAT."
SLSSH
GIGAN IS FAR TOO IMPORTANT TO ME TO RISK IN A BATTLE LIKE THIS, OTHERWISE HE'D BE HERE.
BUT REGARDLESS, MY TECHNOLOGY, YOUR GIFTED BRAINS... WE ARE TRULY A PERFECT MATCH, WOULDN'T YOU AGREE?
YOU NEED US TO KEEP UP THIS CHARADE YOU HAVE GOING. AND YOUR TECHNOLOGY IS STOLEN. FROM WHERE, WE DON'T KNOW. BUT SHOULD THE OWNERS EVER COME LOOKING FOR YOU—

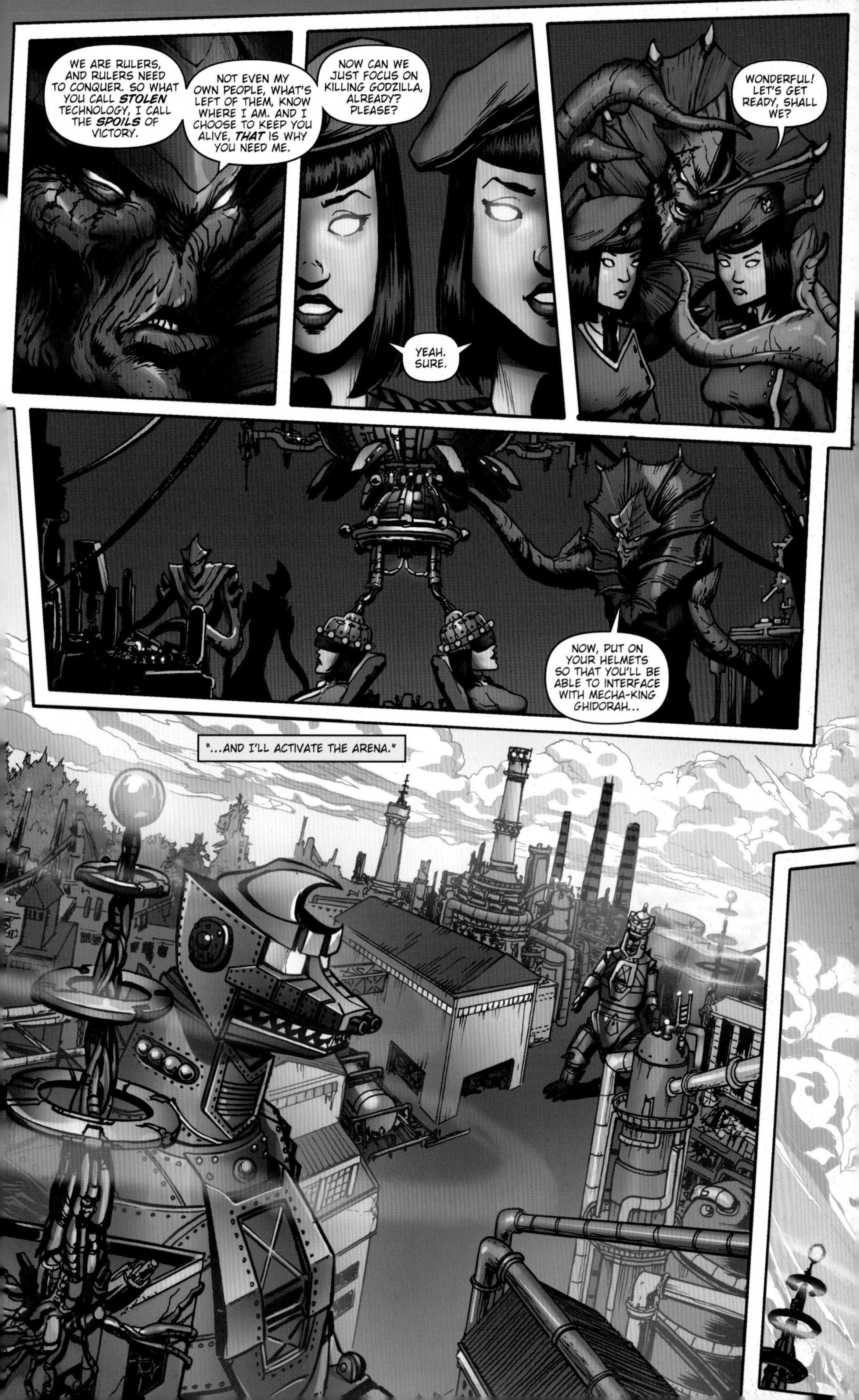
WE ARE RULERS, AND RULERS NEED TO CONQUER. SO WHAT YOU CALL STOLEN TECHNOLOGY, I CALL THE SPOILS OF VICTORY.
NOT EVEN MY OWN PEOPLE, WHAT'S LEFT OF THEM, KNOW WHERE I AM. AND I CHOOSE TO KEEP YOU ALIVE, THAT IS WHY YOU NEED ME.
NOW CAN WE JUST FOCUS ON KILLING GODZILLA, ALREADY? PLEASE?
YEAH. SURE.
WONDERFUL! LET'S GET READY, SHALL WE?
NOW, PUT ON YOUR HELMETS SO THAT YOU'LL BE ABLE TO INTERFACE WITH MECHA-KING GHIDORAH...
"...AND I'LL ACTIVATE THE ARENA."

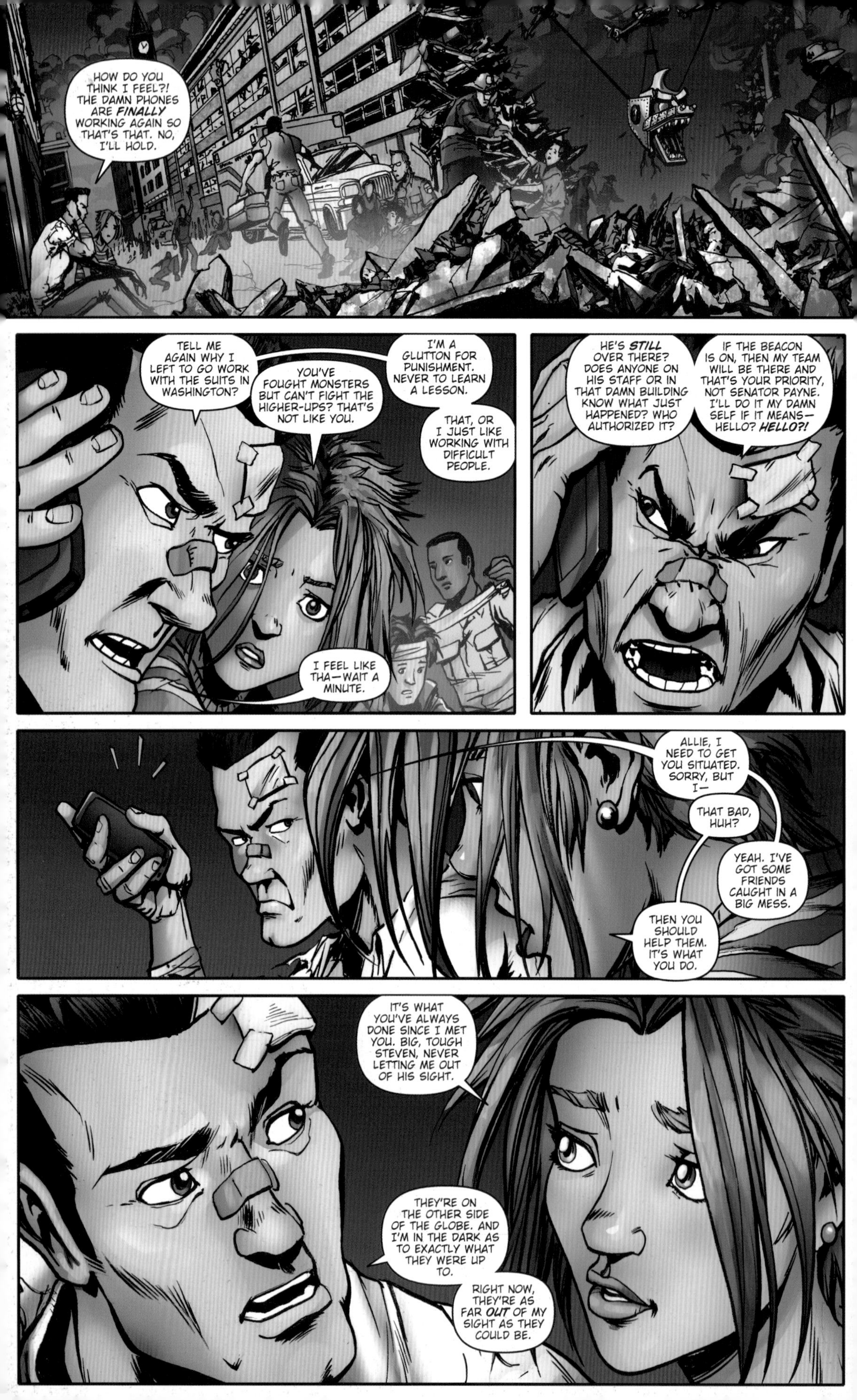
HOW DO YOU THINK I FEEL?! THE DAMN PHONES ARE *FINALLY* WORKING AGAIN SO THAT'S THAT. NO, I'LL HOLD.
TELL ME AGAIN WHY I LEFT TO GO WORK WITH THE SUITS IN WASHINGTON?
YOU'VE FOUGHT MONSTERS BUT CAN'T FIGHT THE HIGHER-UPS? THAT'S NOT LIKE YOU.
I'M A GLUTTON FOR PUNISHMENT. NEVER TO LEARN A LESSON.
THAT, OR I JUST LIKE WORKING WITH DIFFICULT PEOPLE.
I FEEL LIKE THA—WAIT A MINUTE.
HE'S *STILL* OVER THERE? DOES ANYONE ON HIS STAFF OR IN THAT DAMN BUILDING KNOW WHAT JUST HAPPENED? WHO AUTHORIZED IT?
IF THE BEACON IS ON, THEN MY TEAM WILL BE THERE AND THAT'S YOUR PRIORITY, NOT SENATOR PAYNE. I'LL DO IT MY DAMN SELF IF IT MEANS— HELLO? ***HELLO?!***
ALLIE, I NEED TO GET YOU SITUATED. SORRY, BUT I—
THAT BAD, HUH?
YEAH. I'VE GOT SOME FRIENDS CAUGHT IN A BIG MESS.
THEN YOU SHOULD HELP THEM. IT'S WHAT YOU DO.
IT'S WHAT YOU'VE ALWAYS DONE SINCE I MET YOU. BIG, TOUGH STEVEN, NEVER LETTING ME OUT OF HIS SIGHT.
THEY'RE ON THE OTHER SIDE OF THE GLOBE. AND I'M IN THE DARK AS TO EXACTLY WHAT THEY WERE UP TO.
RIGHT NOW, THEY'RE AS FAR *OUT* OF MY SIGHT AS THEY COULD BE.

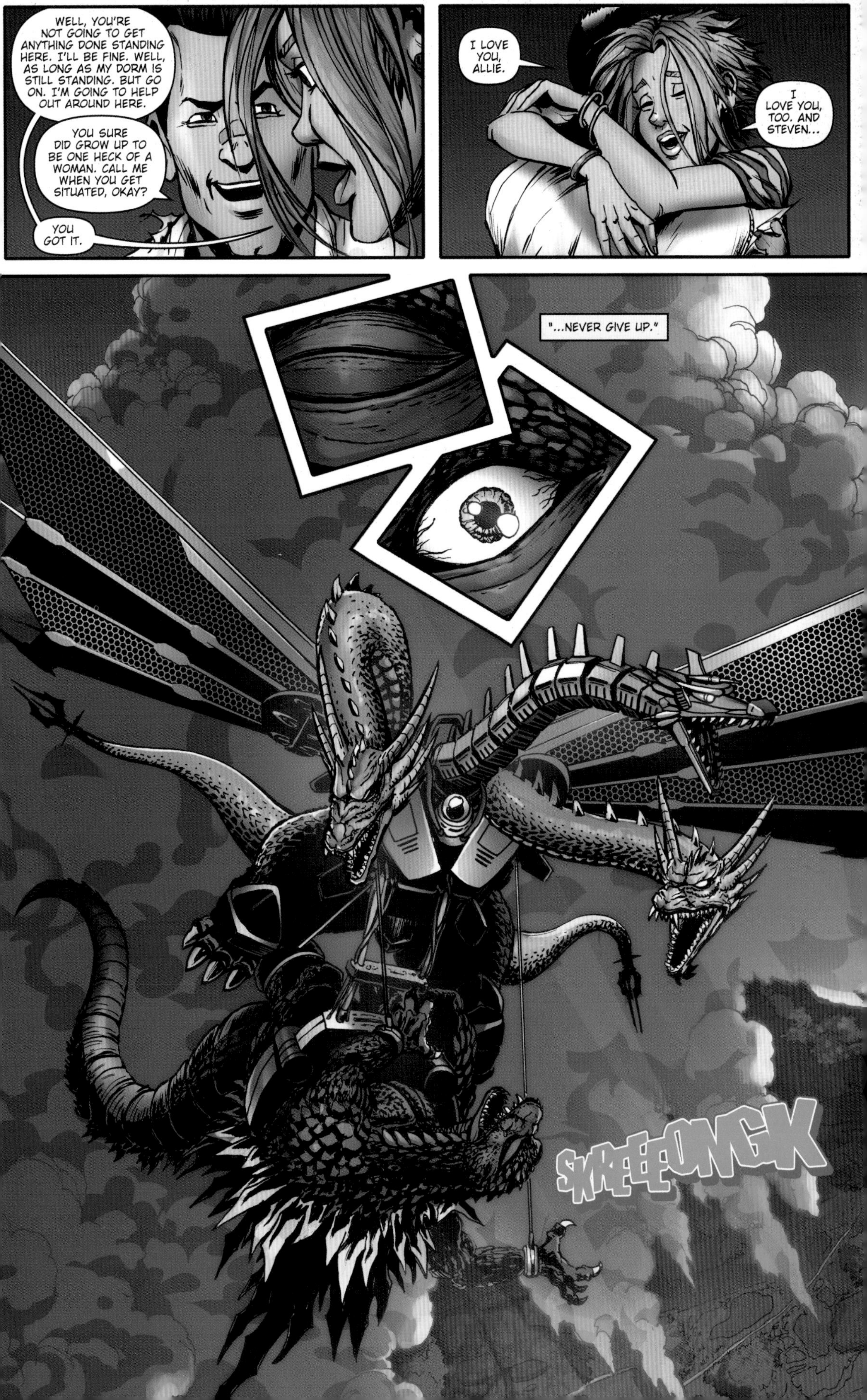
WELL, YOU'RE NOT GOING TO GET ANYTHING DONE STANDING HERE. I'LL BE FINE. WELL, AS LONG AS MY DORM IS STILL STANDING. BUT GO ON. I'M GOING TO HELP OUT AROUND HERE.
YOU SURE DID GROW UP TO BE ONE HECK OF A WOMAN. CALL ME WHEN YOU GET SITUATED, OKAY?
YOU GOT IT.
I LOVE YOU, ALLIE.
I LOVE YOU, TOO. AND STEVEN...
"...NEVER GIVE UP."
SKREEEONGK

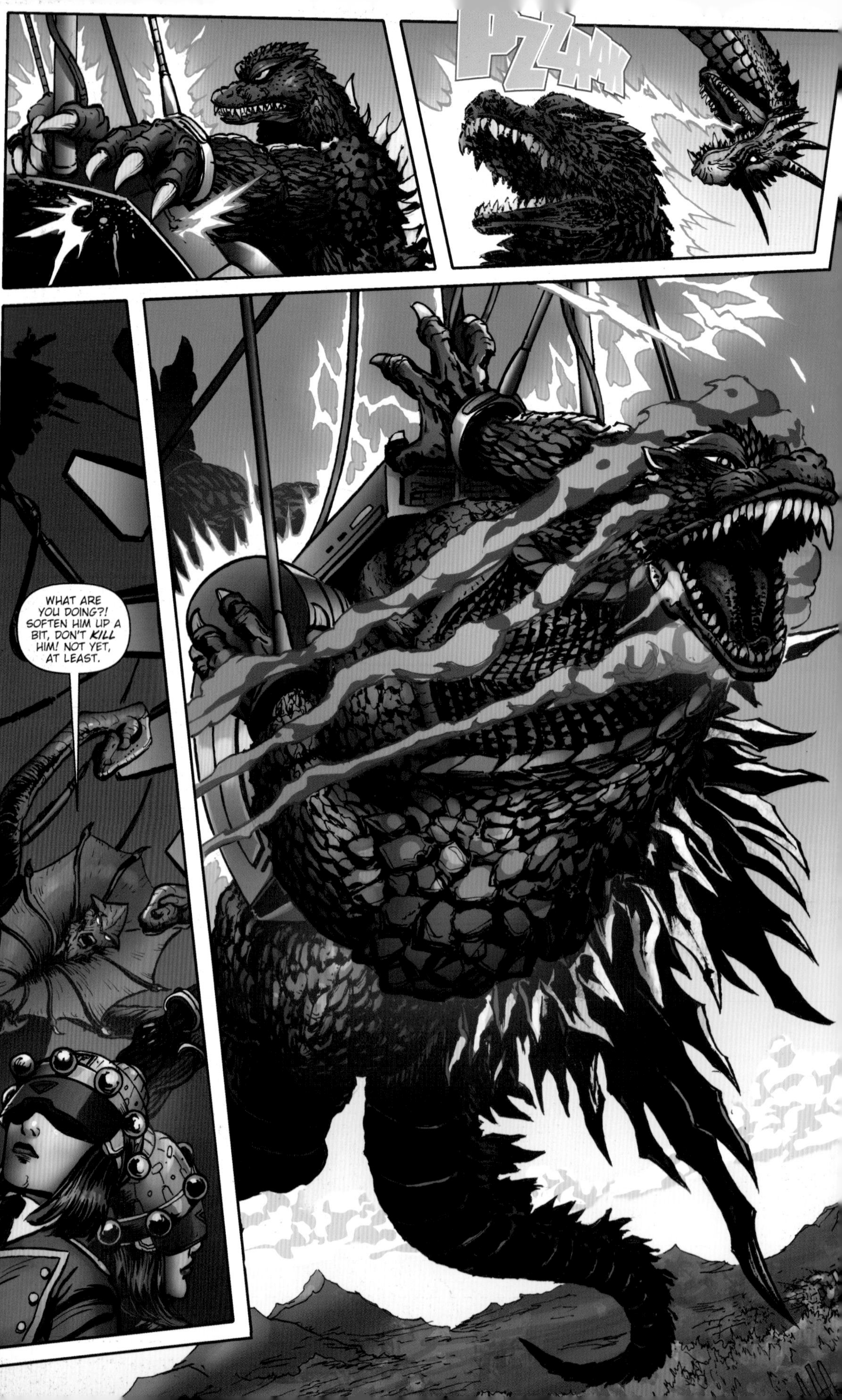
PZZAAK
WHAT ARE YOU DOING?! SOFTEN HIM UP A BIT, DON'T KILL HIM! NOT YET, AT LEAST.

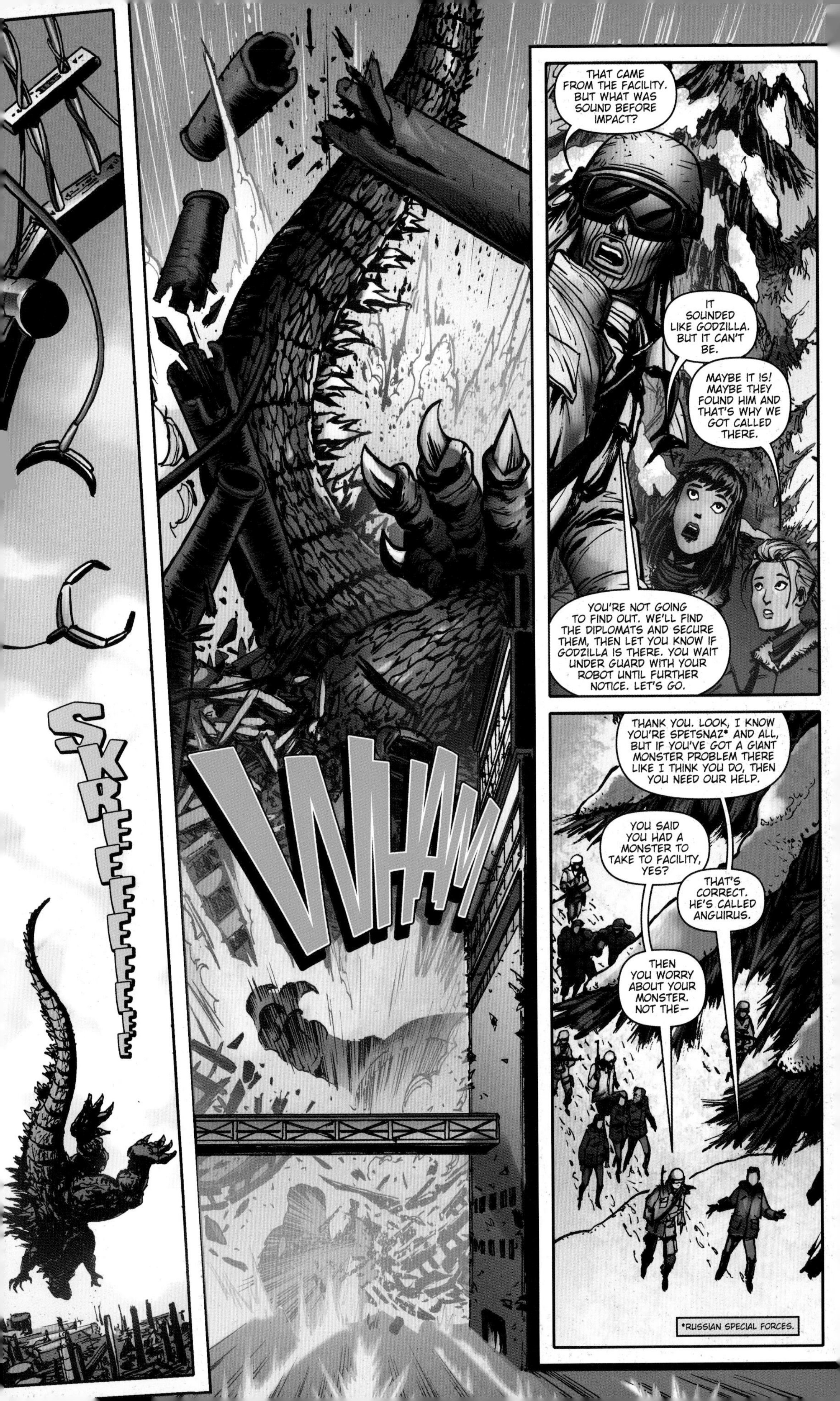
SKREEEEEEE
WHAM
THAT CAME FROM THE FACILITY. BUT WHAT WAS SOUND BEFORE IMPACT?
IT SOUNDED LIKE GODZILLA. BUT IT CAN'T BE.
MAYBE IT IS! MAYBE THEY FOUND HIM AND THAT'S WHY WE GOT CALLED THERE.
YOU'RE NOT GOING TO FIND OUT. WE'LL FIND THE DIPLOMATS AND SECURE THEM, THEN LET YOU KNOW IF GODZILLA IS THERE. YOU WAIT UNDER GUARD WITH YOUR ROBOT UNTIL FURTHER NOTICE. LET'S GO.
THANK YOU. LOOK, I KNOW YOU'RE SPETSNAZ* AND ALL, BUT IF YOU'VE GOT A GIANT MONSTER PROBLEM THERE LIKE I THINK YOU DO, THEN YOU NEED OUR HELP.
YOU SAID YOU HAD A MONSTER TO TAKE TO FACILITY, YES?
THAT'S CORRECT. HE'S CALLED ANGUIRUS.
THEN YOU WORRY ABOUT YOUR MONSTER. NOT THE—
*RUSSIAN SPECIAL FORCES.

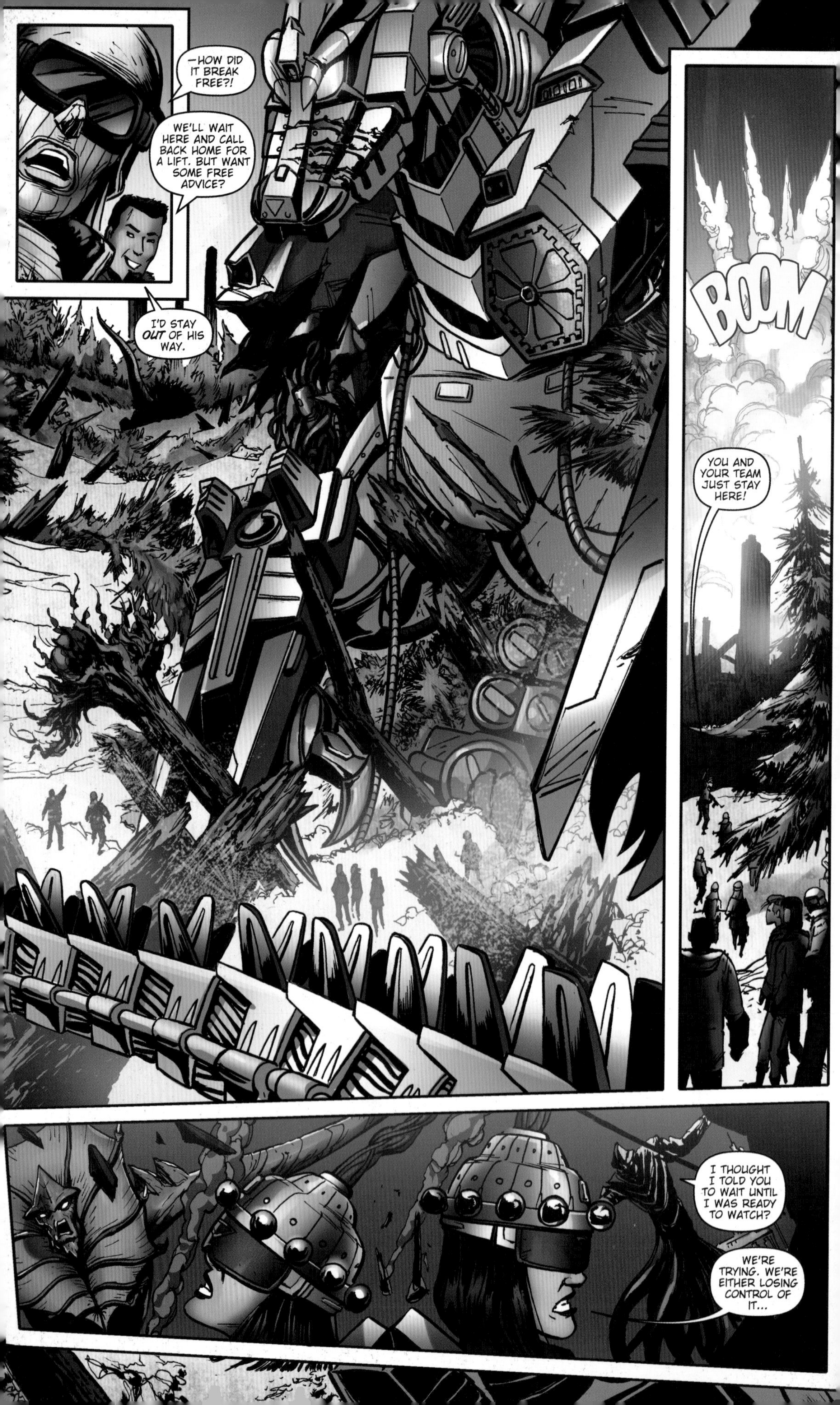
—HOW DID IT BREAK FREE?!
WE'LL WAIT HERE AND CALL BACK HOME FOR A LIFT. BUT WANT SOME FREE ADVICE?
I'D STAY OUT OF HIS WAY.
BOOM
YOU AND YOUR TEAM JUST STAY HERE!
I THOUGHT I TOLD YOU TO WAIT UNTIL I WAS READY TO WATCH?
WE'RE TRYING. WE'RE EITHER LOSING CONTROL OF IT...

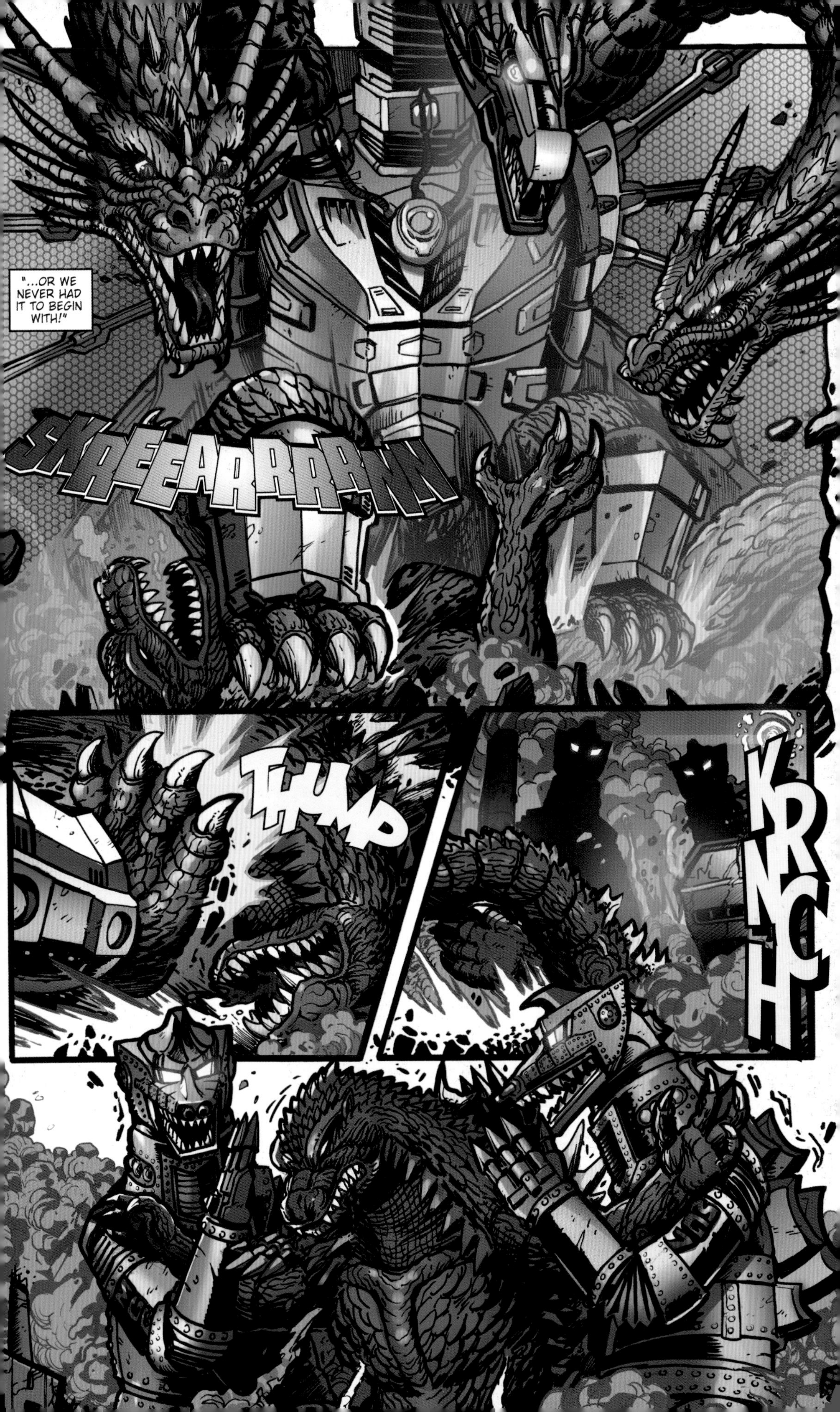
"...OR WE NEVER HAD IT TO BEGIN WITH!"
SKREEARRRRNN
THUMP
KRNCH

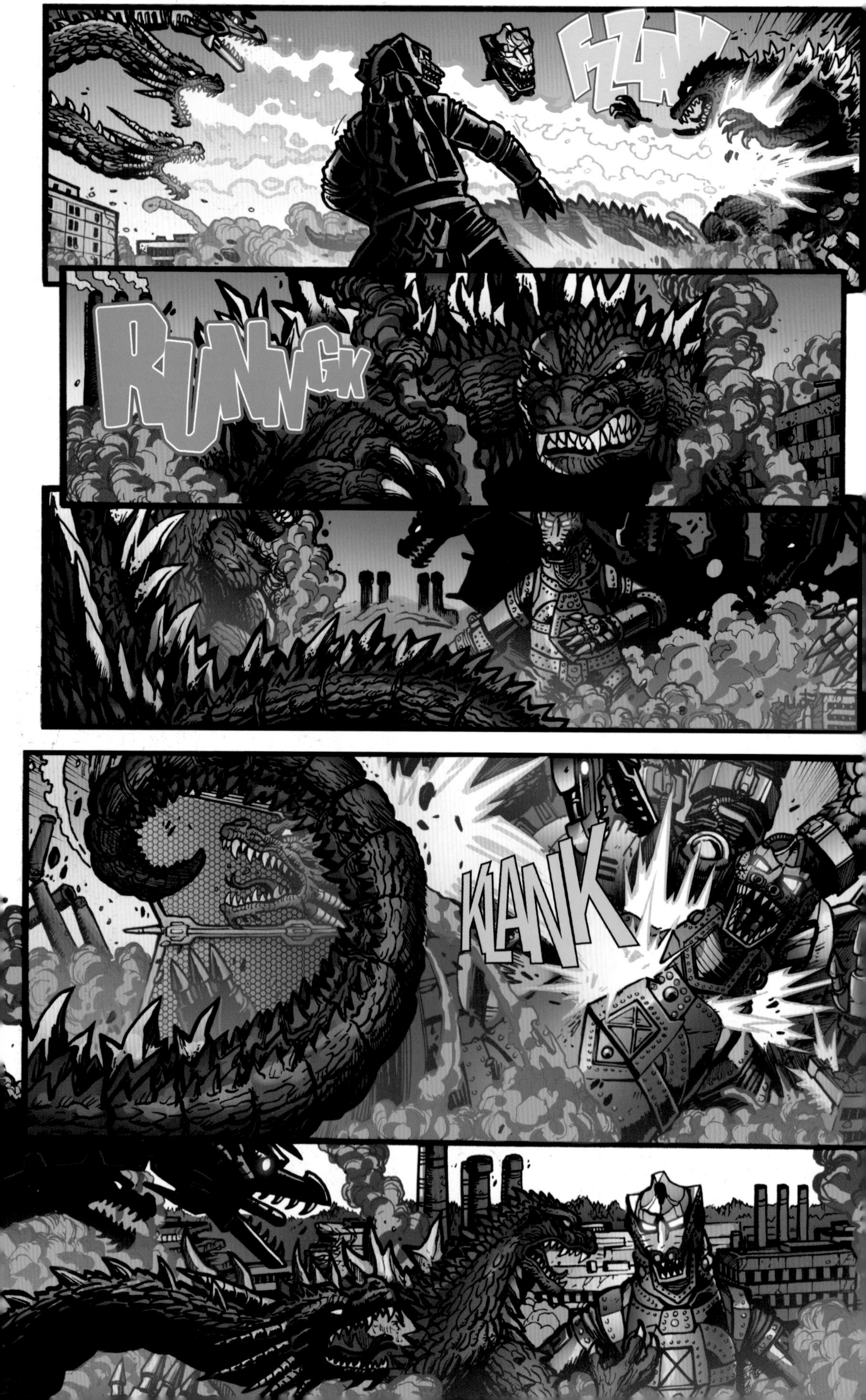
FZZAK
RUNNGK
KLANK

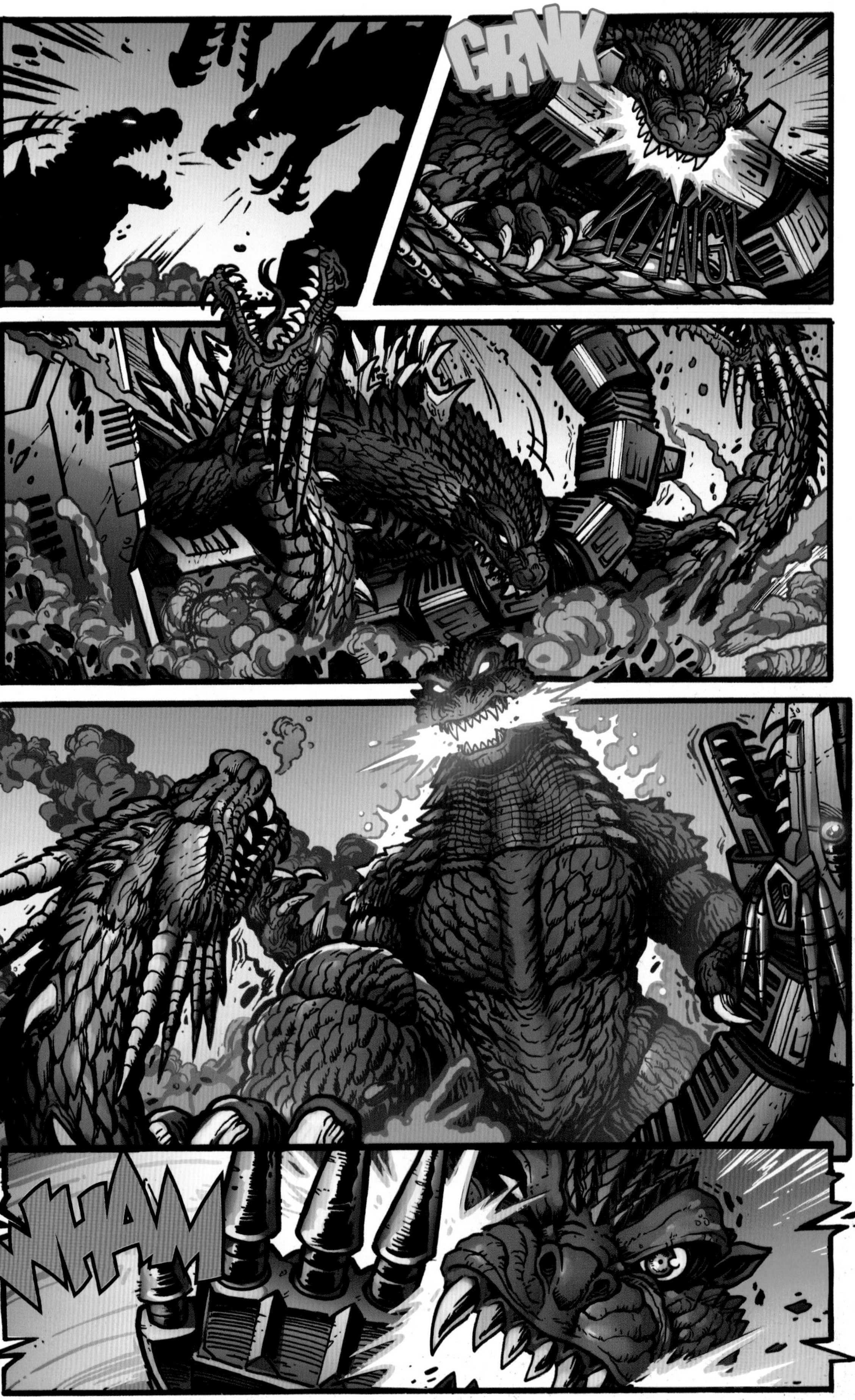
GRNK
KLANGK
WHAM

FWAM
THOOM

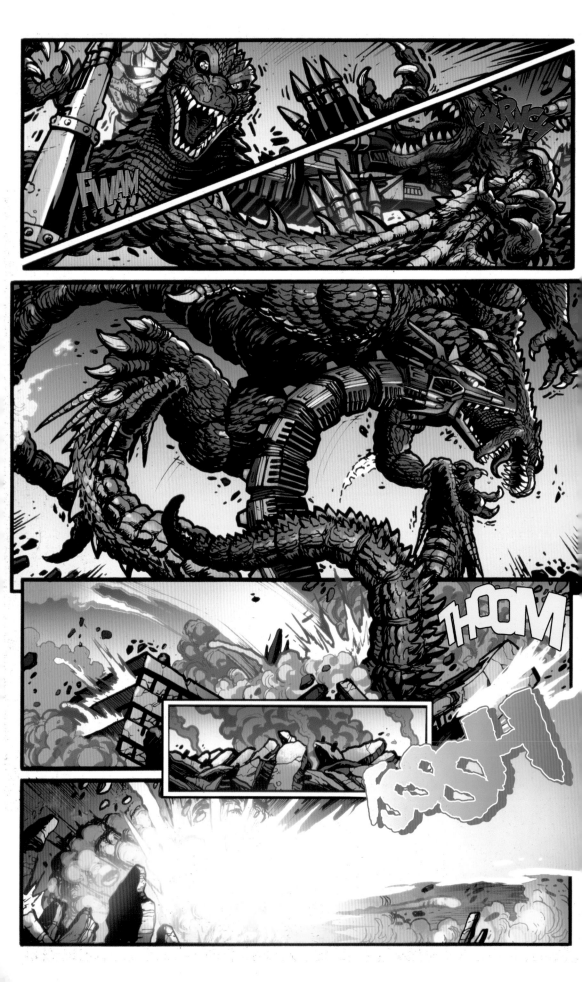

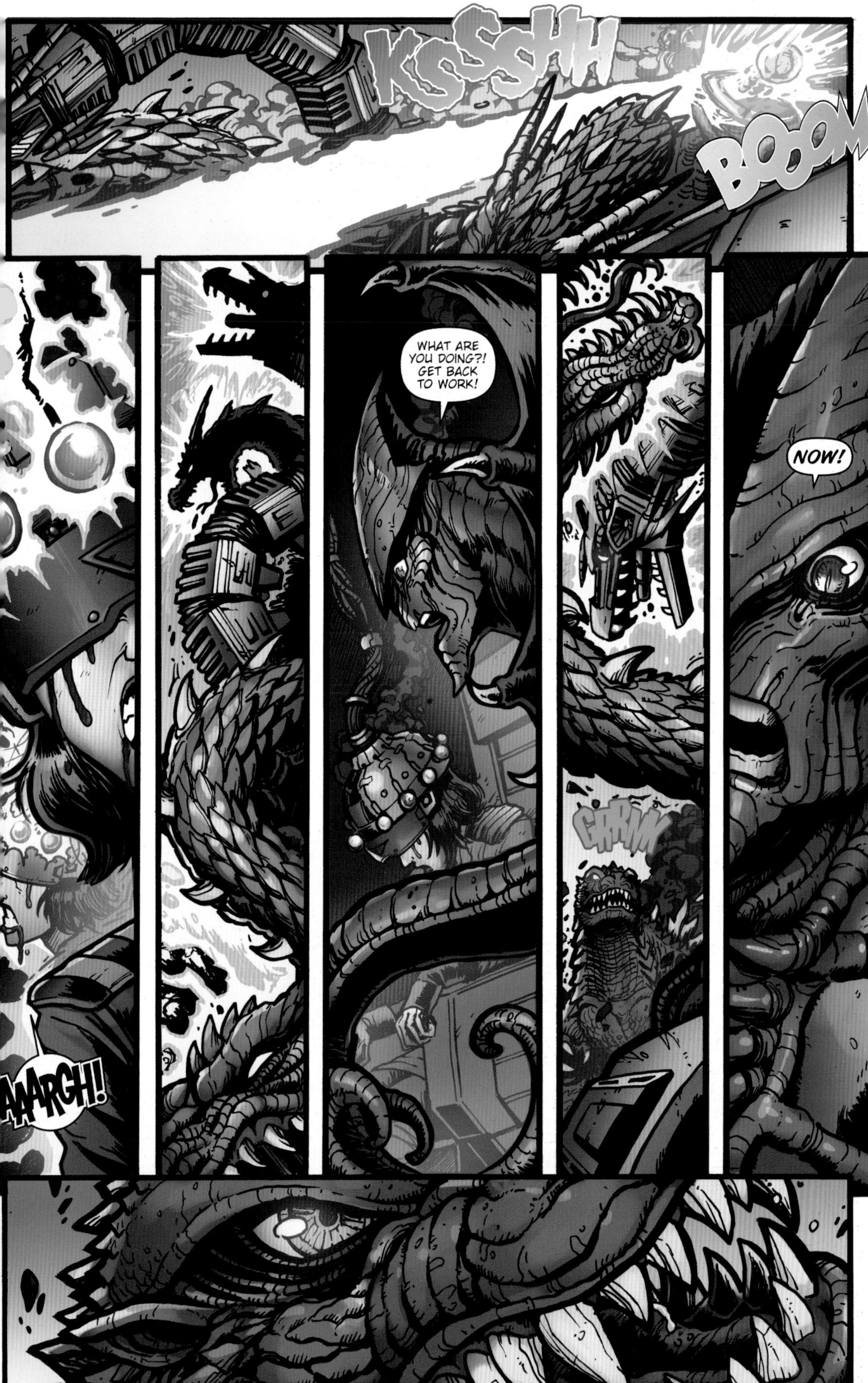
KSSSHH
BOOOM
AAARGH!
WHAT ARE YOU DOING?! GET BACK TO WORK!
GRRM
NOW!

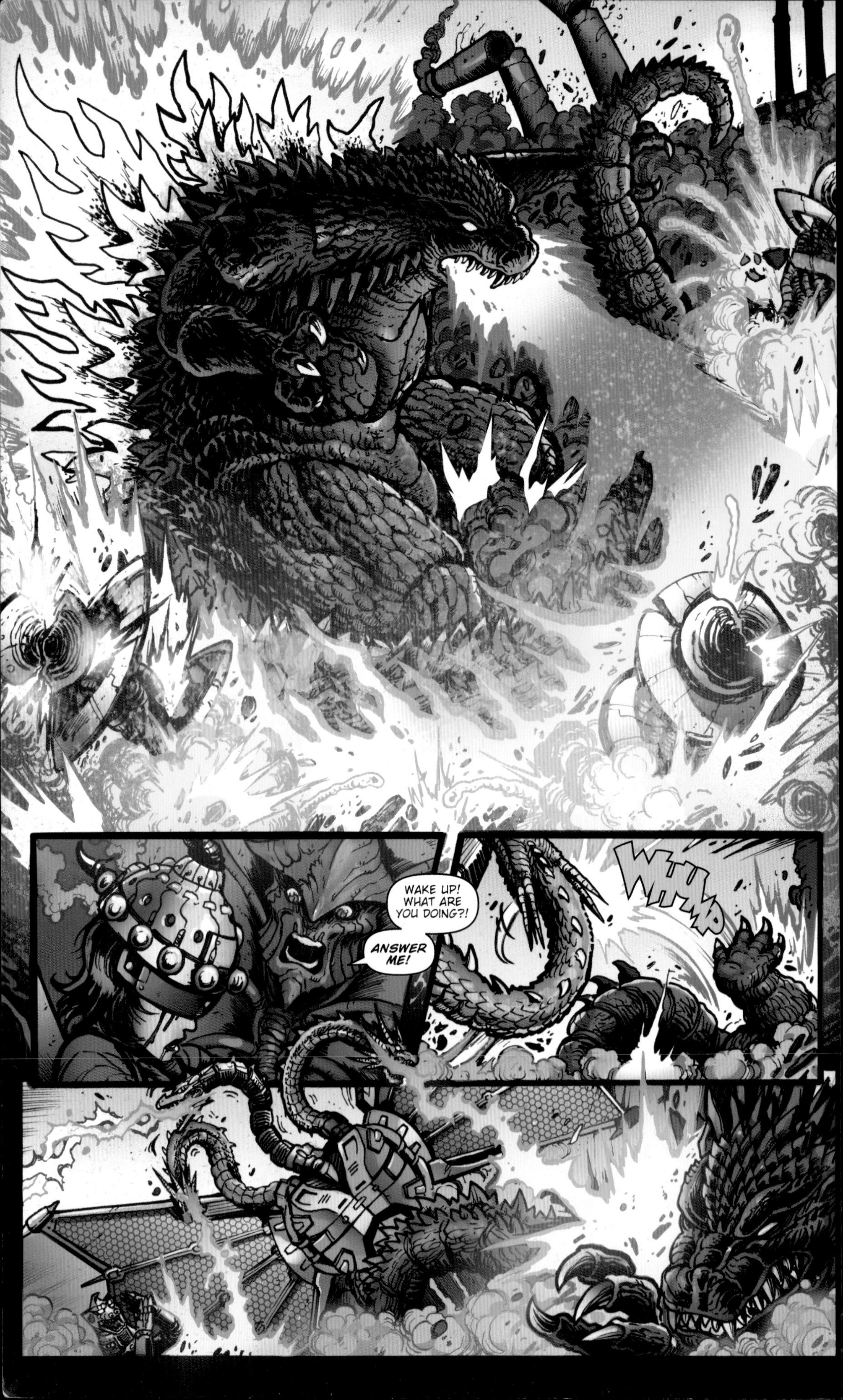
WAKE UP! WHAT ARE YOU DOING?!
ANSWER ME!
WHUMP

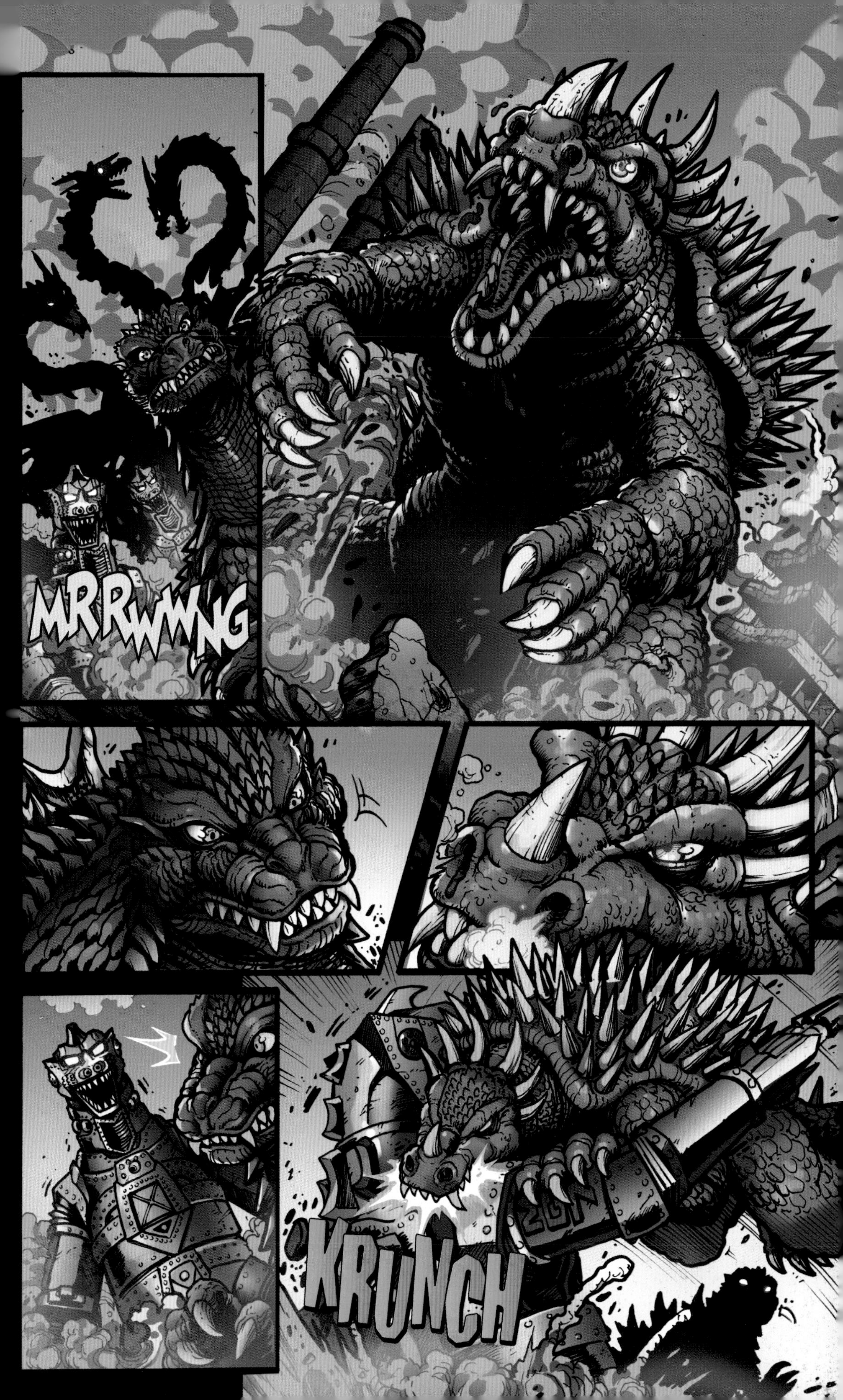
MRRWWNG
KRUNCH

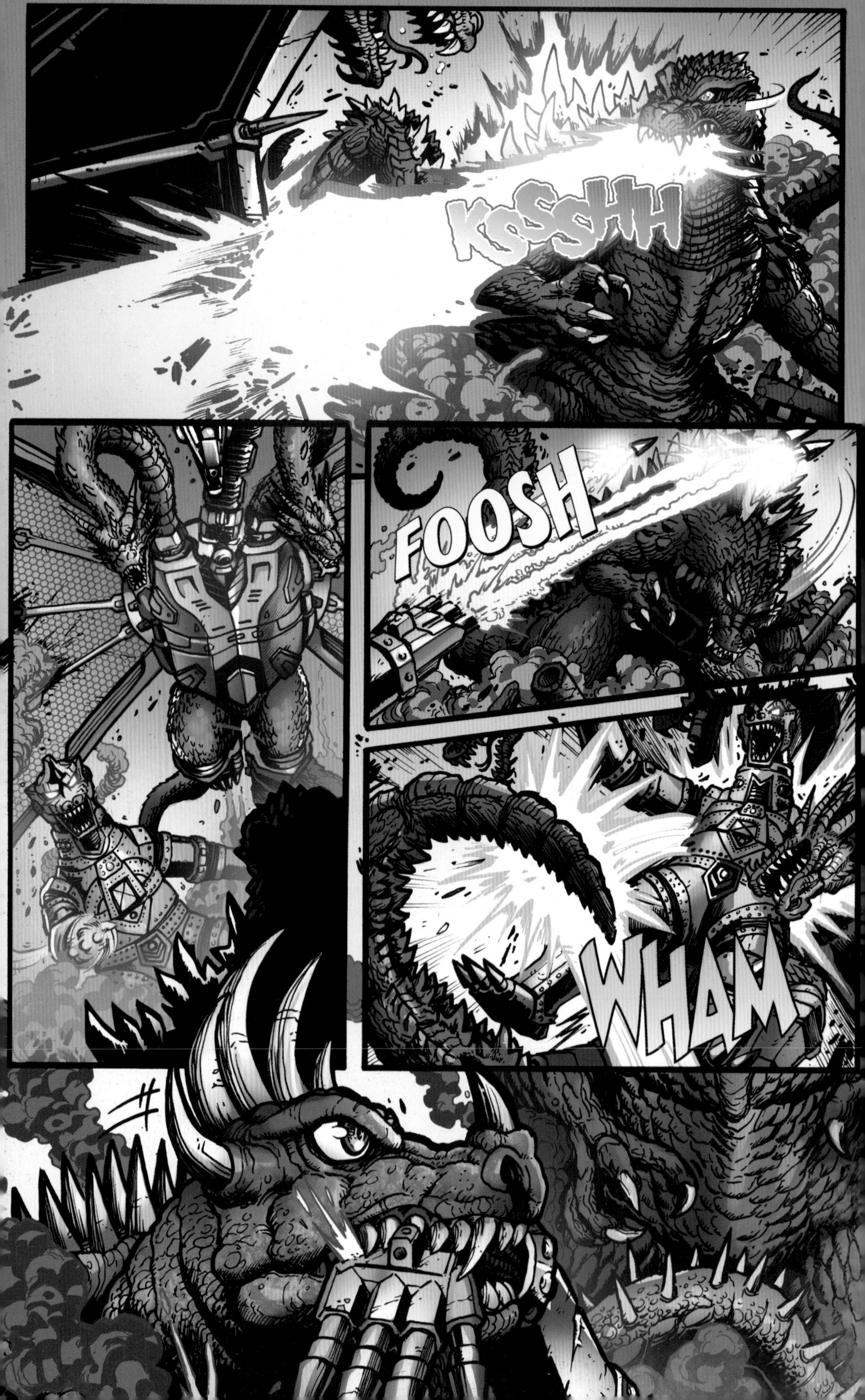
KSSSHH
FOOSH
WHAM

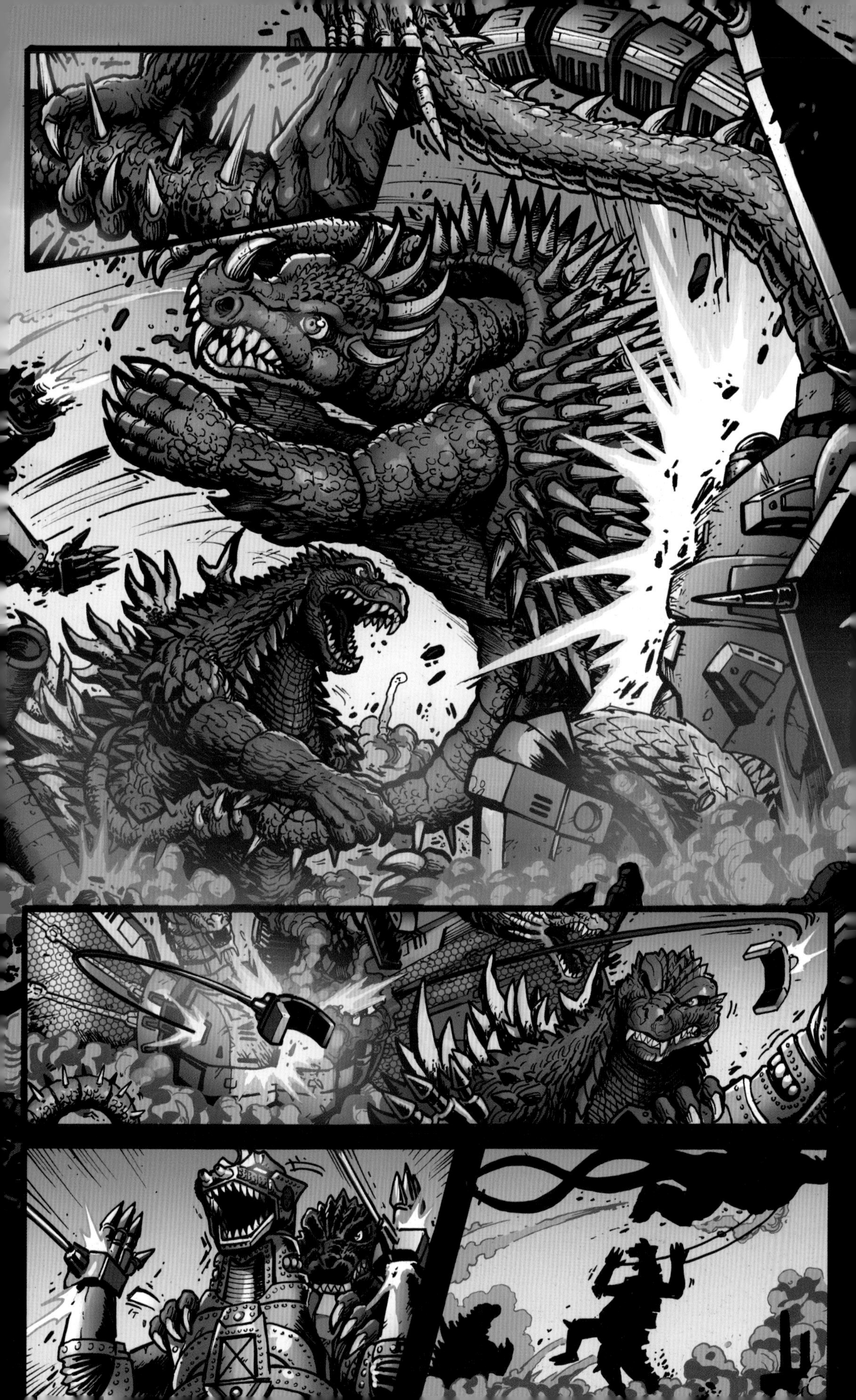

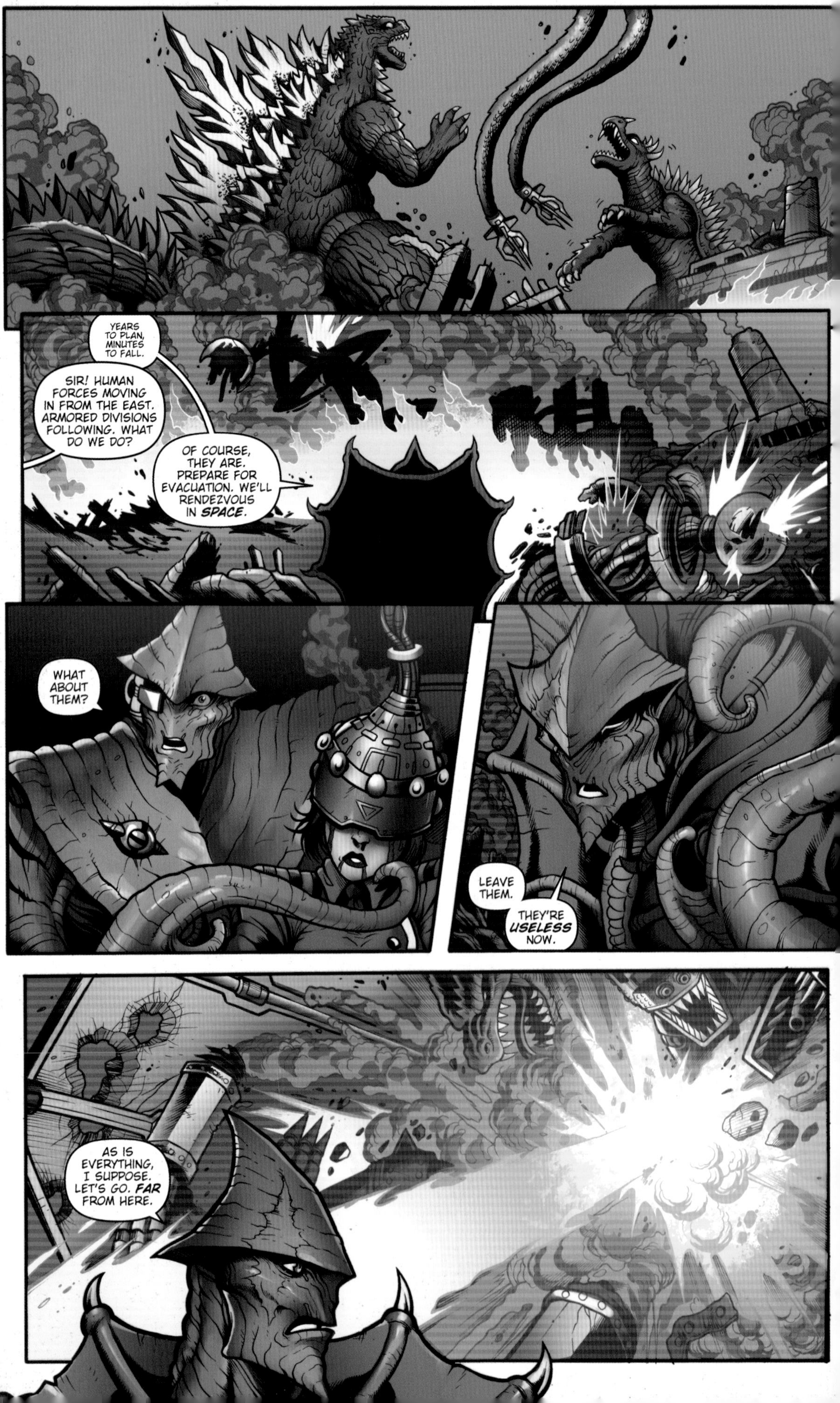
YEARS TO PLAN, MINUTES TO FALL.
SIR! HUMAN FORCES MOVING IN FROM THE EAST. ARMORED DIVISIONS FOLLOWING. WHAT DO WE DO?
OF COURSE, THEY ARE. PREPARE FOR EVACUATION. WE'LL RENDEZVOUS IN *SPACE*.
WHAT ABOUT THEM?
LEAVE THEM.
THEY'RE *USELESS* NOW.
AS IS EVERYTHING, I SUPPOSE. LET'S GO. *FAR* FROM HERE.

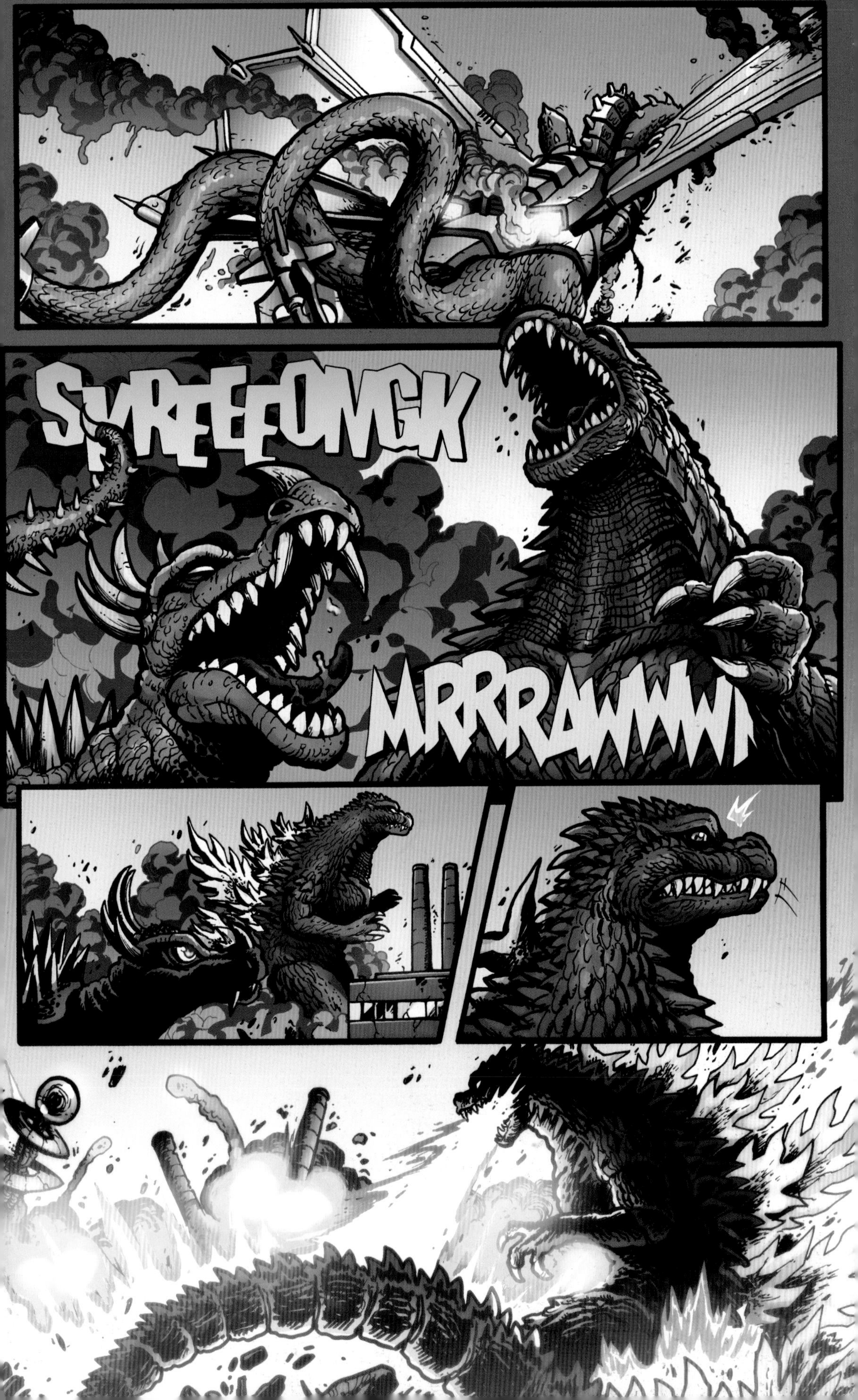
SKREEONGK
MRRRAWWW

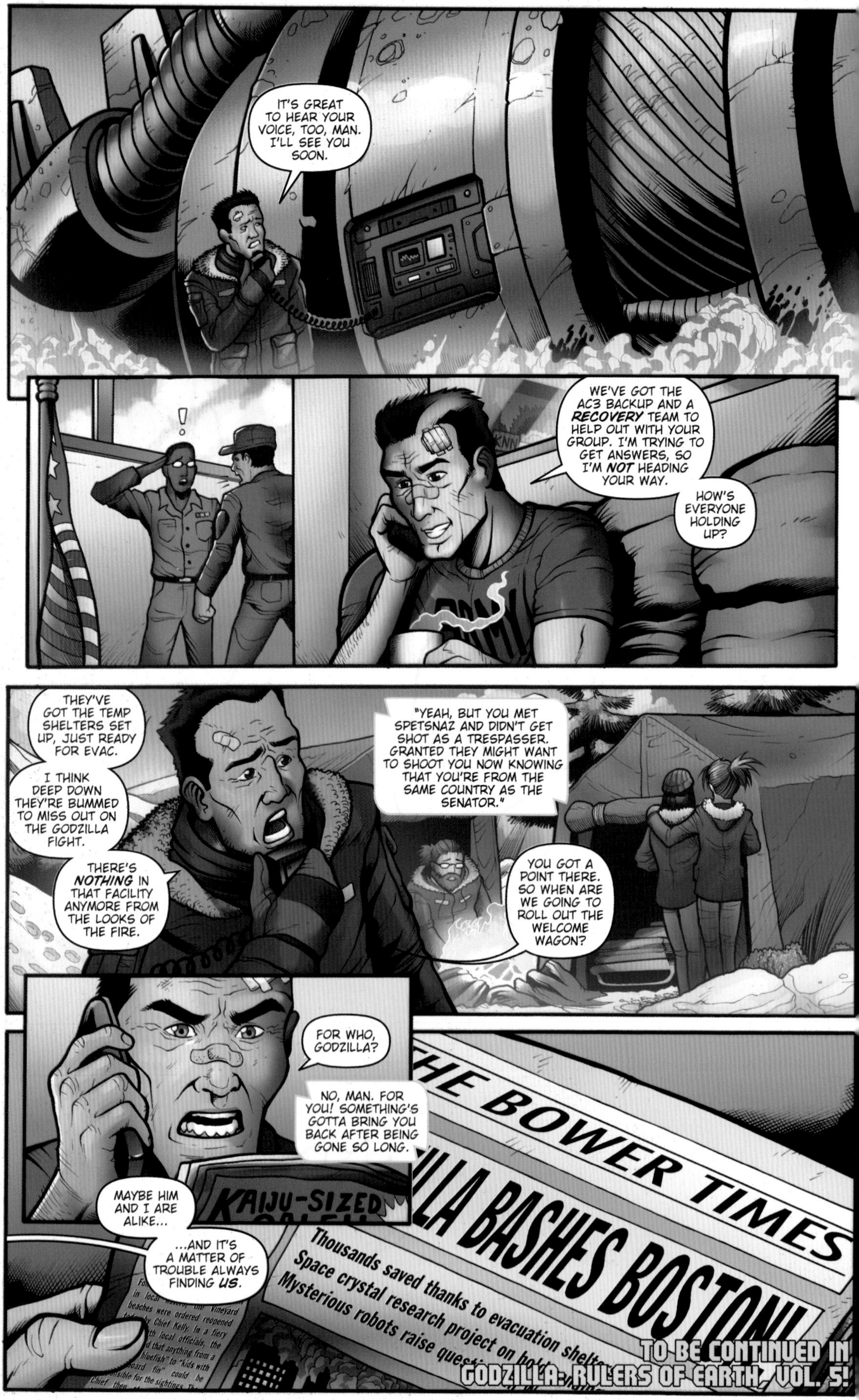
IT'S GREAT TO HEAR YOUR VOICE, TOO, MAN. I'LL SEE YOU SOON.
!
WE'VE GOT THE AC3 BACKUP AND A RECOVERY TEAM TO HELP OUT WITH YOUR GROUP. I'M TRYING TO GET ANSWERS, SO I'M NOT HEADING YOUR WAY.
HOW'S EVERYONE HOLDING UP?
THEY'VE GOT THE TEMP SHELTERS SET UP, JUST READY FOR EVAC.
I THINK DEEP DOWN THEY'RE BUMMED TO MISS OUT ON THE GODZILLA FIGHT.
THERE'S NOTHING IN THAT FACILITY ANYMORE FROM THE LOOKS OF THE FIRE.
"YEAH, BUT YOU MET SPETSNAZ AND DIDN'T GET SHOT AS A TRESPASSER. GRANTED THEY MIGHT WANT TO SHOOT YOU NOW KNOWING THAT YOU'RE FROM THE SAME COUNTRY AS THE SENATOR."
YOU GOT A POINT THERE. SO WHEN ARE WE GOING TO ROLL OUT THE WELCOME WAGON?
FOR WHO, GODZILLA?
NO, MAN. FOR YOU! SOMETHING'S GOTTA BRING YOU BACK AFTER BEING GONE SO LONG.
MAYBE HIM AND I ARE ALIKE...
...AND IT'S A MATTER OF TROUBLE ALWAYS FINDING US.
KAIJU-SIZED
THE BOWER TIMES
ZILLA BASHES BOSTON!
Thousands saved thanks to evacuation shelte
Space crystal research project on hol
Mysterious robots raise questi
TO BE CONTINUED IN GODZILLA: RULERS OF EARTH, VOL. 5!

ART GALLERY

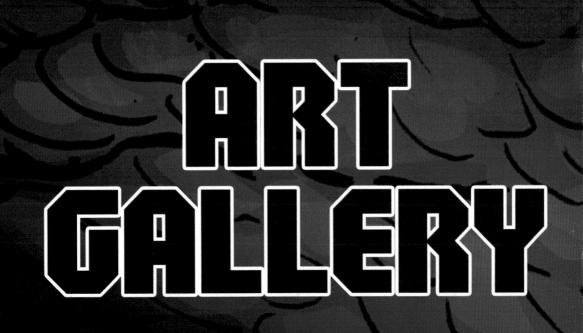

ART BY JEFF ZORNOW

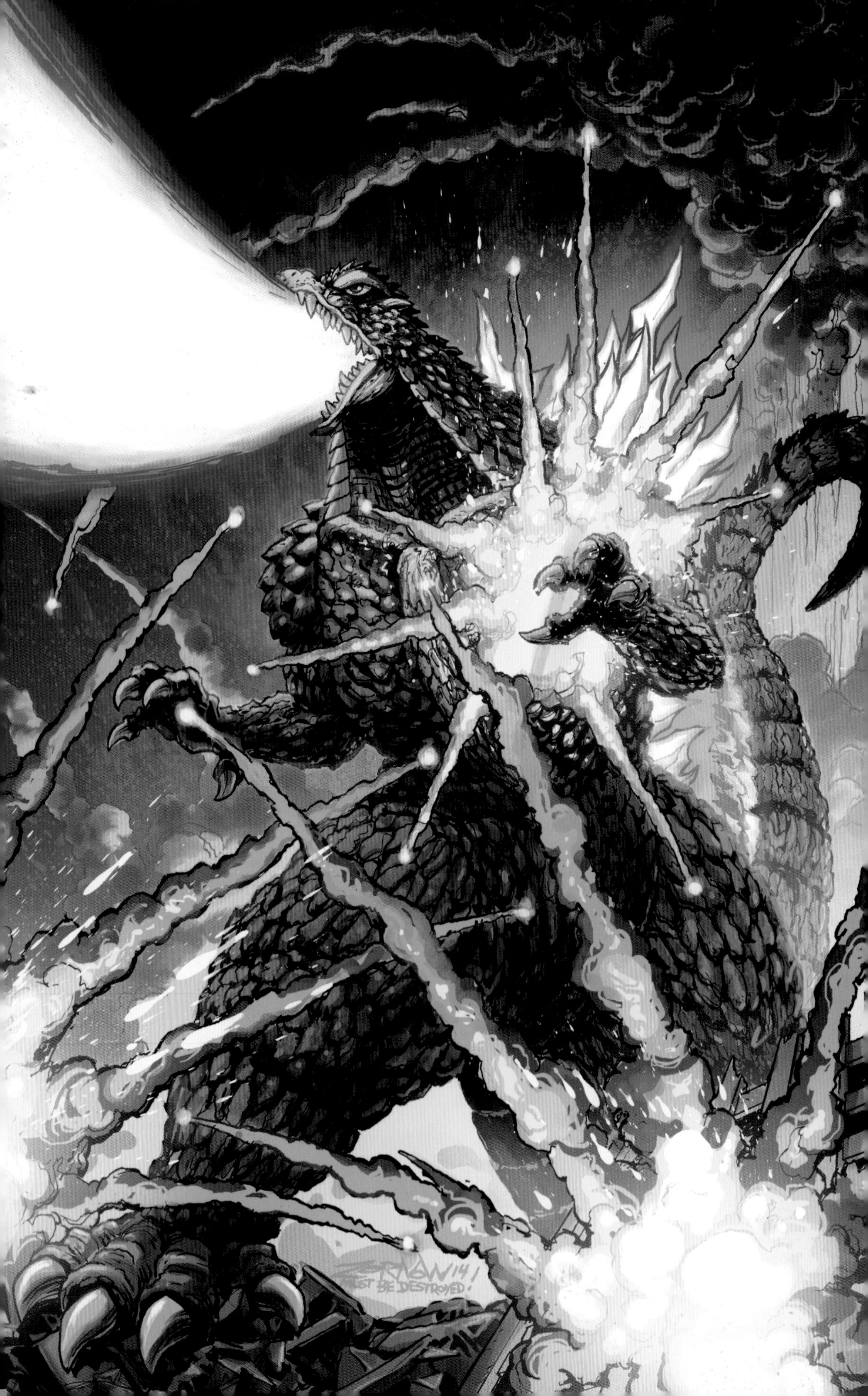
ZORNOW '14!
MUST BE DESTROYED!

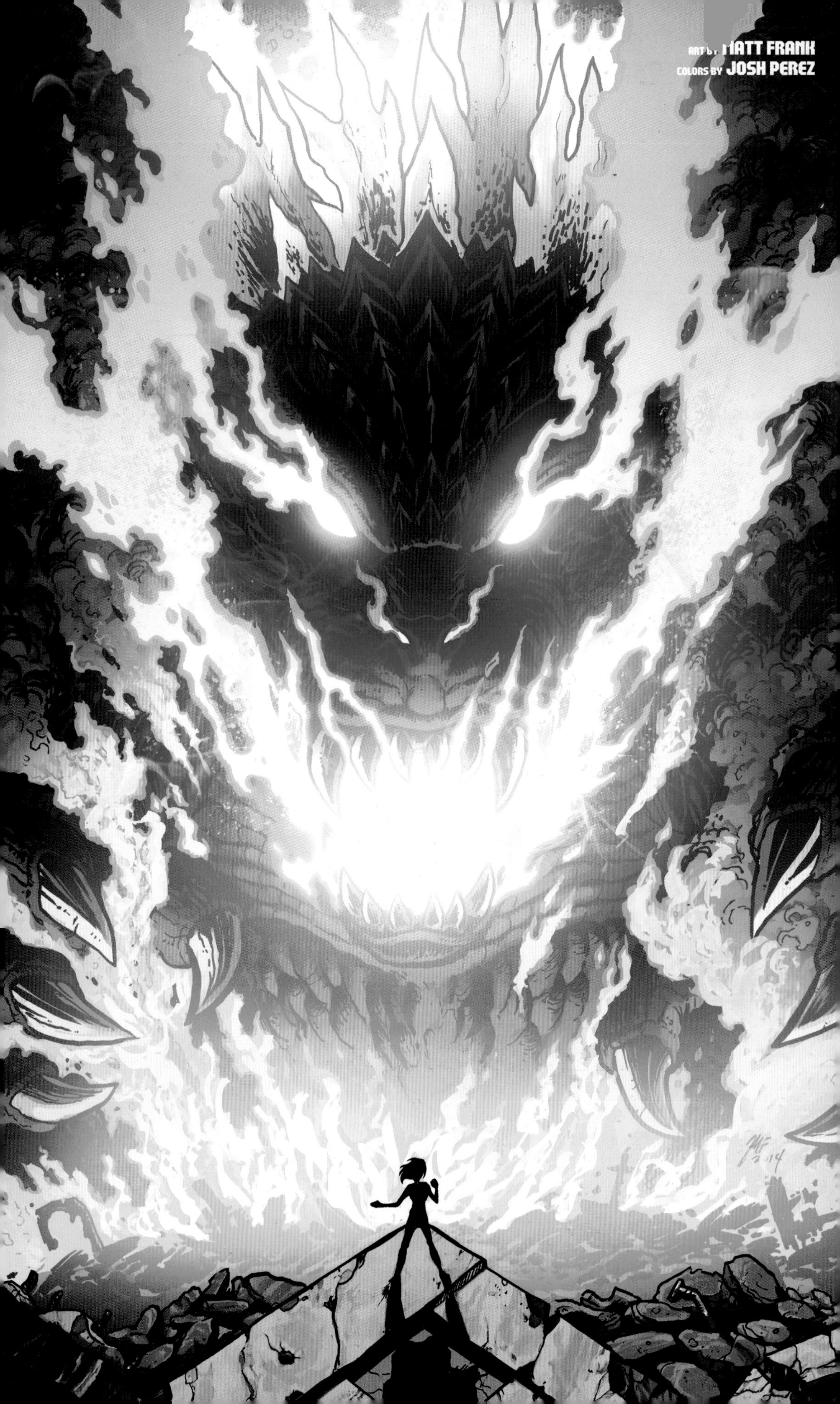
ART BY MATT FRANK
COLORS BY JOSH PEREZ

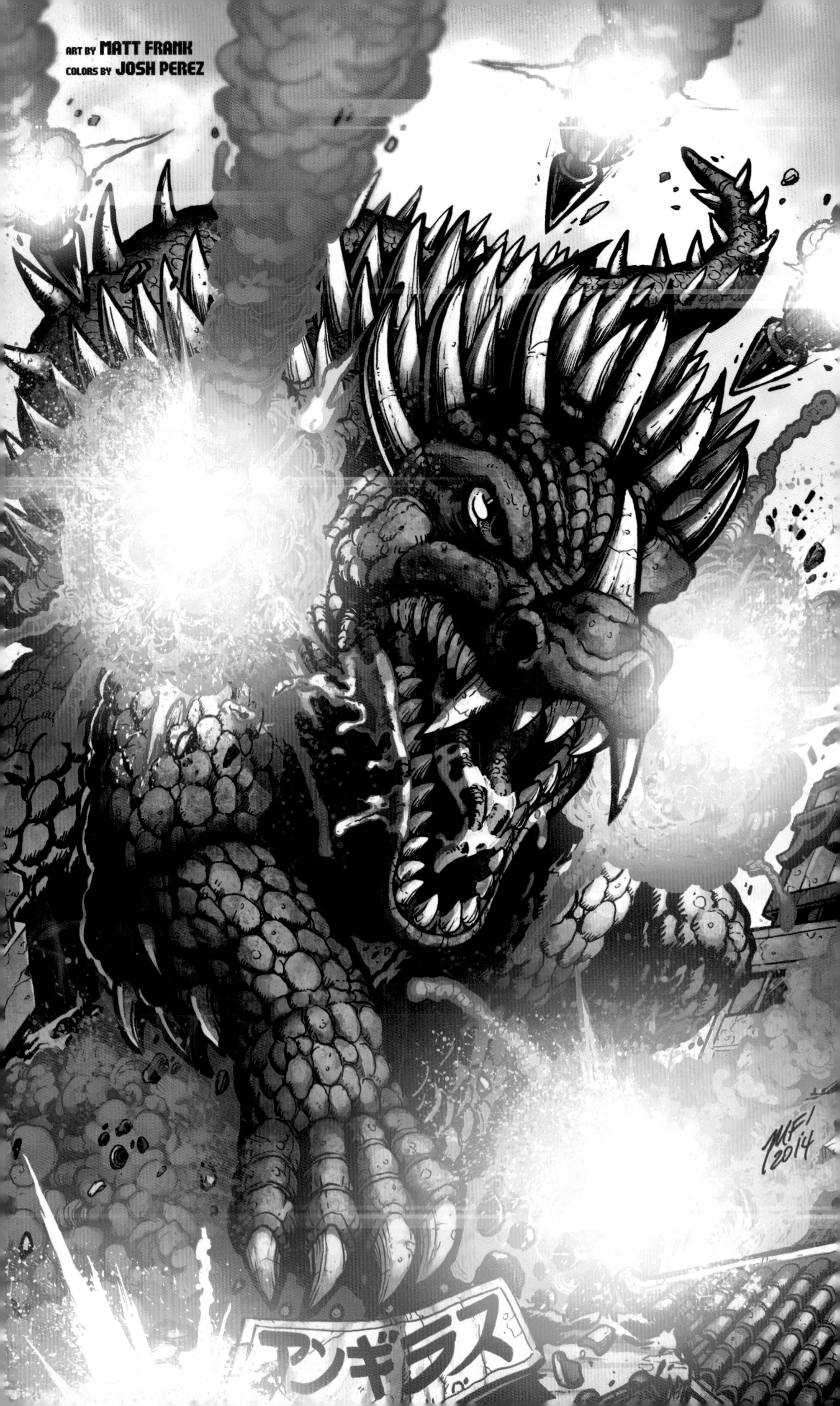
ART BY MATT FRANK
COLORS BY JOSH PEREZ
MF 2014
アンギラス

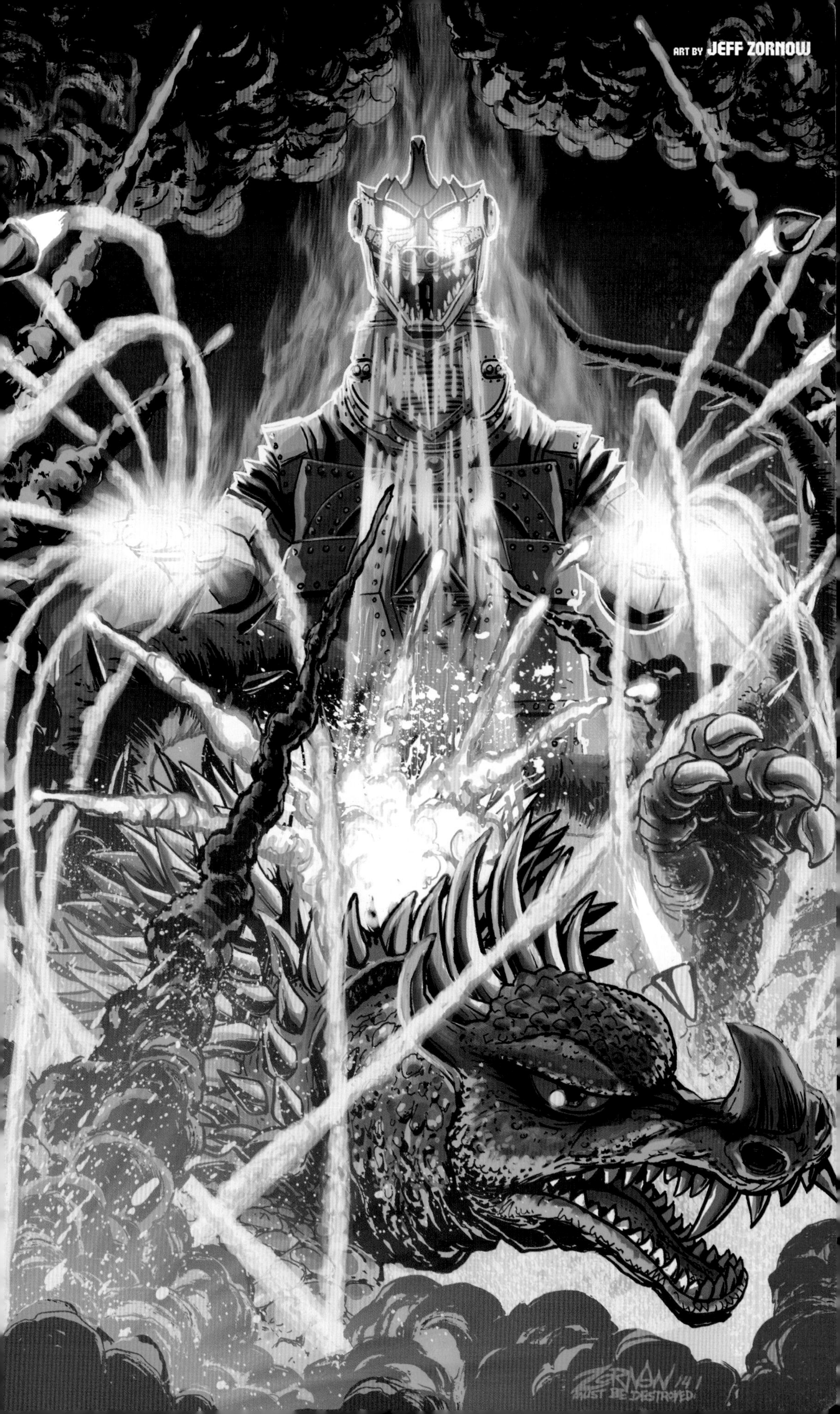
ART BY JEFF ZORNOW

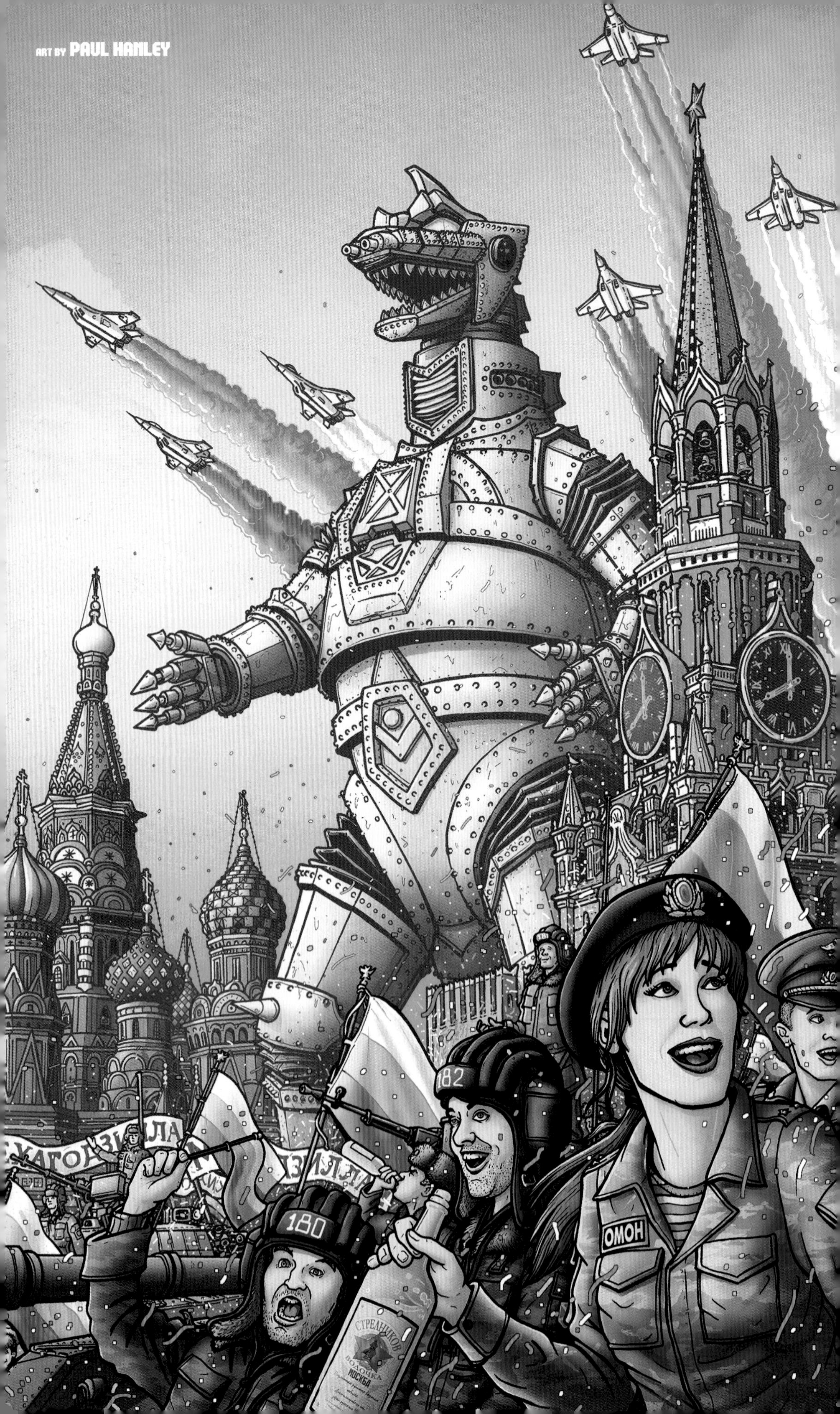
182
180
ОМОН

ART BY PAUL HANLEY

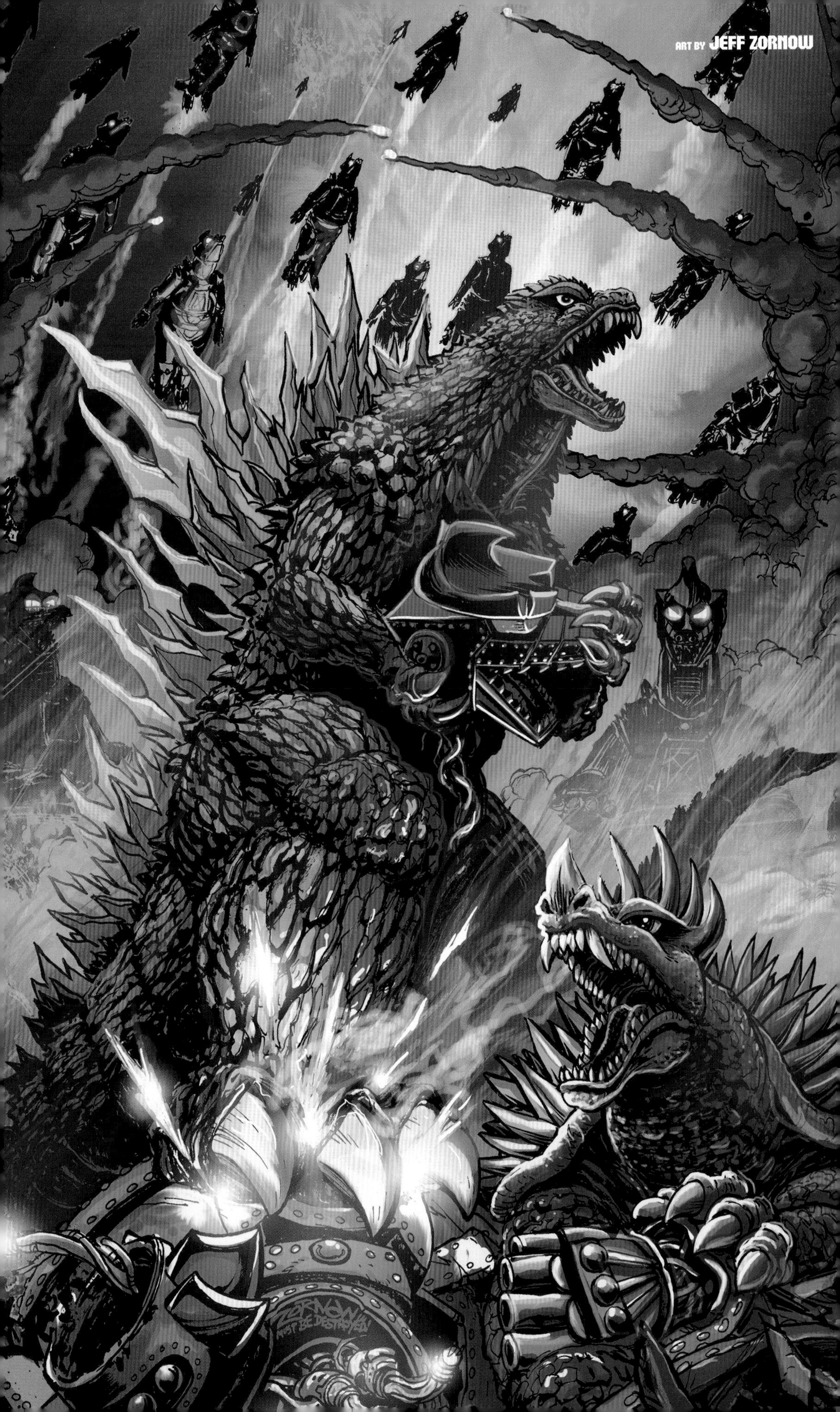

ART BY **JEFF ZORNOW**

ART BY MATT FRANK

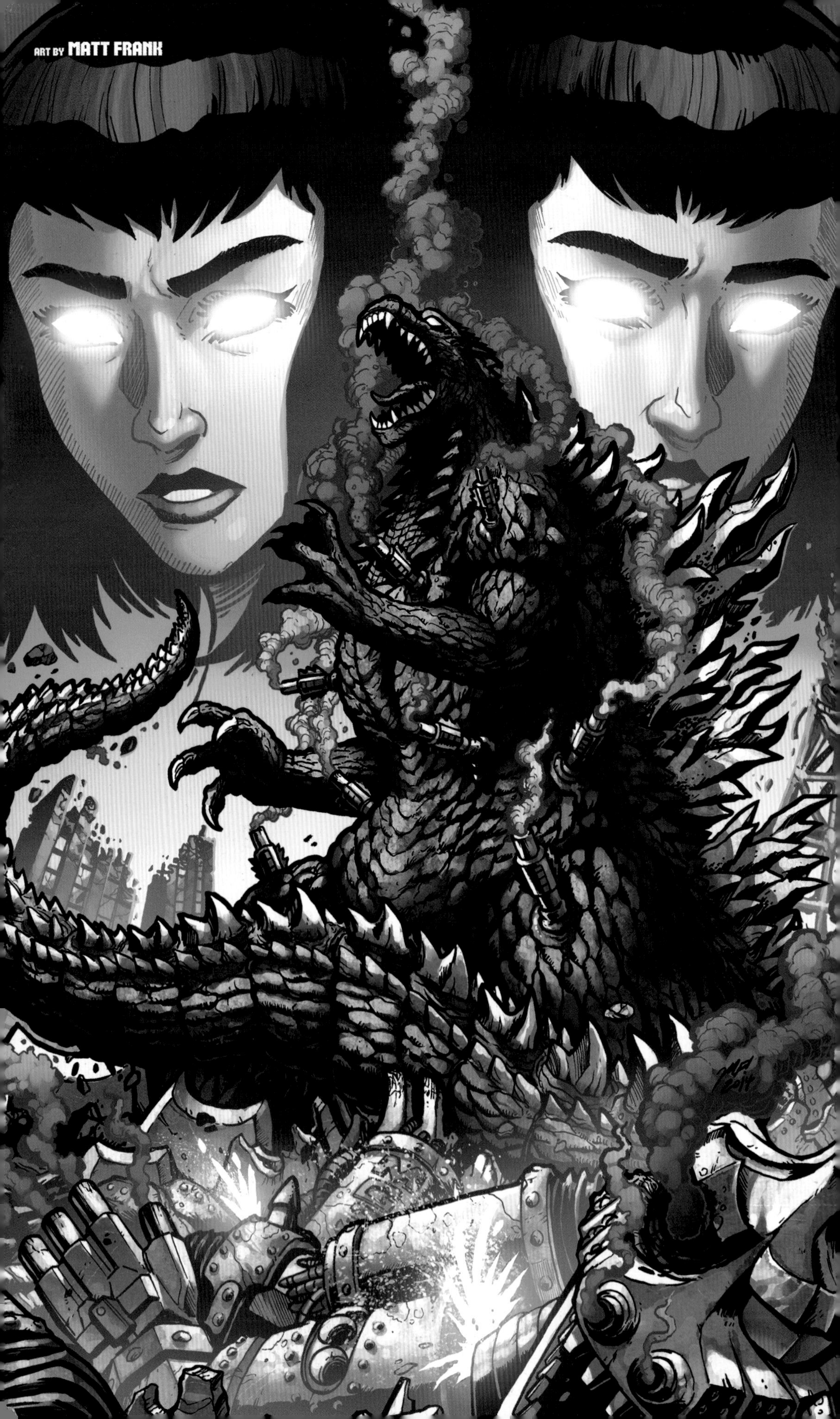

ART BY **JEFF ZORNOW**

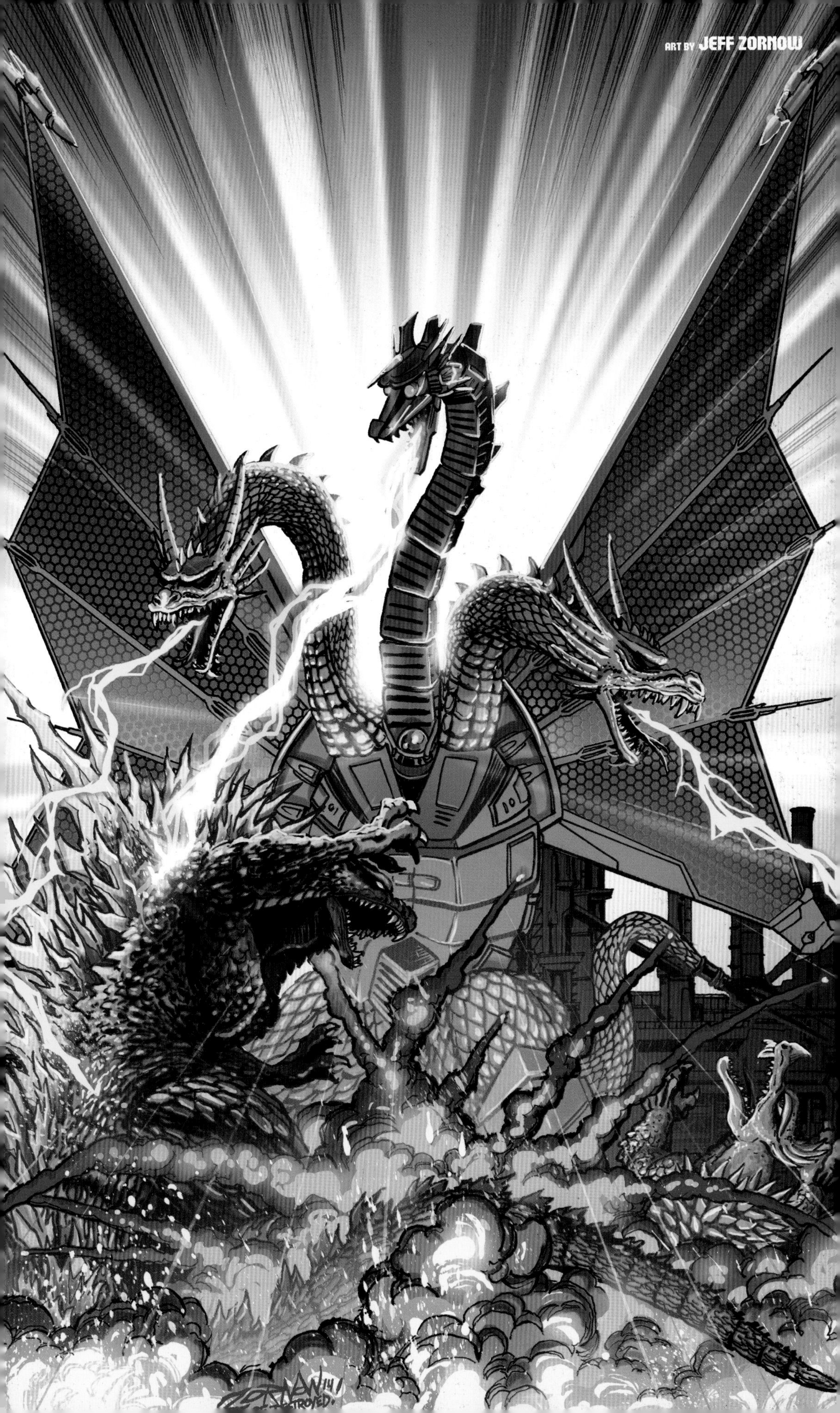

ARTIST CONCEPTS

Since issue #13 takes place four years after the events of issue #12, the cast needed to reflect that in their appearance. New looks for Lucy Casprell and Kristina Sumres were rendered, as well as new uniforms for working at the Monster Islands facility; one that combined a military look with that of a zookeeper. Matt Frank and Jeff Zornow each produced new character sketches, with series colorist Priscilla Tramontano offering her take on Kristina as well.

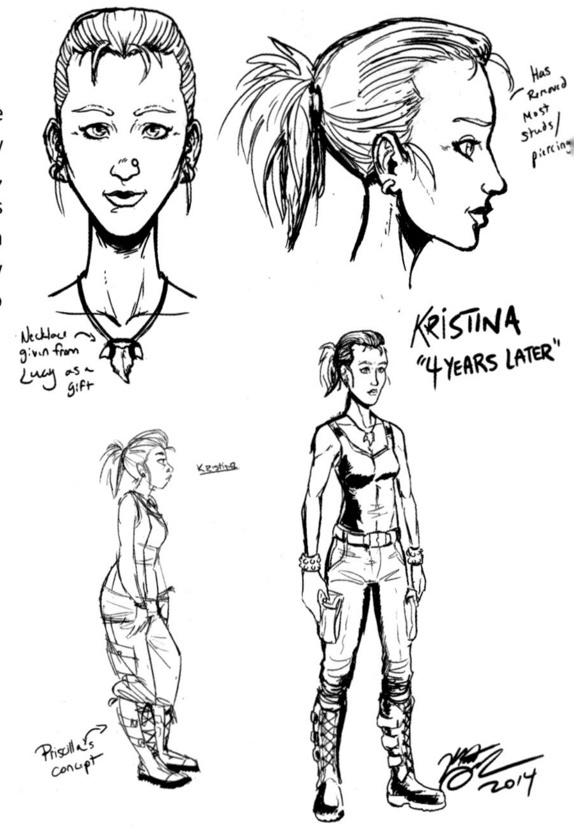
Has Removed Most studs/ piercing
Necklace given from Lucy as a gift
KRISTINA
"4 YEARS LATER"
Kristina
Priscilla's concept
2014

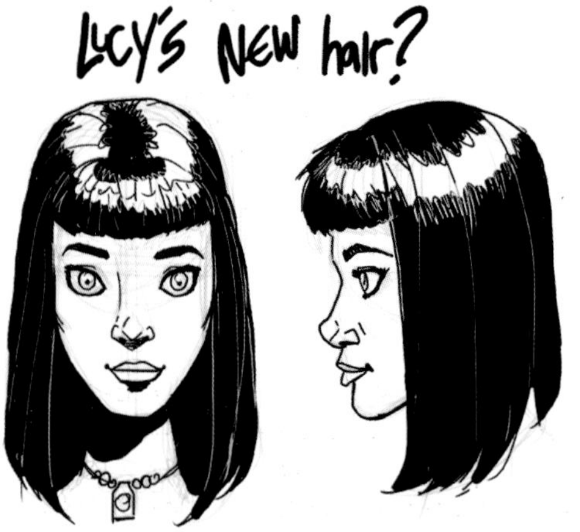
LUCY'S NEW hair?

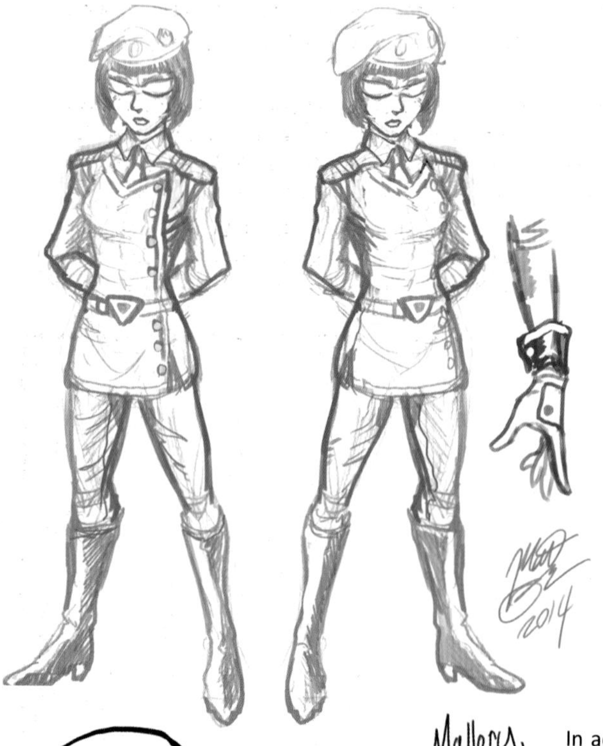
2014

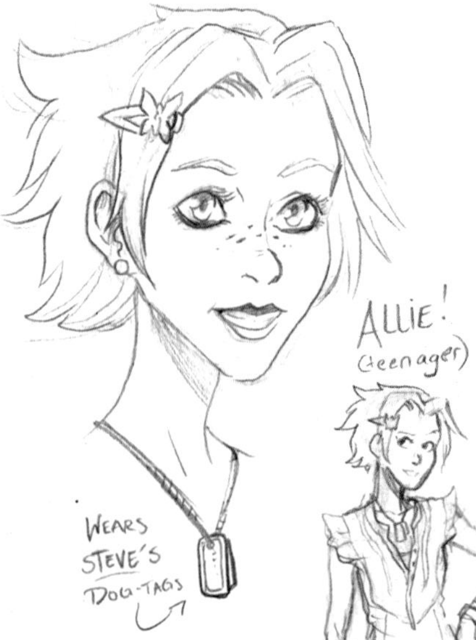
WEARS STEVE'S DOG-TAGS

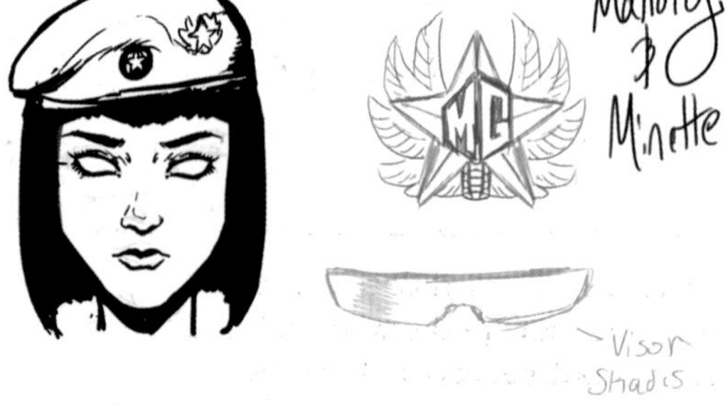
Mallory & Minette
Visor Shades

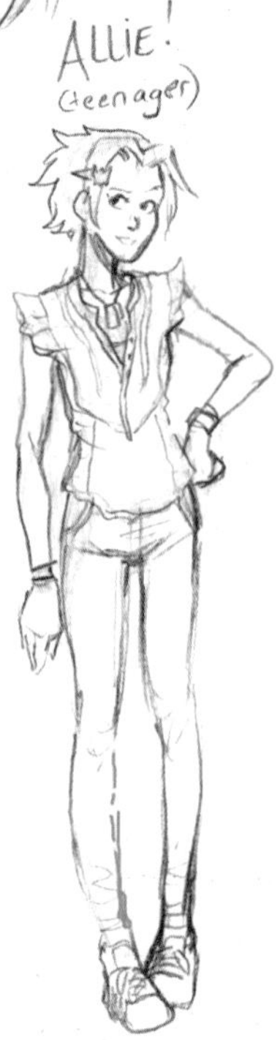
ALLIE!
(teenager)

In addition to Steven Woods, three more characters from IDW's first Godzilla series (*GODZILLA: KINGDOM OF MONSTERS*) have appeared. The evil psychic twins Minette and Mallory (left) were updated to have a military look, while Allie (right), the young girl befriended by Steven Woods years ago, now returns as a young adult.

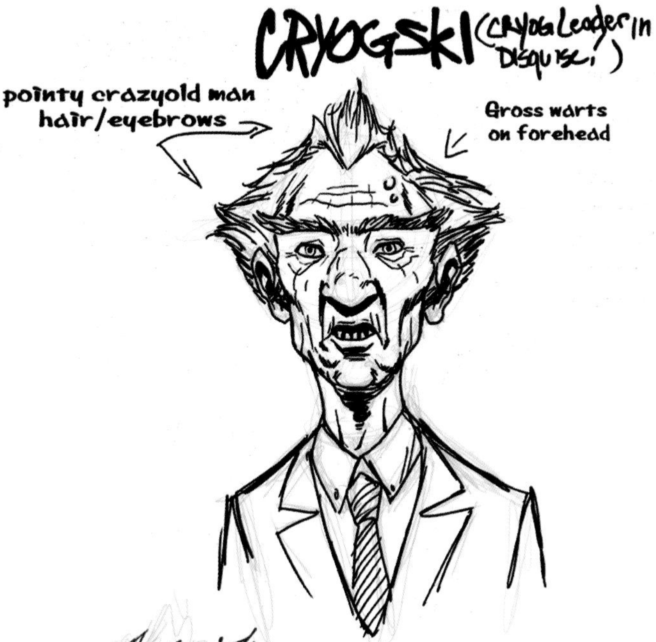
CRYOGSKI (CRYOG LEADER IN DISQUISE)
pointy crazyold man hair/eyebrows
Gross warts on forehead

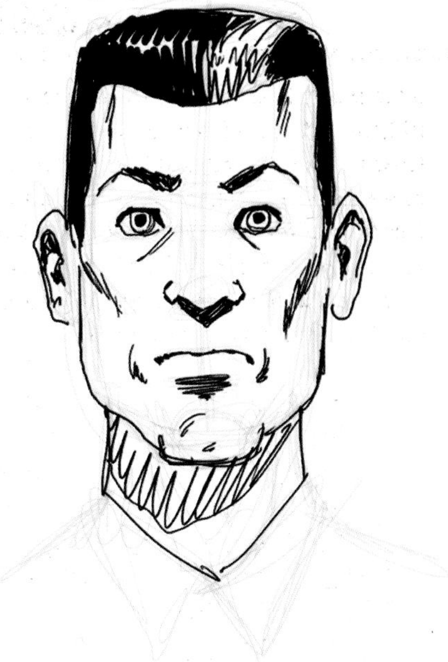

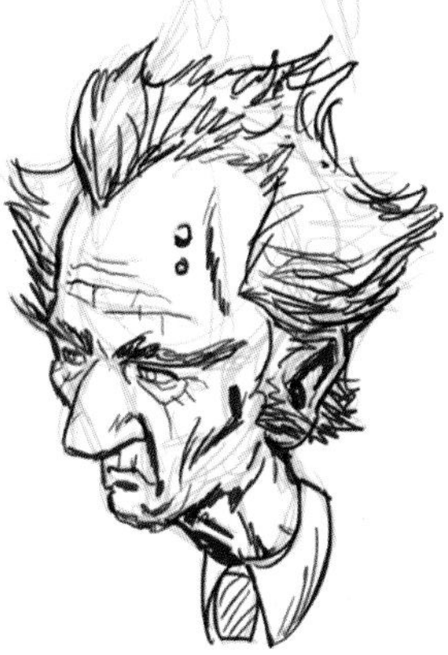

The story called for the Showa era version of Mechagodzilla to be used, but the design had to be one of an alien origin. What better way to bring on the classic monster design than with the Cryog aliens and their ability to change their appearances? Dyachenko (above-left) was simply called "Cryogski" until a better name was selected for him, but the thought was that his human form would be a creepy old man, one that represents political and financial crimes. Notice how his hairline follows the same pattern as the Cryog's pointy heads.

Not quite as old, but definitely showing a little gray, was Steven Woods (above-right). The story finds him retired from active service with the Counter-Kaiju Reaction teams due to an injury suffered in issue #12. Rather than fight monsters, Woods now finds himself fighting Senators and government policies. Since he was to be reunited with his young friend Allie, Woods was drawn to resemble more of someone's father than leader.

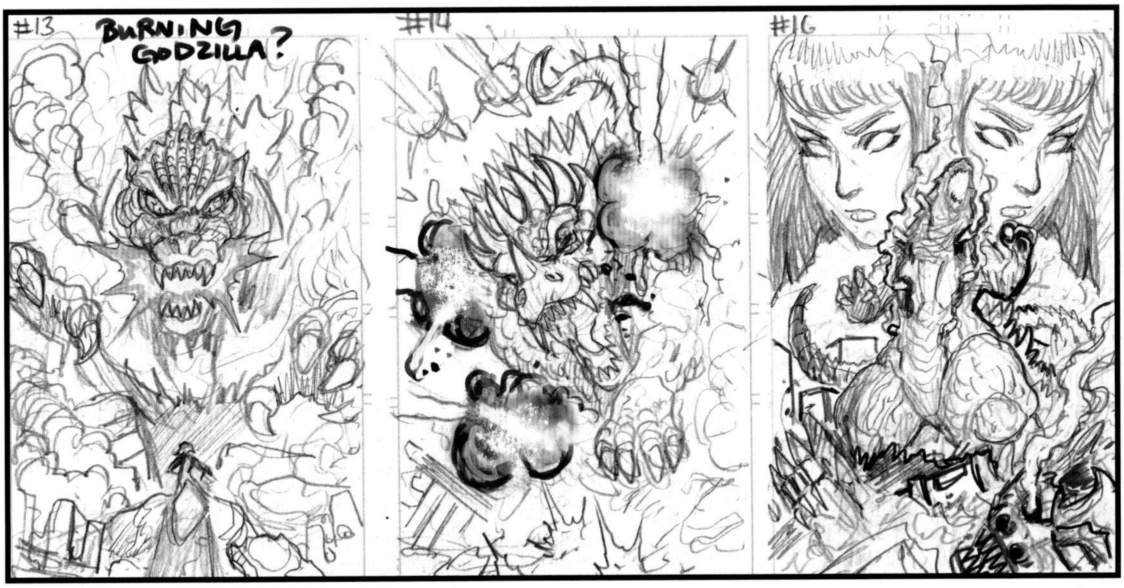
#13
BURNING GODZILLA?
#14
#16

Above: Matt Frank's cover sketches for *GODZILLA: RULERS OF EARTH*. Note the text on the #13 concept. When Godzilla first appears in Lucy's nightmare, the original idea was for him to have his glowing, steaming, "burning" effect that he did in 1995's *Godzilla vs. Destoroyah*.

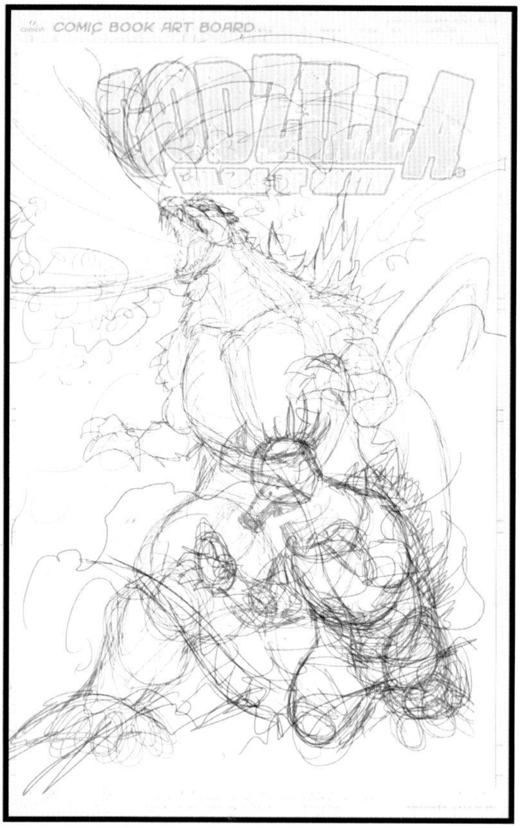
COMIC BOOK ART BOARD
GODZILLA

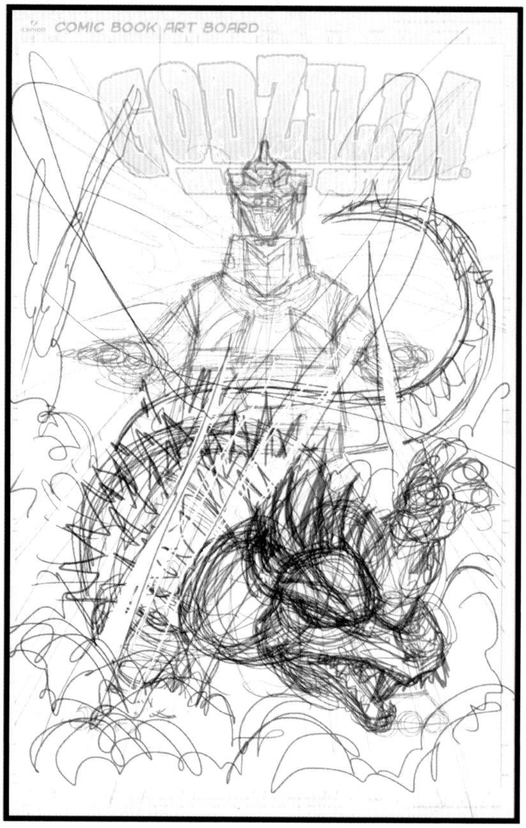
COMIC BOOK ART BOARD
GODZILLA

This page: A collection of concept sketches for *GODZILLA: RULERS OF EARTH* by Jeff Zornow.

Opposite page: Jeff's sketch for Godzilla's return (albeit in Lucy's nightmare) in issue #13.

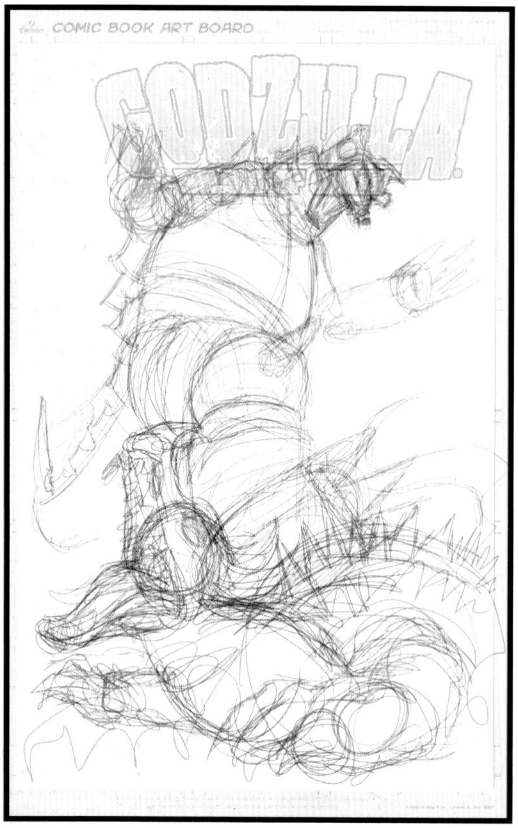
COMIC BOOK ART BOARD
GODZILLA

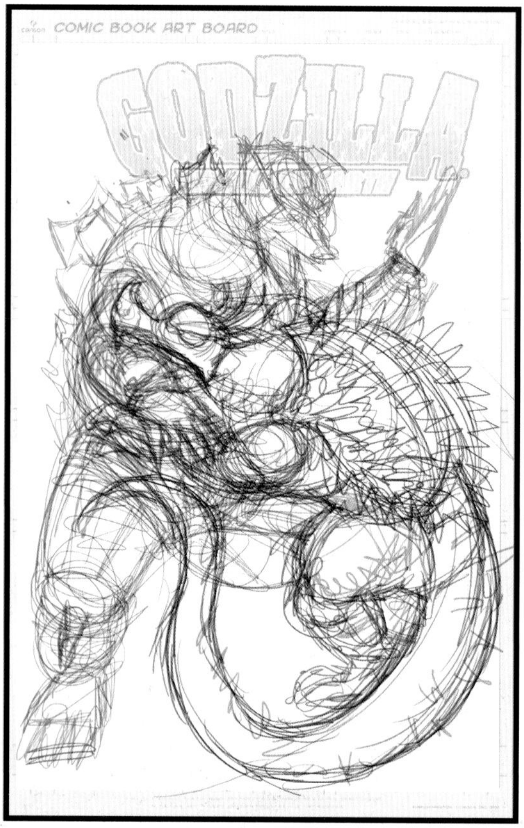
COMIC BOOK ART BOARD
GODZILLA

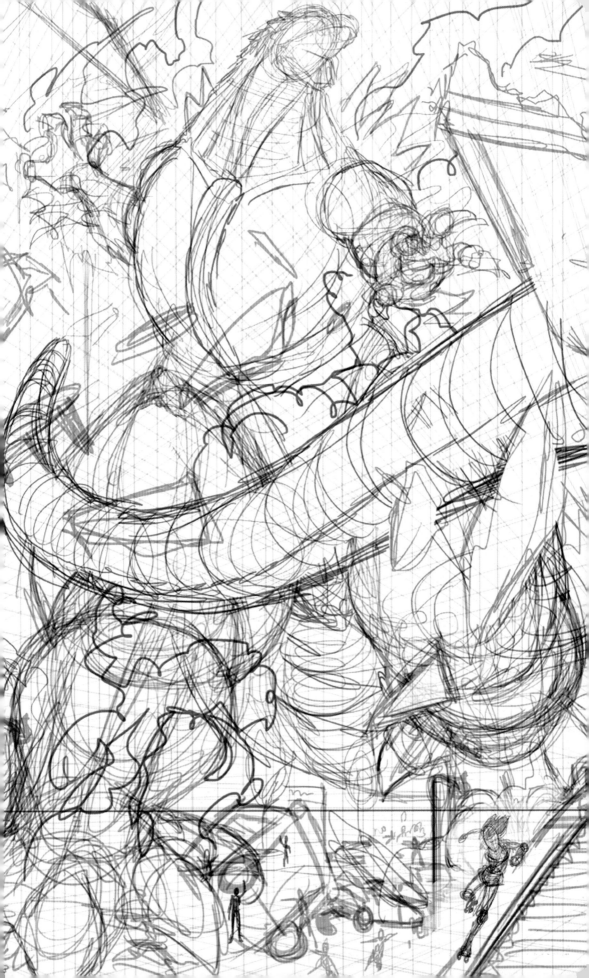

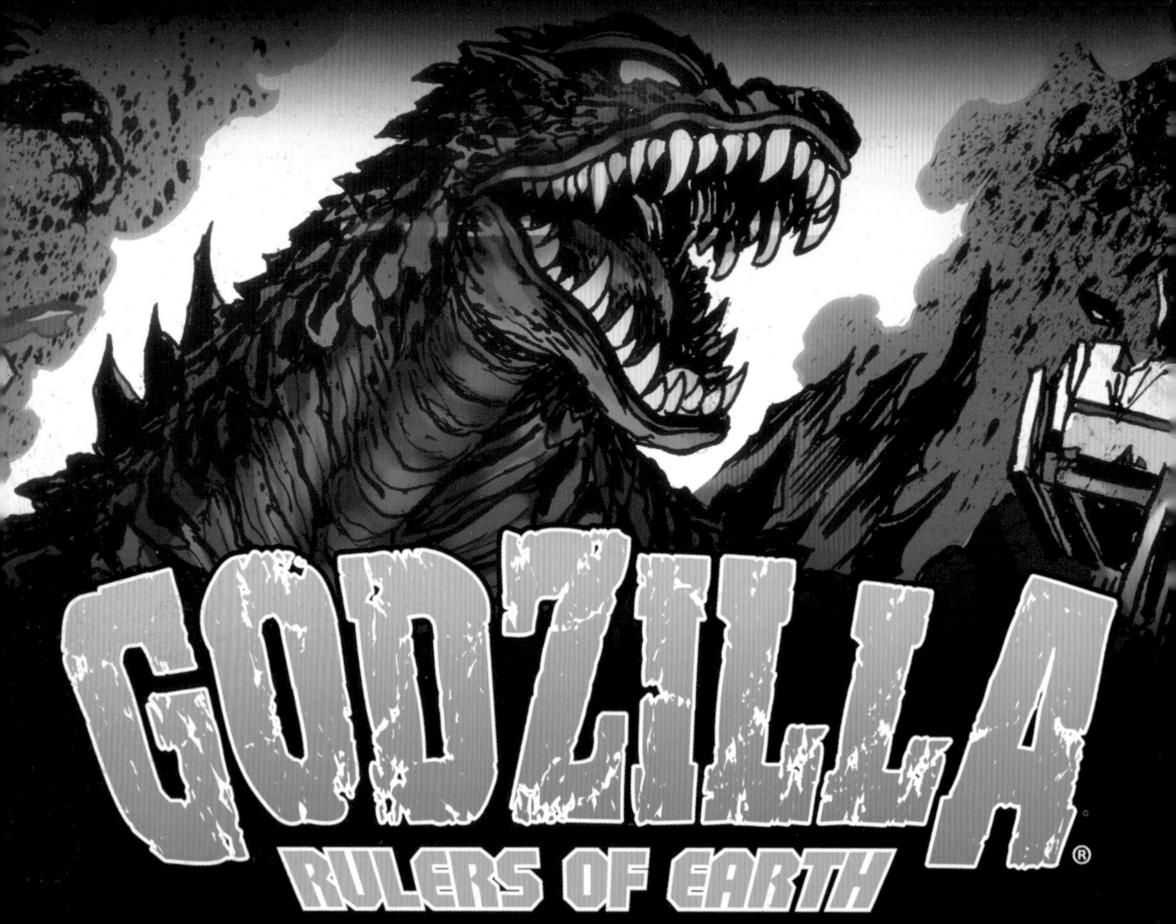
GODZILLA®
RULERS OF EARTH

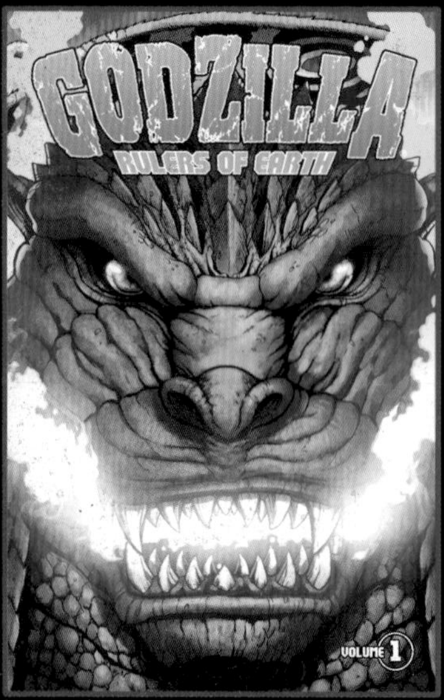
GODZILLA
RULERS OF EARTH
VOLUME 1

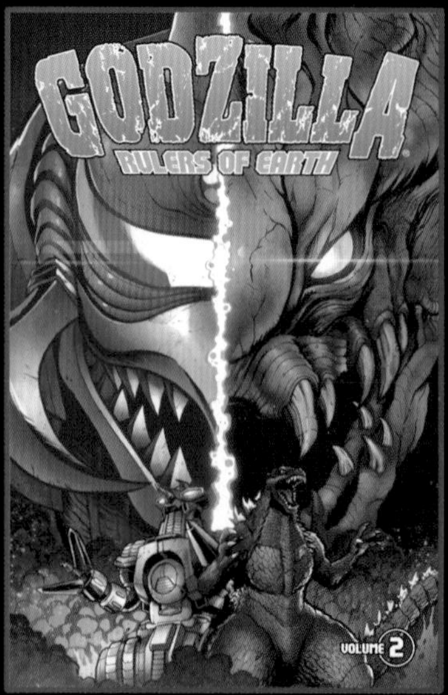
GODZILLA
RULERS OF EARTH
VOLUME 2

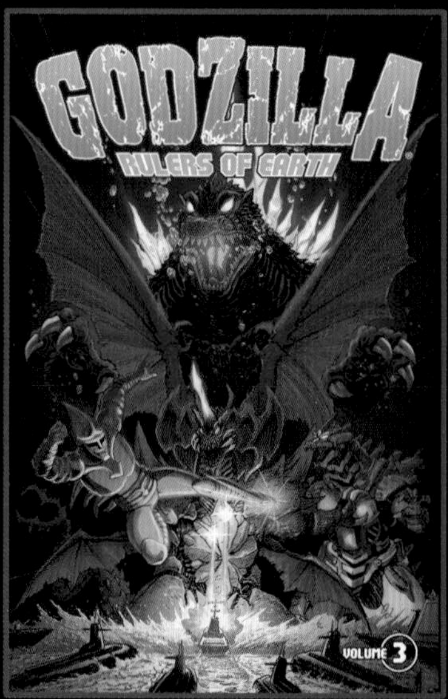
GODZILLA
RULERS OF EARTH
VOLUME 3